TEACHING THE EDUCABLE
MENTALLY RETARDED

Practical Methods

Photo by
CAMERA CRAFTS STUDIO

(Third Edition, Second Printing)

TEACHING THE EDUCABLE MENTALLY RETARDED
— Practical Methods —

By

MALINDA DEAN GARTON, A.M.
Assistant Professor and Supervising Teacher, Emerita
Intermediate Educable Mentally Retarded
Thomas J. Metcalf School
Illinois State University
Normal, Illinois

CHARLES C THOMAS • PUBLISHER
Springfield • Illinois • U.S.A.

Published and Distributed Throughout the World by
CHARLES C THOMAS • PUBLISHER
BANNERSTONE HOUSE
301-327 East Lawrence Avenue, Springfield, Illinois, U.S.A.

© *1961, 1964, and 1970 by* CHARLES C THOMAS • PUBLISHER

ISBN 0-398-00654-7

Library of Congress Catalog Card Number: 71-126477

First Edition, First Printing, 1961
First Edition, Second Printing, 1962
Second Edition, First Printing, 1964
Second Edition, Second Printing, 1965
Second Edition, Third Printing, 1967
Second Edition, Fourth Printing, 1968
Second Edition, Fifth Printing, 1969
Third Edition, 1970
Third Edition, Second Printing, 1974

*With THOMAS BOOKS careful attention is given to all details of
manufacturing and design. It is the Publisher's desire to present books
that are satisfactory as to their physical qualities and artistic possibilities
and appropriate for their particular use. THOMAS BOOKS will be true
to those laws of quality that assure a good name and good will.*

Printed in the United States of America
00-2

To the memory of my parents, MARY M. (WIER) DEAN *and* DAVID ANDREW DEAN, *who directed my early endeavors and inspired me to ever search for the good, the true, the beautiful, and when found, to savor it fully.*

PREFACE

Teaching the Educable Mentally Retarded is restricted in its scope to problems directly related with instructing the educable mentally retarded, or slow learner. This nontechnical book consists of information, suggestions, examples, and practical methods of teaching from the pre-readiness stage through the work-study and vocational workshop areas.

The content of the book includes methods, materials, and literature found helpful, and procedures evolved through personal experimentation in the classroom. The characteristics, objectives in education, curriculum outlines, and methods for achieving success are described. Many illustrations are included throughout the book. References at the end of the chapters provide sources of further detailed information.

This book is written for all of those who work with the retarded or slow learner in any capacity. These experiences, suggestions, examples, and methods should help provide a better understanding of the educable mentally retarded child and youth. It presents practical plans for assisting the retarded to retain and use the material to which he is introduced during his school tenure.

These methods should guide the inexperienced teacher in planning and carrying out her daily schedule. They should help the experienced teacher who enjoys and finds satisfaction in new plans, materials, and methods. They should also inspire the teacher of the regular class to include plans for the slow child so that he, too, may achieve some success.

Malinda Dean Garton

ACKNOWLEDGMENTS TO THE
THIRD EDITION

I wish to express my gratitude to the friends and educators who have helped me to express my concern for the mentally retarded in this revised Third Edition of *Teaching the Educable Mentally Retarded—Practical Methods.* I wish especially to express appreciation to the administrators and staff of Lyons Township High School for the many courtesies shown to me on my recent visit there: Dr. Donald R. Reber, Superintendent; Mr. Edward Zimdars, Principal, South Campus; Mr. Richard Ellis, Principal, North Campus; Mr. C. Lewis Martin, Director, LaGrange Area Department of Special Education;

Also, Miss Magdelene D. Wittmayer for her information about testing and for her escort service; Mrs. Evelyn Leonard, Librarian, for assistance in finding materials in the professional libraries at both South Campus and North Campus and for the telephone calls;

Also Mr. Roland P. Piller, Special Education, North Campus, who was courteous and helpful in providing information, arranging LADSE workshop sequences, and taking photographs; Mrs. Mary M. Lockhart, LADSE, North Campus, who kindly presented briefs of her program as her pupils prepared lunch and then assisted in setting up displays for photographs; Dr. Richard E. Yena, Prevocational coordinator, LADSE, who made a special trip to the library to give information and offer assistance;

And, Mrs. Helen McCallum Stehlik, Special Education, both North and South Campus, who arranged displays showing her freshmen girls homemaking class activities in cooking, health, and grooming; Mr. John Russell, Industrial Arts instructor, who arranged sequences for photographing class activities;

Mr. Richard D. Starnes, Special Education, South Campus and North Campus, arranged with Mrs. Pamela Harding's class for photographs of their work-study activity, mimeographing, collating, and preparing materials for use in the school; Mr. Starnes also conducted a tour of the cafeteria work-study program and took photographs of that activity.

I wish to thank my son, Martin William Garton, and his wife, Myrna S. Garton, for suggesting the visit to the special rooms at LaGrange and arranging the initial conferences to the various classes and workshops for the slow learners, so that the time was pleasant and interesting. Mr. Garton also photographed the activities in Mr. Russell's and Mrs. Stehlik's classes.

My thanks to those in other schools who at various times and places have been kind enough to arrange for tours and to give information concerning their schools. Among those are Mr. George G. Baird, McLean County Sheltered Workshop, Bloomington, Illinois; Mr. Russell Horn, Dixon State School, Dixon, Illinois; Mr. William Duvall of the Arkansas Children's Colony, Conway, Arkansas; Dr. Harold Love, Arkansas State Teachers College, Conway, Arkansas; Lt. Col. Elmer T. Lian, USAF, Ret., Grand Forks, N.D. Sheltered Workshop.

My sincere gratitude to Mr. and Mrs. G. Emery Taylor, Denton, Texas, for arranging the tour of Denton State School, and to Mr. E. W. Killian, Director of the School, who devoted an afternoon to explaining the purpose of the various departments, and then personally conducted Mr. and Mrs. Taylor and me on a tour of the new, well-equipped buildings.

My gratitude for good counsel, suggestions, materials, and encouragement from my sister, Mrs. Lillie Dean Wise, Oklahoma City; and Mrs. Louise O'Neal Parker, Assistant Professor and special education health nurse at Illinois State University, with whom I was associated in the laboratory school for thirteen years; also to Mr. Lowell J. Kuntz, Assistant Professor and Supervisor of Music, Illinois State University;

And to Dr. Linnea M. Anderson, Professor of Special Education, North East Missouri College, Kirksville, Missouri, who was Director of Special Education, University of North Dakota, Grand

Forks, when I served as Visiting Professor of Special Education for three summer sessions. Dr. Anderson has shared experiences, evaluation of materials and methods, and provided a valuable tour of the George Zeller Zone Center, Peoria, Illinois; through her arrangements I was privileged to be one of the first in the Midwest to lecture by telephone to college classes. I delivered three lectures to Dr. Anderson's special education classes at the University of North Dakota by telephone from my office in Cincinnati.

My appreciation to Mrs. Mary Burg, Cincinnati, Hamilton County, Ohio, Supervisor of Special Education, with whom I had the privilege to serve as a teacher for six years, for her many helpful suggestions, words of encouragement, and for two photographs of classroom scenes; also to the executive heads of Finneytown School District, Cincinnati: first, Mr. Telford A. Whitaker; later, Dr. Malcolm D. Evans; and the principals of Whitaker Elementary School, Finneytown School District, Cincinnati: first, Mr. James Hogan; later, Mr. Duane Puckett, for allowing me freedom to carry out my ideas for a sound program for the slow learners, for their faithful support in many matters, for allowing me to develop the teacher aide program in my class, as well as new methods and materials, and to experiment with new materials from other sources.   M. D. G.

ACKNOWLEDGMENTS TO THE SECOND EDITION

I WISH to express my appreciation to all those who have assisted in any way in the preparation of the book, including the following:

Miss A. Grace Hiler, Assistant Professor of English, University High School, Illinois State University, for her editorial assistance, invaluable criticism, and encouragement during the final preparation of the manuscript.

Mrs. Vera Moon, Special Teacher of Dependent and Delinquent Children, Gift Avenue School, Peoria, Illinois, who first encouraged the writing of this book and gave suggestions concerning its scope;

Miss Dorothy M. McEvoy, Assistant Professor and Teacher of the Deaf, Metcalf School, Illinois State University, who gave helpful advice and encouragement;

Miss Lillie Mae Rickman, Assistant Professor and Associate Principal of Metcalf School, Illinois State University, for understanding consideration during the final preparation of the manuscript;

Nelson R. Smith, Assistant Professor and Official Photographer, Illinois State University, and his helpers for their patience and skill in capturing representative poses of the children in the classroom and other illustrative materials for the book;

Wilbur Ludwig, commercial artist, Bloomington, Illinois, for his patience and care in preparing the ink illustrations;

Miss Gloria Reyes, Jose Abad Santos Memorial School, Philippine Women's University, Manila, P.I., for introducing the "Tinikling" dance to the children;

Silver Burdett Company, Morristown, N. J., for permission to use directions for the "Tinikling" from *The Philippine Progressive Music Series*, Primary Grades, copyright 1948;

My student teachers from 1950 through 1963, who helped make my teaching an even more rewarding experience, with special mention to D. Wayne Ruble, Kay Eich Wilhelmi and Juanita Lynn;

Also to Kay Lindenbaum Crane, Emmajo Luke McPherson, Eileen Joyce Seymour, James Seay, Carolyn Jones Dobbins, Joan Lane, Carol Touzinsky, Barbara Thiessen, Dorothy Hafstrom, and Carol Brubaker Kaliher for bulletin board materials and arithmetic devices;

Also Karen Reedy, Dianne Thiessen, Alice Moxey, Jacqueline Dudnick, Virginia Huisinga, and Colleen Mauterer for reading parts of the manuscript and giving helpful suggestions.

I wish to express appreciation to Mr. M. William Garton for preparing the ink drawings of the xylophone and the looms for the revised edition; and to Mr. James Hogan, principal of Whitaker Elementary School, Finneytown, Ohio, for permission to use his working drawings of the standing rug loom which were made to Mrs. June Jentz' specifications.

M. D. G.

CONTENTS

Chapter   *Page*

Chapter   *Page*

TEACHING THE EDUCABLE
MENTALLY RETARDED

Practical Methods

1

OBJECTIVES FOR THE EDUCABLE MENTALLY RETARDED

THE PURPOSE OF THE PROGRAM

THE overall aim of the program for the retarded, or slow learner, is the same as for the education of any child. The basic philosophy is to assist the child: to develop to his fullest capacity; to achieve the social and economic independence his ability will allow; and to become a responsible citizen.

The President's Committee on Mental Retardation has made great progress since the first recommendations several decades ago. The 1968 and 1969 reports have shown the popular and professional acceptance of these children. These recommendations state the growing concern regarding the necessity for help and acceptance for the retarded. Agencies have found it necessary to change their methods of handling these children.

The 1968 report, *The Edge of Change*, shows that the program for mental retardation must be a part of the "new community planning, manpower training and use, education policy, population study, and human resource planning."

Many studies have shown the most rapid learning comes in the earliest months and years. The report to the President in 1968 also states, "The range of an individual's intelligence is set in earliest childhood. It can be blunted in those same early years by a limiting, harsh, negative environment."

3

With the new community awareness of need, and the readiness to help, the teacher must be ready to provide expert and loving training to the children entrusted to her care. The tasks must be tailored to the children's individual needs and abilities. The teacher must also consider that each child has many needs, and therefore should have many experiences to develop abilities to solve the problems. His training time will be short, so the most constructive use should be made of each day.

The teacher's concern should be to know the child's past, his present problems and pressures, and try to develop means to help him overcome these difficulties. She should prepare experiences to assist him in overcoming his fears and frustrations; to help in instilling self-confidence and emotional stability, and in developing good attitudes and habits toward daily tasks. These factors will aid the retarded adult to succeed in a vocational training program and to maintain a feeling of confidence and self-respect. This type of training program is important for the final success in becoming self-sufficient.

Part of the training should include some knowledge of our cultural and historical heritage. Each new generation must be made aware of the value of personal rights and the problems concerned with human values. These facts and values should be definitely taught and stressed for they are not automatically absorbed.

DEVELOPING SELF-CONFIDENCE

The development of each child's abilities to the extent of his capabilities is furthered by a flexible plan permitting growth in all areas. This will ensure satisfaction and happiness, vocational, social, and economic success commensurate with his abilities. To accomplish these goals the child must have well-structured lessons. These lessons should be presented in an interesting manner, with the material well spaced and reinforced for retention, with added repetition at suitable intervals to aid in retention.

Suggestions follow for developing self-confidence and social competence.

    1. Acting as hosts and hostesses.

    2. Building and operating a play store, taking turns as manager and customers.

3. Cultivating hobbies: picture taking, model making, stamp collecting, rock collecting, arrowhead collecting, etc.
4. Dramatizing events, giving puppet shows, social dramas, peep shows, shadow plays, pantomimes, and historical plays.
5. Learning about homemaking, buying food, clothing, furnishings, equipment, cars, repairing.
6. Learning to cook, clean house, do laundry, to take care of foods, clothing, and equipment.
7. Having proper contacts with a doctor, nurse, dentist, health center, Red Cross center, a hospital, a guidance center; daily inspection of hands, skin, hair, teeth, nails, until firm habits are established; checking and keeping charts on weight and height, and general health.
8. Developing language through using the telephone, making introductions, and practicing conversation.
9. Learning to enjoy music by listening to records, singing, playing an instrument.
10. Participating in rhythmic games, dancing, physical education class, swimming.
11. Learning crafts: weaving, painting, ceramics, carving, modeling, plastics, semiprecious stones for jewelry.
12. Reading for information from newspaper want ads, sales, signs, catalogs, and reading for pleasure.
13. Watching TV, sharing experiences, talking about current events, viewing films, having personal contacts with community workers.
14. Performing experiments under careful supervision.
15. Participating in class discussions.
16. Keeping a library corner in order in the classroom.
17. Learning the use of pictures, maps, graphs, charts, specimens, and models.
18. Writing letters of friendship, invitation, and thank you notes.
19. Studying to discover how community workers affect one another in their various work areas.
20. Collecting seed. This is a good fall activity. A colorful bulletin board showing different kinds of seed will stimu-

late interest in learning about plants and their uses. This makes an excellent basis for a society study unit.

21. Planting seed is a good springtime activity. The large lima beans usually bring nice plants a few days after planting. The beans may be started between damp layers of cotton on a tin lid, or planted in individual boxes of soil. The small milk cartons make nice boxes when washed and trimmed. Grapefruit, orange, and lemon seed will sprout and grow but take longer to germinate.

22. Potato "eyes" will sprout and grow when cut out of the potato. Tops of carrots and turnips produce leaves if kept in a shallow dish with moisture around them. A sweet potato anchored in the top of a glass is interesting to watch as it produces a long green vine.

23. Cuttings from the philodendron produce nice plants to watch grow. If the cuttings are placed in glass containers, the children can see the roots grow as well as the leaves. When well rooted, the little plants may be transferred to individual cartons of dirt. They make attractive gifts, especially when wrapped in paper decorated by the children.

DEVELOPING ECONOMIC SELF-SUFFICIENCY

To assist the educable mentally retarded, or slow learner, to become successful in a vocation, training must be given to develop good work habits, good attitudes, and a pleasing personality. He can be taught the value of money, of planning, of seeking proper authorities for counseling on family affairs, on legal matters, and for his medical needs.

The educable mentally retarded child must be adequately taught to know how to apply for a job, and to know what he must do to keep the job so that he may become economically self-sufficient.

The teacher should encourage the pupils to participate in those activities that will contribute to their feelings of success and security. Some suggestions follow for developing economic self-sufficiency.

1. Maintaining good mental and physical health through games, modeling, a study of nutrition, and personal hygiene.
2. Learning muscular coordination through rhythms, dancing, games, and practice in walking, sitting, and standing correctly.
3. Learning the basic facts and skills in arithmetic.
4. Talking with people about jobs.
5. Using books, magazines, newspapers, records, and films.
6. Spelling useful words.
7. Dramatizing situations related to economic efficiency.
8. Matching objects.
9. Carrying on conversations personally and over the telephone.
10. Buying supplies.
11. Keeping records.
12. Telling stories to the class.
13. Reading stories silently and orally.
14. Reading signs.
15. Learning to follow directions.
16. Learning about banking procedures, such as cashing checks, paying notes, interest, and taxes.
17. Using charts, diagrams, and patterns.
18. Learning about applying for a job.

DEVELOPING CITIZENSHIP

The teacher should help the educable mentally retarded child to prepare to assume civic responsibility. He should learn something about the laws of the town, the state, and the nation in which he lives. He should respect property, both public and private. He should develop the desire to be of service to his fellow man, to know how to vote, to know what he is voting about, and then to go and cast his ballot.

The following activities are suggested to assist the pupils to develop a sense of responsible citizenship.

1. Studying about the city, county, state, national, and world affairs, through viewing pictures, films, television, graphs, charts, and reading magazines, newspapers, books, and examining other media.

2. Locating through field trips, studying the uses of, and listening to talks by personnel of: libraries, parks, museums, YWCA, YMCA, recreation centers, the zoo, fire station, police station, city hall, county building, social security office, other schools, factories, banks, internal revenue office, stores, hospital, special service organizations, and similar places.
3. Doing errands.
4. Writing to secure information or to continue a friendship.
5. Reading for information or pleasure.
6. Discussing the responsibility for paying bills on time and loans of a personal nature.
7. Paying taxes when due should be explained and enlarged upon at each promotional level. Pupils should understand that everyone pays taxes in some form: for candy, ice cream, books, pencils, school buildings, the jail, the streets, the city workers salaries, the governor of the state, the President. The taxes are collected in many ways. Everything that belongs to the people that is destroyed must be replaced so the people must pay more taxes to replace it.

Vocational Placement. The educable mentally retarded or slow learners have a special place in the economy of our country. There are many essential jobs in every community and in industry for which they are especially well endowed by temperament and ability.

These people must be given the experiences from earliest childhood to maturity to prepare them for real life situations. Their daily activities and experiences comprise their program. They must learn to follow directions, to work under supervision, to be punctual, to be honest, to assume responsibility for completing a task, to be congenial, to control both words and actions, and to attend to their own affairs.

Where the teacher accepts the responsibility of instilling respect for authority and developing good mental health along with the teaching of the basic skills and social graces, the pupils will likely be employable. Industrial leaders have stated that the employment possibility of the mentally deficient is based largely upon their emotional stability and their ability to take orders from supervisors and to carry out directions.

Not all children classified as being educable mentally retarded will be able to utilize all of the training that is offered. However, to the extent that each person is able to do so, his life and the lives of his family are benefitted.

SUMMARY

It seems obvious that the teacher is responsible for providing helpful, happy, healthful, successful experiences for the educable mentally retarded. The teacher's aim through the use of these activities is to assist the development of self-sufficiency, social competence, economic efficiency, and good citizenship in each child to the best of his ability.

REFERENCES

1. Dunn, Lloyd M.: *Exceptional Children in the Schools.* New York, Holt, Rinehart, Winston, 1963, pp. 90-93.
2. Ayrault, Evelyn West: *You Can Raise Your Handicapped Child.* New York, Putnam, 1964.
3. *Children Limited,* 420 Lexington Ave., New York, 10017. (News published every other month by the NARC.)
4. Cruickshank, William M., and Johnson, G. Orville, Eds.: *Education of Exceptional Children and Youth,* 2nd ed. Englewood Cliffs, N.J., Prentice-Hall, 1967.
5. Cullum, Albert: *Push Back the Desks.* New York, Citation, 1967.
6. Egg, Maria: *When a Child is Different.* New York, John Day, 1964.
7. Hudsor Margaret W., and Weaver, Ann A.: *To Be A Good American.* A Pacemaker Book. Palo Alto, Fearon.
8. Johnson, G. Orville: *Education for the Slow Learners.* Englewood Cliffs, N.J., Prentice-Hall, 1963, pp. 48-49.
9. Lemee, Harry A.: Social adjustment for the intellectually handicapped. *School and Community,* 54(3):10-11, 1967.
10. Love, Harold: *Exceptional Children in a Modern Society.* Dubuque, Iowa, William C. Brown, 1967.
11. Nolen, P. A., and others: Behavioral modification in a junior learning disabilities classroom. *Exceptional child,* 34(3):163, 1967.
12. Perry, Natalie: *Teaching the Mentally Retarded Child,* rev. ed. New York, Columbia Univ., 1965.
13. President's Committee on Mental Retardation: *Hello World.* Washington, D.C., U.S. Government Printing Office, 1969.

14. President's Committee on Mental Retardation: *The Edge of Change.* Washington, D.C., U.S. Government Printing Office, MR68.
15. Rosenzweig, L. E., and Long, T.: *Understanding and Teaching the Dependent Retarded Child.* Darien, Conn., Education Pub., 1960.
16. Vargason, Glenn A.: Facilitation of memory in the retarded. *Exceptional Child,* 34(8):589, 1968.
17. Webster, John D., President's Committee on Mental Retardation: *How to Get a Job.* Washington, D.C., U.S. Government Printing Office, 1968.
18. Witty, Paul A., Ed.: *The Educationally Retarded and Disadvantaged.* NSSE, Chicago, Univ. of Chicago, 1967.

2

ETIOLOGY AND HISTORY OF MENTAL RETARDATION

T HE etiology and history of the retarded is interesting and voluminous. Until a few years ago this was not true. The people who wanted to help the retarded, or feebleminded as they were then called, were pioneers and experimenters in this important field of study. The handicapped person was regarded as a curse, an evil fellow, or a punishment upon the parents for some great secret sin. The causes of these conditions were considered by many to be supernatural.

This chapter offers a brief review of the etiology of some familiar forms of retardation, and of the lives of some of the persons whose work and influence have enabled the teaching of the retarded to arrive where it is today.

ETIOLOGY

The etiology of these handicaps is as varied as the degrees. In non-technical terms some common causes are (1) birth injuries, pre-natal, para-natal, post-natal; (2) germ plasma defects; (3) injuries and disease, (4) other causes—RH factor, enzyme deficiency, PKU or phenylketonuria, thyroid deficiency, hydrocephalus, and the solid skull.

Some of these conditions, if discovered at an early stage and properly treated, can be prevented from doing serious damage to the brain. The RH factor is shown by blood tests of the prospective parents. A transfusion of whole blood at birth, or even before birth, may save the child. Now the mother may be inoculated after an RH birth to avoid the next child carrying the antibodies.

The presence of phenylketonuria, or PKU, can be determined at the age of two weeks by a simple diaper test of the infant's urine. This test is known as "Folling's Reaction." Dr. Asbjorn Folling of the University Hospital of Oslo, Norway, discovered this in the early 1930's. It was not widely noticed and studied until about 1950. Another test for PKU can be made soon after the infant's birth. This is a simple blood test, with blood taken from the infant's heel. Early detection of PKU is important, as the deterioration of the brain cells begins with the lack of proper diet. There are foods available low in phenylalanine that provide correct nutrition and allow the child to develop mentally. The diet continues throughout the early years, to three or four years of age, sometimes longer. Tests at regular intervals keep track of the progress of the child's system in overcoming the condition. There are other enzyme deficiency diseases. Two are galactosemia and galactose, both are easily recognized in early infancy. They, and phenylketonuria, may be controlled by special diets, and brain damage may be avoided.

The child with hydrocephalus may often have a tiny valve and tube surgically imbedded in the cranium. This prevents excess fluids from building up in the brain cavity and causing damage to the brain. The fluids are drained into the blood stream. The child whose skull is solid, instead of being capable of expansion with growth, may now be treated surgically, and brain damage is kept to a minimum.

Germ plasma defects are being explored. One of the late discoveries is that of Dr. Jerome Lejeune, Director of Genetics, University of Paris, of the chromosomal abnormality in many cases of mongolism.

It is known that during the early weeks of pregnancy, Rubella, or German measles, may cause brain injury to the child. A child does not appear to be very ill with the German measles. The young mother who cares for this child may contract the measles during this critical first few weeks of a pregnancy and cause many congenital afflictions to the unborn child including deafness, blindness, and mental retardation. A vaccine has been developed to immunize against Rubella which is now being widely administered to children in an attempt to prevent the disease from spreading.

This vaccine is not the same as that given for the immunization against the so-called common red measles or rubeolla, which has been used since 1961. Many complications also result from this type of measles. In any event, a physician should be consulted when a child is feverish, has a sore throat, or a cough. The study of the cause of brain injury and of mental retardation covers a wide area. The student who is interested in this problem should pursue the problem in depth, which is not the purpose of this text, consult the references provided at the end of this chapter, and current literature in the library.

HISTORY

The retarded individual has been known from earliest history. In many countries the retarded was considered as something to be destroyed, abandoned, treated as insane, laughed at, or hidden away in the home or in an institution.

Teaching the mentally retarded started in Europe in the early nineteenth century. Most of those interested were physicians and teachers. The leader in this movement was a physician, Dr. Jean Marc Itard, of France. He worked for five years attempting to train and humanize a boy who had been found living in a forest. The boy is known as Victor, the Wild Boy of Aveyron.

Dr. Itard tried to teach Victor to talk, to want to live as others lived. He finally placed the boy in an institution, and felt that he failed. Others had watched the experiment with interest. They persuaded Dr. Itard to write a report of his experiences and methods with Victor. These friends thought Dr. Itard had accomplished many things for Victor.

One of the friends was a student of Dr. Itard's, Dr. Edward Seguin. He was also a teacher and a surgeon. He studied Dr. Itard's methods and started working with the retarded. He made some changes in the methods and emphasized the training of the muscles and the senses.

Dr. Edward Seguin came to the United States in 1848. He assisted in establishing new hospitals and homes for the retarded.

Seguin's work was so well received that when in 1876 an Association was formed that is now the American Association on Mental Deficiency, he was chosen as its first president.

Dr. Deteressa Maria Montessori became interested in the retarded in Rome. She was a helper at a psychiatric clinic in Rome where she found mentally retarded children interned with the insane. She determined to do something to alleviate their condition. In 1897 she began her self-teaching system with some of these unfortunate children. She used sense and muscle training as a basis for her teaching. Out of this interest the Montessori method of training any young child was incorporated in many educational systems.

Dr. Ovide Decroly, a physician of Brussels, Belgium, was a student of Seguin's methods. He used many games for the sense and muscle training with attention to the child's social and physical needs. Dr. Decroly had as an apprentice, Alice Descoeudres, who believed in his methods but devised numerous activities to make the knowledge an integral and useful part of the child's life. She used the idea of working around a topic, or the unit idea. Her principles and philosophy are embodied in her text, *Education of Mentally Defective Children,* which is now out of print.

Dr. Alfred Binet was a scientist and an experimental psychologist, who worked with the mentally retarded. He constructed the tests for measuring intelligence according to an age scale. The tests have been refined and revised and are used as a standard means for the evaluation of intelligence potential.

There are many others who have contributed to the general knowledge of the many facts of mental retardation. They have shown the importance of improving the care and educational procedures of the retarded of all ages and stages of ability. Space would not permit naming the many outstanding workers in the field of mental retardation today.

REFERENCES

1. Baumesiter, Alfred A., Jr.: *Mental Retardation: Appraisal, Education and Rehabilitation.* Chicago, Aldine, 1967.
2. Clark, C. A.: The prevention of Rh-immunization. In Crow, James F., and Neel, James V., Eds.: *Proceedings of the Third International Congress of Human Genetics.* Baltimore, Johns Hopkins, 1967, pp. 83-91.
3. Cruickshank, William M.: *The Brain Injured Child in Home, School, and Community.* Syracuse, Syracuse Univ., 1967.
4. Descoeudres, Alice: *The Education of Mentally Defective Children,* translated from the Second French Edition by E. F. Ross. New York, D.C. Heath, 1928.
5. Dunn, Lloyd M.: *Exceptional Children in the Schools.* New York, Holt, Rinehart, Winston, 1963.
6. Hellmuth, Jerome, Ed.: *Learning Disorders,* Vol. I. Seattle, Special Child Publications, 1965.
7. Hellmuth, Jerome, Ed.: *Learning Disorders,* Vol. II. Seattle, Special Child Publications, 1966; Vol. III, 1967.
8. Ingram, Christine P.: *Education of the Slow Learning Child,* 3rd ed. New York, Ronald, 1960.
9. Itard, Jean-Marc-Gaspard: *The Wild Boy of Aveyron,* translated by George and Muriel Humphrey. New York and London, Century, 1932.
10. Jervis, George A., Ed.: *Expanding Concepts in Mental Retardation: A Symposium.* Springfield, Thomas, 1968.
11. Kirk, Samuel A.: *Educating Exceptional Children.* Boston, Houghton Mifflin, 1962.
12. Koch, Richard, Fishler, Karol, Schild, Sylvia, and Ragsdale, Nancy: Clinical aspects of phenylketonuria. *Mental Retardation,* 2:1, 1964.
13. Lin-Fu Jane S.: *Rubella.* Washington, D.C., Children's Bureau, Superintendent of Documents, 1968. (An explanation of German measles and its effect on the fetus.)
14. *Mental Retardation,* 7(2), 1969. (Entire issue of *MR* has special articles in relation to cause, treatment, and prevention of retardation. The issue is dedicated "In Memoriam to Robert Francis Kennedy 1925-1968.")
15. Minnesota Public Welfare Department: *A World of the Right Size.* St. Paul, Minn, 1966.
16. Myklebust, H. R., Ed.: *Progress in Learning Disabilities,* Vol. I. New York, Grune and Stratton, 1968.

17. NARC: *Measles Fact Sheet.* New York, National Association for Retarded Children Publishing Co., 1968.
18. Phillips, Irving, Ed.: *Prevention and Treatment of Mental Retardation.* New York, Basic Books, 1966.
19. Rosenblith, Judy F., and Allinsmith, Wesley: *The Causes of Behavior: Readings in Child Development and Educational Psychology,* 2nd ed. Rockleigh, N.J., Allyn and Bacon.
20. Rothstein, Jerome H.: *Mental Retardation.* New York, Holt, Rinehart, Winston, 1967.
21. Rubella: What becomes of baby born with rubella? *Medical World News,* 9(7):65, 1968. (A report from Sydney, Australia, of a 25-year follow-up study.)
22. Sarason, Seymour B.: Mentally retarded and mentally defective children: major psychosocial problems. Chapter 9 in Cruickshank, William M., Ed.: *Psychology of Exceptional Children and Youth.* Englewood Cliffs, N.J., Prentice-Hall, 1955.
23. Sarason, Seymour B.: *Psychological Problems in Mental Deficiency,* 3rd rev. ed. New York, Harper and Row, 1959.
24. Scott, Florence: *Protect from PKU,* 2nd ed. Portland, Ore., State Board of Health, 1968. (Prompt dietary treatment is necessary to prevent mental retardation.)
25. Siegel, Morris, Fuerst, H., and Duggan, W.: Rubella in mother and congenital cataracts in child: Comparative data in periods with and without epidemics from 1957 to 1964. *JAMA, 203(9):* 632-636, 1968.
26. Standing E. M.: Montessori: *Her Life and Work.* Fresno, Calif., Academy Library Guild, 1959.

3

CHARACTERISTICS OF THE
EDUCABLE MENTALLY RETARDED

THESE questions are often asked: What do you mean by an educable mentally retarded child? What are some of his predominant characteristics? What of this person's future?

DEFINITION OF MENTAL RETARDATION

The definition prepared by Heber and his committee for the American Association on Mental Deficiency is published in their Journal of September 1961, A Monograph Supplement. "Mental Retardation refers to subaverage general intellectual functioning which originates during the developmental period and is associated with impairment in one or more of the following: (1) maturation, (2) learning, and (3) social adjustment."[1]

The report states that though the upper age limit of the *developmental period* cannot be precisely specified, for practical purposes it may be regarded as about sixteen years. *Maturation* is interpreted as "the rate of sequential development of self-help skills of infancy and early childhood such as, sitting, crawling, standing, walking, talking, habit training, and interaction with age peers."[1]

"Learning ability refers to the facility with which knowledge is acquired as a function of experience."[1] "Social adjustment . . . during the pre-school and school years . . . is reflected, in large measure, in the level and manner in which the child relates to parents, other adults and age peers."[1]

Supplementary term categories in the behavioral areas are defined as follows:

Personal-Social Factors

Impairment in interpersonal relations. This category is intended to reflect deficiencies in interpersonal skills. The individual with an impairment in interpersonal relations does not relate adequately to peers and/or authority figures and may demonstrate an inability to recognize the needs of other persons in interpersonal interactions.

Impairment in cultural conformity. . . . behavior which does not conform to the social mores, . . . does not meet the standards of dependability, reliability, and trustworthiness; behavior which is persistently asocial, anti-social, and/or excessively hostile.

Impairment in responsiveness. . . . an inability to delay gratification of needs and a lack of long range goal striving or persistence with response only to short term goals. . . .[1]

Sensory Motor Factors discussed are: motor skills, auditory skills, visual skills, speech skills.

In studying this definition one should note that the condition of mental retardation is associated with one or more of the three categories of disability as applied to the description of "the current status of the individual."

Kirk, Karnes, Kirk in "You and Your Retarded Child," define the educable mentally retarded child in terms of not being able to profit from a regular school program. They recommend placement in a special class and conclude that he can in most cases "become self-supporting at the adult level."

Duhl defines a mentally retarded person as—

1. . . . an individual who according to professional evaluative disciplines and criterial, has failed to demonstrate his ability to live up to expectations in the intellectual and social spheres when he is compared with those of his chronological age. 2. The mentally retarded include all persons who have a condition of which the etiology is organic or inorganic, but always exhibit a deficit in the intellectual sphere.[1]

---

[1] Reprinted by permission of the *American Journal of Mental Deficiency.*

An educable mentally retarded child is defined by the Illinois Commission for Handicapped Children as "any child whose rate of mental development, as measured by individual psychological examinations, has been retarded from birth or early age, but who requires and may expect to benefit from special education facilities designed to make him economically useful and socially adjusted."

The mentally retarded is variously named in different states and countries, as the slow-learner, the mildly retarded, those with potential for competitive employment, the moderately mentally deficient, those with mental subnormality, high grade retardates, marginal-independent, independent, borderline mental deficiency, educable but mentally handicapped, educationally subnormal, the educable retarded. In addition to these terminologies there are many others.

The next lower range of ability is called the sheltered, the trainable, the moderately retarded. The third lower range of ability is called the self-help trainee, the custodial, the unskilled potential, or the severely retarded. The lowest range of retardation is that of the gross or profound type, that needs total care and is not capable of self-maintenance.

DISCOVERING THE EDUCABLE MENTALLY RETARDED CHILD

The evaluation of each child is going on every day, through pre-natal days, through the birth, and the days, months and years of childhood. It is only when something unusual happens, when the expected rate of development does not occur, that one becomes aware of the almost anxious continuous evaluation that goes on concerning a child.

With the parents of the retarded child this moment of truth may arrive very early in the child's life. The first examination may reveal certain stigmata. There may be a refusal to eat; inability to retain food; a peculiar odor of the diaper; failure to notice objects; inability to sit, crawl, stand, walk, or to speak at the usual time. These are warning signs of trouble ahead.

Some parents refuse to heed the warning advice of their doctor or clinicians. They go from place to place seeking a nostrum that will "make the child snap out of it." The parent who is able to accept the child's evaluation is fortunate. The energy and love of the parent can be turned toward giving this child security, encouragement, and the proper early training. The child will respond by being happy, friendly and making progress commensurate with his ability.

A retarded child may be discovered at school age through the family doctor, the public health service, a social agency, or siblings enrolled in school, or through a teachers recommendation for a child in school. The parents may be aware of facilities for their retarded child and initiate placement in a special room. After the child is known to the school, arrangements are made to start a series of tests.

A case history of the child and the family will be made. This should include family health, physical and medical history, home conditions, reasons for referral, and eventually school records.

The school psychologist will administer several individual tests to determine the child's mental and social maturity. The tests usually include the Stanford-Binet, The Weschler Intelligence Scale for Children, or the Merrill-Palmer Test, Peabody Picture Vocabulary Test, Draw-A-Man Test, The Arthur Performance Test. The Vineland Social Maturity Test is really a report by the parents of the ability of the child at various ages. There are many other tests and some are in highly specialized areas of the senses. These are all administered as they are required by thoroughly trained psychologists.

Achievement Tests. At the end of the year, or for a special evaluation of pupil achievement, the teacher may use a standard test such as the Metropolitan or the California Achievement. The Metropolitan Readiness Test usually is difficult enough for the primary group, while the Primary II Test covers the ability range of the intermediate group. The pupil of better ability should have a more challenging test. For the junior high and high school pupils, tests should be given at a grade level that will not prove frustrating and will show the pupils ability.

It is not necessary to follow the time limits set in the test manuals. These pupils will usually become tired or reach a place beyond which they are unable to proceed, before the allotted time is completed. The results compared to a previous test give the teacher an idea of what each child has learned, as well as the rate at which he is learning.

There is usually a scatter in each area of the test. In arithmetic the problem solving will have a low score because of the reading difficulty and the abstract thinking required. The skill processes will be high in simple addition and subtraction; low in multiplication and division.

Test results for reading are low in marking opposites, and in answering comprehension questions. They are high in word form recognition. Writing is generally average for the pupil's chronological age. Spelling achievement is usually low.

The Illinois Test of Psycholinguistic Abilities is a battery of nine sub-tests on the basic language abilities. It may be administered to children from two to eight years of age by trained personnel.

The Sociogram. Another form of evaluation is the sociogram. This is the social evaluation of any one by his peers. It is used in a simple form in the classroom and is a valuable aid in spotting potential trouble makers and in avoiding unnecessary friction among the pupils. A later chapter illustrates and explains how to prepare, administer, and evaluate a sociogram.

Mental Age. The mental age of the child is an important factor to consider in all planning for training. From three to six years Mental Age, there should be nursery school and kindergarten activities. From six to seven MA, reading readiness and beginning reading and numbers. Emphasis is usually on the home and school activities. From seven to nine MA, interest begins to extend to the community. From nine to eleven MA, work should center around the community, job possibilities, our country, our responsibilities at home, at school, in the community, to our nation. From eleven MA on, the activities should be occupational and vocational centered, with job training, securing, and holding emphasized. Birch and Stevens present a chart showing the MA derived from IQ and CA, in *Reaching the Mentally Retarded.*

CHARACTERISTICS

Too often we think of the educable mentally retarded child as just slightly different from the normal child. We should be aware of his special characteristics and behavioral patterns in order to find him and help him. Left without special help, he becomes lost and frustrated in competition with the usual children in school, work, or play.

EDUCABILITY

The most important and constructive characteristic of the educable mentally retarded (that group of persons obtaining I.Q. scores between about 50 and 80) is the fact that he is capable of being educated and trained to maintain himself independently as an adult.

Sensitivity to Surroundings. The retarded child is usually quite sensitive to either hostile or friendly surroundings. He seems instinctively to know when the teacher accepts him, when the visitor is friendly, or when the visitor is merely tolerating him. Teachers, parents, and visitors should realize that this child must be loved for what he can do, instead of being rejected for what he is unable to do. Acceptance is important for the preservation of the child's dignity and the achievement of self-realization. Many children are rejected at home and must rely on the school to fulfill this need for praise and love.

Each child should have praise and love given to him daily by his teacher. He should be made to feel that what he has accomplished is important to his teacher. After a while the child will begin to feel satisfied with himself. When he is freed from the strain of apprehension of failure and rejection, he will likely succeed in some area to compensate for former failures.

Without acceptance by the adults in his life, the child will show resentment in tantrums, sulking, inattention, hyperactivity, defacing property, destroying work papers, crying, or arguing. Special training and experience are necessary to understand how to approach the child. The teacher or worker must know when to be firm, when to ignore an act, and when to move to another activity to forestall unpleasant situations.

Slow Reaction Time. Most mentally retarded children have a slow reaction time. They seem unable to become interested in a new idea without adjusting to the idea. The teacher should give them time to put away materials from a previous class, admire the products of the previous period, and settle down to anticipate the new experience. As the child becomes accustomed to school's routine, and to the many activities around him, this habit of procedure will carry him from one activity to the next. This is useful in later work habits.

Short Attention Span. The mentally retarded child may look at, or listen to, almost anything for brief periods. The teacher will discover the attention will wander from an enjoyable activity, yet he will not wish to relinquish the activity.

The less interest the child has in an activity the more easily he is distracted. Therefore, all of the materials used in teaching the retarded must be at the child's level of interest and comprehension; the activities must be geared to his short attention span; and, the material must be within his ability to complete with a reasonable degree of satisfaction. As he continues to study and develop, his attention span will increase too, so eventually he will be able to complete vocational training, secure a job, and be a satisfactory worker.

2.   Bulletin board for September showing children's contributions.

Language Limitations. The mentally retarded do not observe closely, they see few details. Many do not observe that the tree has branches or leaves, that the leaves have tiny veins, unless these details are pointed out to them. They speak in single words, the "me" is the center of everything. To help overcome this deficiency in learning and in their knowledge, they must be shown many things and the likeness and differences must be pointed out repeatedly. They must have it called to their attention that there are many colors, that things are big and small, near and far away, that one should be on time, to know about time and space values, to recognize many objects, so that an oral vocabulary may be established.

This procedure is difficult in a group with a wide chronological and mental age spread. It will require a longer time to develop where the instruction is necessarily on an individual basis. Sarason explains that the greatest difficulties for the retarded are in the "use and comprehension of verbal and numerical symbols. It is through the medium of words that thinking develops and that the comprehension of abstract meaning occurs."

A serious defect of mentally retarded children is their inability to communicate. They do not understand most of the words used in ordinary conversation. Prepositions are especially baffling. Children who do not respond readily to a direction may not understand the meaning of a term used, such as *over, under, between,* or *below.*

Each situation is a new and difficult experience for this child. The teacher should remember that even though the child knows how to spell *can,* she should not expect him to spell *pan.* Even though he knows the sound of the beginning consonant *p* and the ending *an,* he needs much help in associating and blending the sounds into a word.

Lack of Initiative for Planning. Mentally retarded children are the followers of the world. Ingram states, "these children have less ability to learn from experience." Sarason explains that the "judgment of the subnormal as well as her creative ability is limited." When working with the retarded most teachers and parents have found that time is not understood nor is the value of planning. If the teacher announces on Monday that the class will have a party on Friday, then every day all week, the party is the topic of conversation with the questions centering on, "When is the party?"

The inability to determine the importance of situations as well as having poor judgment and less ability to learn from experience are necessary considerations in planning with the group for any event. The idea of quantities, number, and time must be understood to plan even a single party at school. Someone must teach these boys and girls, these young men and women, how to plan, how to become helpers in the home and community, and how to avoid following plans that lead them into trouble.

Limited Imagination. The educable mentally retarded tend to be practical. They seem to be unable to do work requiring originality. However, they are able to imitate and to vary the finished product with fanciful or playful additions.

The educable mentally retarded have some facility at *fancy*, which Fernald defines as being a mental image found upon capricious or whimsical association or resemblence. They frequently perseverate with some art or craft pattern. They will repeat the same form over and over for weeks or months. In story telling or sharing time in the primary the sentences are short or fragmentary. Only the most obvious facts are reported. One little girl reported day after day, "My daddy works—office." Then she would stand on one foot and kick back with the other foot, finally saying, "My Mommie works—home. HMMM." Then after a pause, "Me at school." She was chronologically seven, but about three mentally. In four months time she was bringing Mother Goose records from home to share with the class. The sentences continued that year to be short and broken. They later improved with practice and help. Another girl reported each Monday on one fact, the family did or did not attend church on Sunday.

As the child matures he becomes more aware of his environment and his vocabulary increases. He is able to express his experiences in longer sentences and use a greater variety of words. The stories remain essentially factual. The TV and movie programs are usually taken for the truth. At junior or senior high level the retarded are usually able to separate the make-believe from the fact.

Limited Use of Concepts. The educable mentally retarded are seldom able to distinguish between essential and non-essential factors in trying to solve personal or financial problems.

They find it difficult to apply separate qualities to the solution of problems. They have difficulty in making a transfer of learning from one area to another. Wallin states: "A concept is, in effect, a condensation of experiences into a shorthand of thought, a 'rolled-up judgment.'" Since the retarded child seems to lack the ability to condense, classify, transfer and generalize, his use of the language will necessarily be limited. Abstract terms, such as *four*, *multiply*, *sympathy*, are difficult to understand. In developing concepts, the teacher should not only be explicit but use simple language. She should use a variety of experiences and demonstrations to ensure comprehension and retention.

Inability to Evaluate Efforts. The mentally retarded have little ability to evaluate their own efforts. The teacher should give deserved praise to strengthen confidence in their ability to perform designated tasks. Conversely, she should also quietly point out defects in workmanship and give help to develop better skills.

Narrow Range of Interest. Frequently the children of this group, because of poor ability to observe and make use of previous experiences, are lacking in a knowledge of common events and places, as well as in good manners, morals and ethical conduct. The teacher should provide for special instruction and activities to promote the attainment of these qualities.

Their range of interest may be stimulated and enlarged by field trips, by telling stories, by films, film-strips, music, making up little plays, making interesting bulletin boards, tours of the school building, school grounds, experiments, and class discussions. The teacher should frequently call the pupils attention to the environment, and to outstanding as well as to small events.

Difficulty in Recognizing Boundaries. The mentally retarded child usually does not recognize boundaries. This characteristic applies to his dealings with such things as physical and moral issues or property rights. The boundary of the child's playground may be outlined with shrubbery; yet he is unable to realize that the property outside of that boundary belongs to someone else.

This child may walk about the classroom to get a drink and start back to his seat. On his way he may see a pencil on a desk

3. Bulletin board for a study of the community.

that he needs for his seat work. He picks it up and carries it to his desk, where he uses it to work his problems. Afterwards, although he no longer needs it, he does not return it to the owner.

The educable mentally retarded child does not readily recognize the shapes of objects, such as circles, squares, or oblongs. He has difficulty in associating the name and the shape of the object. This same difficulty appears when he is asked to identify his cap, gloves, or a painting in an unfamiliar setting. However, when he does recognize his belongings, he is usually fiercely possessive.

Difficulty in Distinguishing Right from Wrong. The inability to distinguish right from wrong frequently causes the mentally retarded to become involved in actions leading to the juvenile court. The teacher must realize that, because these children are usually unable to generalize, they should be taught definitely that certain actions are *right* or *wrong*. The teacher needs to be alert to grasp every opportunity to impress upon the mentally retarded the highest social and moral values. Ingram states that the retarded are "limited in ability to anticipate consequences," which is shown in their lack of comprehension of the results of going with the wrong friends, or of carrying out a dare such as throwing a rock at a window, or using unseemly language in public places.

These young people argue wildly and get into fights because they are not able to tolerate any opposition. When they argue they do not advance reasons, they usually just call back and forth something like, "It isn't," "It is." They have one name for an object and if a person calls that object by any other term they think it is wildly hilarious and an occasion for ridiculing the person.

Emotionally Unpredictable. The mentally retarded seem to be lacking in some factor that produces emotional stability. The unexpected situation throws them into near panic. The accident, or the practical joke causing a near injury is sure to provoke laughter. The tack on the chair on which the person sits, is considered very funny. An episode like that may upset the group for half an hour, and require an entire change of program before order is restored.

Jokes must be very simple and to the point, for the meaning to be caught. Witty remarks are lost as the words convey no meaning. Their fun is in the ridiculous, the clowning, the unexpected. Sometimes they are very sympathetic and will take the part of one of the group that is being mistreated either by one of the class or by an "outsider." Tattling is common until junior high school age. The younger child will become agitated over an insult or slight, and will come to tell the teacher about it. Sometimes many of his classmates will accompany him, and will add their versions of the story.

Ability to Be Loyal. Once the mentally retarded person has accepted the teacher or employer, he has a strong sense of loyalty and attachment for that person. Once a place has been found for a mentally retarded youth to work, he usually stays there. This capability of remaining loyal to an employer keeps the retardate on the job and he becomes a useful contributing adult. If he is treated with fairness and consideration, he will remain with that person as long as he is allowed to do so.

Ability to Acquire Habits. The educable mentally retarded are strongly bound by habits. The teacher should be careful to prepare all activities in such a manner that the material is presented the first time in the way she wishes the project to be completed. It is difficult to change the procedure of teaching these children to do anything once a habit has been formed.

They must be taught habits of personal cleanliness, physical fitness, social acceptability, and emotional stability. They must learn how to get along with people. They must learn to observe and use the ordinary social amenities. They must learn how to communicate and how to use the different methods of transportation. They must understand the relationship between the weather and proper clothing. They must acquire the habit of seeking help and information from reliable sources when they are unable to solve their own problems.

Physical Maturation. The physical maturation of the mentally retarded approximates that of the normal child. The emotional needs and pressures of both groups of children are similar. Because the retarded child has a limited vocabulary for verbal expression, his feelings become crowded with repressions and frustrations. Consequently, his emotional problems are often greater than those of the normal child. The mentally retarded child requires consistent daily help in attaining manipulative skills. Kephart emphasizes the necessity of teaching the directions, the center of the child's body, left and right, across, up and down. There are many exercises from arm movements across the blackboard to walking a beam to improve bodily coordination.

WHAT IS THE FUTURE OF THE EDUCABLE MENTALLY RETARDED

These boys and girls will develop into homemakers, parents, voters, taxpayers, and consumers. How useful they are to our own town, state, and nation depends largely upon the training they receive during their formative years. Their employment possibility is based upon emotional stability and the ability to take orders and to carry out directions.

SUMMARY

The teacher should realize that the educable mentally retarded have many characteristics that should be considered when she plans activities for them. Because they observe few details of any object or incident, they fail to understand a situation, to recognize an object, or to find a solution to a problem. They are unable to interpret others' actions or to speculate on the results of their own actions. Good habits must be formed through the teacher's presentation of many lessons and dramatizations demonstrating right from wrong.

REFERENCES

1. Allen, Robert M., and Allen, Sue P.: *Intellectual Evaluation of the Mentally Retarded Child: A Handbook*. Los Angeles, Western Psychological Services, 1967. A variety of tests and their uses with retarded children and adults are discussed.

2. American Association on Mental Deficiency: *A Manual on Terminology and Classification in Mental Retardation*, 2nd ed. prepared by R. Heber, Monograph Supplement to the *American Journal of Mental Deficiency*, 1961.

3. Barbe, Walter B.: Who are the educationally retarded? *Education, LXXXV:451*, 1965.

4. Baumeister, Alfred A., Ed.: *Mental Retardation: Appraisal, Education, and Rehabilitation*. Chicago, Aldine, 1967.

5. Baumgartner, Bernice B.: *Guiding the Retarded Child*. New York, John Day, 1965.

6. Birch, Jack W., and Stevens, Godfrey D.: *Reaching the Mentally Retarded*. Bloomington, Ill., Public School, 1955.

7. Blake, Kathryn A., and Williams, Charlotte L.: Induction and deduction: retarded, normal, and superior subjects concept attainment. *Amer J Ment Defic, 73(2):226*, 1968.

8. Bowers, E. M.: *Early Identification of Emotionally Handicapped Children*. Springfield, Thomas, 1960.

9. Buddenhagen, R. G., and Sickler, Priscilla: Hyperactivity: A forty-eight hour sample plus a note of etiology. *Amer J Ment Defic, 73(4):580*, 1969.

10. Drew, Clifford J., and Espeseth, Vernon K.: Transfer of training in the mentally retarded: A review. *Exceptional Child, 35(2): 129*, 1968.

11. Duhl, Leonard J.: Mental retardation: A review of mental health implications. *Amer J Ment Defic, 62:5*, 1957.

12. Dyer, Venita: An example: Reinforcement of principles in a classroom for emotionally disturbed children. *Exceptional Child, 34(8), 597*, 1968.

13. English, Horace E., and English, Ava C.: *Comprehensive Dictionary of Psychological and Psychoanalytical Terms*. New York, Longmans, Green, 1958.

14. Flavell, J.: *The Developmental Psychology of Jean Piaget*. New York, Van Nostrand, 1963.

15. Gold, Martin G., and Douvan, Elizabeth M.: *Adolescent Development: Readings in Theory and Research*. Rockleigh, N.J., Allyn and Bacon, 1969.

16. Johnson, G. Orville, and Blake, Kathryn A.: *Learning Performance of Retarded and Normal Children.* Syracuse, Syracuse Univ., 1960.
17. Johnson, Doris, and Myklebust, Helmer: *Learning Disabilities.* New York, Grune and Stratton, 1967.
18. Kaufman, Harvey: The Slosson Intelligence Test as a screening instrument with a rehabilitation population. Correlates with Wechsler Adult Intelligence Scale. *Exceptional Child,* 35(9): 745, 1969.
19. Kerlinger, Fred N.: *Foundations of Behavioral Research.* New York, Holt, Rinehart, Winston, 1964.
20. Long, John D., and Masat, Larry J.: Implications of the Illinois Test of Psycholinguistic Abilities for teachers of educable mentally retarded. *ETMR, CEC,* 2(3):107, 1967.
21. McCarthy, James J., and McCarthy, Joan F.: *Learning Disabilities.* Rockleigh, N.J., Allyn and Bacon, 1969.
22. Meeker, Mary N.: *The Structure of Intellect: Its Interpretation and Uses.* Columbus, Ohio, Merrill, 1969.
23. Melby, Ernest O.: *The Teacher and Learning.* Washington, D.C., The Center for Applied Research in Education, 1963.
24. Morgan, H., and others: *Feelings are Important to Learning.* Washington, ACEI.
25. Piaget, Jean, and Inhelder, Barbel: *The Psychology of the Child,* translated by Helen Weaver. New York, Basic Books, 1969.
26. Rohrs, Frederick W., and Haworth, Mary R.: The 1960 Stanford-Binet, WISC, and Goodenough Tests with mentally retarded children. *Amer J Ment Defic,* 66:6, 1962.
27. Sarason, S. B., and Doris, John: *Psychological Problems in Mental Deficiency,* 4th ed. New York, Harper and Row, 1969.
28. Stevens, Harvey A., and Heber, Rick, Eds.: *Mental Retardation: A Review of Research.* Chicago, Univ. of Chicago, 1964.
29. Strother, Charles R.: *Discovering, Evaluating, Programming, for the Neurologically Handicapped Child: With Special Attention to the Child with Minimal Brain Damage.* Chicago, National Society for Crippled Children and Adults.
30. Tarnpol, Lester, Ed.: *Learning Disabilities: Introduction to Education and Medical Management.* Springfield, Thomas, 1969.
31. Terman, Lewis M., and Merrill, Maud: *Stanford-Binet Intelligence Scale.* Boston, Houghton Mifflin, 1960.
32. Wallin, J. E. Wallace: *Education of Mentally Handicapped Children.* New York, Harper and Brothers, 1955, pp. 245-266.

33. Weber, Elmer W.: *Educable and Trainable Mentally Retarded Children.* Springfield, Thomas, 1962.
34. Wechsler, David: *The Measurement and Appraisal of Adult Intelligence,* 4th ed. Baltimore, Williams and Sildens, 1958.
35. Weston, Donald: Application of psychoanalytic concepts in evaluation of pre-school retarded children. *Ment Retard,* 2:(1), 1964.
36. Willey, Roy DeVerl, and Waite, Kathleen Barnette: *The Mentally Retarded Child: Identification, Acceptance, and Curriculum.* Springfield, Thomas, 1964.
37. Witty, Paul A., Ed.: *The Educationally Retarded and Disadvantaged.* The sixty-sixth Yearbook of the National Society for the Study of Education, Part I. Chicago, Univ. of Chicago, 1967.
38. Young, Milton A.: *Teaching Children with Special Learning Needs: A Problem Solving Approach.* New York, John Day, 1967.

4

TEACHING TECHNIQUES AND GENERAL EXPERIENCES

GENERAL EXPERIENCES

Special Training Is Necessary for the Teacher. The teacher, friends, and relatives of the educable mentally retarded often forget in their planning or their expectations that these children are sub-normal mentally and that, as such, possess certain inherent disabilities that no amount of training can overcome. The physically handicapped person cannot grow a new hand or leg that has been severed or damaged, but he can learn to get along very well with the use of artificial limbs. The same analogy may be applied to the educable mentally retarded child. He can learn to use the undamaged portion of the brain with the help of well-trained teachers and understanding parents, but he cannot use part of the brain that is not functioning.

The untrained person, through his blundering, hinders the child's progress by disturbing him emotionally. Conversely, the trained person will do everything possible to create successful situations by eliminating feelings of frustration and failure. The school period should be a happy experience. These children are very perceptive of false sentiments and quickly detect anyone who assumes superiority or who does not achieve empathy with them.

Preparation for the First Day of School. The teacher of a group of educable mentally retarded children must plan wisely for each child and for each minute of the day. Before school starts in the fall, she should set up a timetable for such items as report cards, parent conferences, P.T.A. meetings, faculty meetings, room meetings with parents, and professional meetings. This will enable her to prepare adequately for her work ahead of such events.

Supplies for the room should be unpacked and stored ready for use. These should include crayons, pencils, paints, drawing paper, news print, puzzles, games, picture books, building blocks, dominoes, checkers, Lincoln logs, scissors and paste. The teacher will be able with such materials to keep a group of young or intermediate age pupils occupied while she becomes acquainted with them.

The older mentally retarded group are young people who are mature enough to be directed into many activities. Their schedule is usually varied enough to keep them busy the first day.

Pupils' Check List

Pupils' Names	M	T	W	TH	F	M	T	W	TH	F
Larry										
Gary										
Brenda										
Troy										
Sue										
James										
Jeanette										
Steven										
Janice										
Rene										

4. Pupil's check list.

Pupils' Check List. The daily schedule should be prepared ahead of the first day of school and be posted on the chalk board or bulletin board. The pupils names may be prepared on a sheet for dittoing. Names listed with spaces following for daily records, make a simple and convenient form for many check lists and reports.

When the children are known to the teacher before school starts, she may prepare fresh name plates and fasten them to the front of the desks with masking tape. She may also prepare a chart listing duties for the children and a seating chart before the first day of school.

The First Day of School. The teacher should have the room in order and well outlined plans for many activities for the first day of school. That is the most demanding day of the school year. Much of the success of the following weeks depends upon the impression the children receive of the teacher on the first day of school.

If the children's names are on their desks, it is easy to recognize and use their names. This is a good device to help the children get acquainted. They appreciate this recognition.

In order to know each other better the children might relate their vacation experiences. The teacher in turn should be prepared to review her holiday. If she has brought some souvenirs or pictures to share with them, the children will receive greater enjoyment from her report.

A child who is new to the room may be seated near a more mature pupil, who will act as a counselor. The new pupil may ask the counselor for help in pronouncing words or the names of letters in a word. The boys and girls soon understand that this arrangement is not for visiting or playing. Children are often very good teachers, for they remember their own difficulties and are able to put into words an explanation that conveys the idea perfectly to the other child.

The teacher should take time to explain her few basic rules for the group's conduct, the daily schedule of classes and activities, and the room monitors' or helpers' duties.

The teacher should keep the children occupied by attempting to hear some of them read, doing some arithmetic and starting plans for a social study unit. Since the children will be eager to get back into the routine of the school work, they should not be disappointed, but be allowed to do some work at their level of ability.

On the first day of school a tour of the building and the grounds is in order. After new pupils learn what takes place in other parts of the building, they will have less incentive to go wandering about alone.

The children should be shown where to take reports, where to mail letters, where to get the teacher's mail, and where the principal's office is located. They should also get acquainted with the caretaker if he is on duty.

Fire Drill Routine. The route for evacuating the school building in an emergency is usually known in advance of the beginning of school. The teacher should use part of the first day of school to help the children become familiar with the fire drill routine. She should impress upon the children the fact that, since they were just practicing, there is no real danger present.

The various steps in leaving the room and getting safely to the playground should be rehearsed orally several times before the actual attempt to follow through with a drill by the group. There should be at least three complete fire drills the first day. This means the route should be covered exactly each time as it should be done if there was an emergency. The routine, once established, should not be changed in future drills unless an alternate emergency route must be taught as a safety precaution. The children should be taken over the new evacuation route *only* after the first one has been mastered.

The teacher should assign an older responsible child to walk with a younger, fearful, or physically handicapped child in order to reassure and to assist him.

Sometimes the children may be out of the classroom in some other area when a fire drill signal sounds. It should be impressed upon them that they are to go from the building with the person in charge of them at that time. The teacher must make the children understand that *they are not to come back to the home room* for any reason. The teacher should make this a stern command, "Never, never, come back to the room for anything during a fire drill."

A mentally retarded child often becomes attached to some

object—a book, a box of crayons, a shell—and may try to return to the room to retrieve it.

The teacher of the educable mentally retarded should be the one who is responsible for closing the windows and the doors. She should search the rest room so that no child may be left in the building. She should then follow the group out of the room and count the children as soon as possible after they are out of the building. If one child is missing, she should leave the group with a responsible person and return to find the child.

Since a fire drill is an emotional experience for children, they should be closely guided and guarded from the time the fire alarm sounds until they are safely back in the room. The educable mentally retarded children must be so well trained that habit takes over in an emergency; otherwise, they will panic and be a menace to other children as well as to themselves.

Delegating Routine Tasks. The teacher should assign the room duties and assure everyone that these will be rotated so that some time during the year each one will be a helper for each duty.

Each child's name may be printed on a strip of paper with a felt-tipped pen. The strips of paper with the names on them may be attached to the chart listing the room duties. Special adhesive plastic disks, which may be used on the paper, allow the teacher to reassign duties without rewriting the pupils' names. The new teacher will need to try out the pupils for duties. Help the ones you have selected to be successful. Later in the year the pupils may select their own duties helpers.

The room duties may be as numerous as the children in the room or limited to make the helper an envied person. The list might include taking attendance reports to the office, passing the wastebasket, serving lunch, and collecting the lunch money.

The children, who quickly learn where the supplies are kept, are adept at passing out materials as they are needed. Since the children take pride in doing these things, they should be allowed to do as many as they can learn to do well.

Training a child to perform a routine correctly is time-consuming, but it is worth the time and effort in saving the teacher steps, and in giving the child the personal satisfaction derived from this small responsibility.

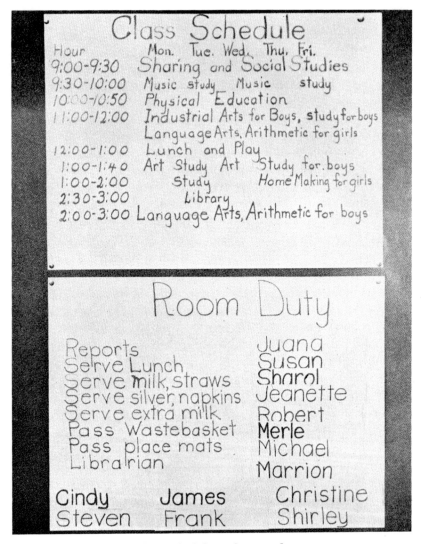

5. Class schedule and room duties.

The appointment of one of the older children as a room librarian offers an opportunity for the use of good writing ability. A child who is willing and able to be gracious, yet persistent, in collecting the books will be a good librarian.

Carrying out room duties helps to develop such qualities as a feeling of confidence in one's ability, satisfaction in carrying out an assignment, dependability, punctuality, and cooperativeness.

Responsibility for Attendance Reports. The teacher should prepare a simple seating chart by using a small pocket chart in which she places the children's name cards in positions corresponding to their seats in the room. The desks have been previously labeled with the children's names.

A pupil helper may take the attendance record and report it to the office. He will soon learn how to check the chart and the desks. He can copy the absentee's name from the desk, remove the corresponding card from the chart and place it on the teacher's desk for her convenience in recording the absentee's name in her record book.

Simple Room Routine. Before school starts each morning, the teacher should have a lesson plan prepared with materials and equipment ready for carrying out the scheduled activities. The materials should be located conveniently to eliminate the necessity of leaving the class unsupervised. Interesting and constructive individual work should be available when the group activity has been completed.

The teacher should be careful to present any work in the same way she expects it to be completed. The routine of the daily activities should be kept simple. Confusion can be avoided by anticipating necessary changes.

As soon as the children gain confidence in the teacher and acquire a feeling of belonging to the group, the teacher may talk to them about room privileges. They should be told that certain things may be done without asking for permission, such as sharpening a pencil, going to the rest room, or getting a drink.

Impress upon the children that one rule must be observed: *Only one child may be walking about at a time.* This helps the children acquire a sense of group responsibility. It also prevents many time-consuming interruptions for the teacher and other members of the class.

Temperature and Ventilation of the Room. The physical aspect of the classroom is important in management and discipline. If the children become restless and start moving about, or a buzz develops, the teacher must interrupt her routine at once and seek the cause. The air in the room may be too hot or too cold, the light for desk work may be too glaring or too dim, or the children may need a change of activity.

Relaxation for the Pupils. The teacher should attempt to reduce tension or restlessness in the pupils by introducing different conditions and experiences. She may adjust the lights or ventilation and proceed to initiate some group activity. This may be a game such as "Do What I Do," in which any activities performed by the leader are imitated by the entire group.

Choral readings and finger plays with rhymes are relaxing. The teacher can read the rhyme, and the children will soon learn it as they act it out. They enjoy chanting a refrain or being an echo. After five or ten minutes of relaxation the pupils should be ready to return to their regular assignments.

Seat Activities. When the children are through with the skill subjects, they often have some time with nothing special to occupy their minds or hands. The teacher should have material available for some purposeful activity.

For the younger group these may include perception materials for training discrimination in likenesses and differences, tracing materials for training letter and number form recognition, and simple games and puzzles.

The intermediate group may have number and word games, clay for modeling, paints and paper for painting, and simple craft activities.

The older groups of mentally retarded should not have a surplus of time, since they are busy with vocational training, as well as with regular academic and non-academic activities.

There should be one definite restriction concerning the use of the above mentioned materials. The children must complete their assigned lessons to the best of their ability before they are free to use the extra materials. The teacher may make quick spot checks to assure herself that the children are not abusing the privilage of this free, quiet activity.

Experiences. First-hand experiences are best remembered by any child. This is especially true of the mentally retarded. There should be practice in the school room with many lifelike situations. The lunch period provides an opportunity for a real experi-

6. The Grocery Store.

ence. Another first-hand situation is the field trip, where processes or objects may be viewed in their natural setting.

Devices may be used in the classroom to imitate first-hand experiences. One such helpful device is the store within the classroom. The children may set up the store with counters, shelves, shopping carts, or bags. They may change the kind of merchandise displayed to provide new experiences. The store may become a grocery store, a pet shop, a hat shop, or a filling station. The shelves and counters may be rearranged to accommodate the new labels and containers or pictures of articles for sale.

By learning how to buy and sell different articles, the children will see a practical use of money and learn the value of knowing how to make correct change. They learn how to interpret weights and measures, how to use the telephone correctly, how to tell time, and how to compare prices and values.

In connection with such studies, auditory and visual aids should be used as frequently as possible. These should include films, filmstrips, recordings, field trips, pictures, and models. The children may also work with many materials and achieve a finished product.

The teacher must be responsible for arousing the interest and understanding for activities she initiates. The educable mentally retarded have little knowledge of materials or topics available for study. Since the children's experiences are usually limited on these matters, the teacher is only hampering the program by prolonged planning with the group; however, she must follow through on ideas suggested by the children wherever it is feasible. By keeping assignments within the level of their ability, she can win their confidence so that she is in a position to offer help where it is needed.

Activities Scaled to Ability. When the teacher starts to work with a new pupil, she has difficulty in determining his ability level in the various areas. She is eager to start him at as high a level as possible. The child usually agrees with any suggestion made by the teacher about where to start reading, whether in first or third grade material. Therefore, he should be tested for correct placement before being given an assignment.

The teacher of the educable mentally retarded in any situation must be alert to the child's need for assistance in academic, as well as in art and craft work. If the academic material or any other activity seems to be causing frustration, she should assist the child to complete the lesson or article.

If this cannot be managed, the child's sense of failure may cause a serious emotional block to his future development. In any case, to help prevent such an occurrence, she should start another activity for him scaled to a lower level. He should be urged and helped to complete this activity so that he feels successful. The teacher's smile of approval for his little achievement will make him want to try again.

Giving Directions. When working with the educable mentally retarded, the teacher should outline and explain the activity step by step until he is able to carry out the work unaided. He will then achieve confidence and satisfaction in performing alone.

To avoid confusion in the children's minds, the teacher should state one thing only and explain that. She should question the children to determine their understanding of the statement or directive. They hestitate to ask questions. They may not want the teacher to know how little they understood of her explanation. They may not be aware of their own lack of understanding. Fre-

7.   Boys working at crafts in the classroom.

quently a commonly used word, such as *over*, needs an explanation which must be taught and retaught until the meaning has become a part of the child's vocabulary. Along with the problem of learning to use simple terms, they have great difficulty in understanding directions.

For their future success as employees, the educable mentally retarded must be taught to follow directions implicity. Since these children need so much assistance in learning any activity or procedure, the teacher must have patience as well as persistence. She must also know the value of securing complete attention before starting to give any instruction.

Procedure for a Group Activity. As the teacher stands in front of the group, she should speak quietly, but firmly, and assume an attitude of expecting attention. She should request that the desks be cleared of all materials. After that has been done and the children are facing her, she is ready to begin her lesson.

The teacher should remember that the mentally retarded's attention span is short. She should be prepared to take instant advantage of that quiet hush when all of the children are looking at her to present something that will provide motivation for them to continue listening. It is also at such times that she may give most effectively the directions which are most likely to be remembered.

This procedure preparatory to any group activity should become automatic with teacher and pupils. These mentally retarded children are creatures of habit, who will work best under direct supervision. The teacher has the responsibility to instill the habit of following directions carefully and of completing assignments. The mentally retarded must acquire good working habits in order to become self-sufficient adults.

Procedure for a Choice of Activities. In speaking to the mentally retarded, the teacher should learn to be careful of her selection of words. A directive should be so plainly stated that the child has no doubt as to whether he has a choice or is expected to actually perform the request, which should be reasonable and consistent with the known performance ability of the child. The teacher should keep in mind the fact that the mentally retarded child is a literal-minded person. For example, if the teacher asks, "Would you like to play 'Green Light, Red Light'?" and the children say "No," she must suggest another game. If the teacher says, "Let us get ready to play 'Green Light, Red Light,'" there will be no confusion and most of the group will enjoy the game.

The teacher must be prepared to abide by the group's decision if she asks for a choice or an opinion. There are many times when the children should be allowed to make a choice. Training is required to help them to know the correct choices to make under various circumstances.

Stimulating Experiences for the Mentally Retarded. An educable mentally retarded child needs stimulation and assistance in understanding everything, far beyond the requirements of the usual child. He needs to learn that he must keep at the task to make progress. The teacher should know that he cannot be hurried or nagged; instead, he should be guided and stimulated. He should be helped to finish anything he starts so that he will have the satisfaction of completing a project. If he becomes tired and the teacher is not securing the response and interest she had planned, perhaps the lack of cooperation is in the teacher's enthusiasm, in the quality of the materials, or in the method of presentation.

To spare the child the feeling of defeat, the teacher should bring the unsatisfactory project to a close as quickly as possible and start on something that does have interest for both her and the pupil. The pupil's interest and enthusiasm will correspond to that generated by the teacher.

The educable mentally retarded, who thrive under kindly, stimulating supervision and teaching, are usually amenable to suggestions. The teacher must organize activities within their ability so that every child has an opportunity to be important. This applies to every area of contact, whether it is art and craft work, physical education, homemaking, shop work, supervised play period, library period, a unit of work, or basic skills. The ego of these children must be bolstered with activities that give them feelings of security and self-respect.

Importance of the Teacher. The teacher must be flexible in her manner of presentation of any activity or experience. She should be willing to accept these mentally retarded as ones worthy of her time in preparing suitable work and activities.

Though the potential of no person may be predicted accurately, due to the many physical, emotional and environmental factors that may be involved, these children, who are functioning within the range of the educable mentally retarded, must be regarded as, and taught as, mentally sub-normal children. If they are handled correctly, the pseudo-retarded may break through their barriers and begin to function closer to their true ability.

The importance of the teacher cannot be over-emphasized. She must be kind, loving, and sympathetic without being sentimental. She must be possessed of unlimited patience and perseverance. She must possess creativeness and enthusiasm, as well as a broad academic background. She may be young or old. These retarded children respect and love a teacher because of her attitude toward them, and because of the security and interesting experiences she gives to them.

DISCIPLINE

Discipline for a New Group. When a teacher is starting with a new class, her future success often depends upon beginning as a strict disciplinarian. After the children learn how to fit into the class routine, how to behave toward each other and the teacher, and how to cooperate and to work as a group, discipline may be relaxed. When the children forget or become careless about rules and liberties, discipline must again be enforced.

Trouble Symptoms. The trained teacher recognizes symptoms of trouble and is always alert to prevent its development. If there are confirmed trouble makers in the class, the teacher should not turn her back to the group. She must know what is going on at all times. She may avoid trouble by directing a special activity which removes the instigator from his immediate environment. The child may return a book to the library, adjust the ventilation, perform some duty in the work room, or work for a while with the paints or clay.

A session with paints or clay has a tendency to relieve pent-up inner feelings, provide for relaxation, and assist the child in regaining control of his emotions. Such activity must be entirely unsupervised to be of any value. The teacher should not seem curious about what the child is doing; however, if the child wishes to share what he has completed by showing it or talking about it, she should take the time to look and listen.

Control of a Group. The teacher can control the group more successfully with gestures and smiles than with spoken commands. She should talk only when the children should listen and speak clearly and only loudly enough to be heard throughout the room. Her directions should be in simple, but detailed form. When children know what the teacher expects them to do, they are usually happy to comply. The child who does not understand and is afraid of failure may be the cause of dissatisfaction among the others in the group.

Value of Praise. The educable mentally retarded child should be encouraged to evaluate his work fairly. He has failed so often that he frequently remarks in advance of presenting his work, "It's not right. It's no good." He says this to preserve his ego if the teacher should find a mistake in his work. If this child has experienced the defeat of being in a regular room, he feels from previous experience that his paper will soon be covered with red marks denoting failure.

The teacher, before pointing out any mistakes on a paper, must find some opportunity to give the child a word of praise and encouragement. He must be reassured that he is loved and appreciated. The two may talk about something not related to school. Such a conversation could be more beneficial that day than an arithmetic lesson.

When the teacher does check the arithmetic paper and finds many examples are incorrect, she should not point out all of the errors at one time. Such mass failure overwhelms the child. If possible, she should find the correct ones and point them out to the child before showing an incorrect answer and explaining why it is wrong.

The teacher assumes the attitude that the child wants to do his work correctly and that he expects her to be the one to help him. She should be matter-of-fact about explaining the process so he understands it. If it is apparent the child is attempting to work with material too advanced for his ability, she should substitute other work sheets for him to do. The child should not be asked to erase incorrect answers to many examples and rework them. He should be given a clean work sheet and allowed to start again.

The teacher's attitude of fairness, interest, and firmness will usually overcome the child's tendency to defeatism in the face of criticism. The child's realization that everyone must learn to accept criticism when work has not been done correctly should lead him to want to remedy his errors and do work that will gain praise.

Difficulties Between Pupils. When difficulties arise between pupils, it is seldom wise to force an issue before the class. The ones who have been having trouble should remain isolated until they have time to lose some of their anger and the teacher has had time to consider the matter objectively.

Since a child needs to save his dignity, the teacher should talk privately with each participant to get his own version of the story. Punishment, to be effective, should be suitable and immediate. After the punishment is completed, the child should resume his place in the class and be reassured by the teacher's attitude and actions that he has her love and interest.

Right and Wrong Behavior. Threats, arguments, and lectures are idle gestures with the mentally retarded. It is necessary to definitely teach that certain acts are good and right and that others are bad and wrong. They should learn that certain acts are socially acceptable, while others are not acceptable. *These children must be led and directed*, for *they are the followers in our world.*

TEACHER-PARENT RELATIONSHIP

Counseling with Parents. The teacher should be thoroughly familiar with the case history of each child in her group. She should know his social and economic background and his medical history, as well as his academic and psychological test results. Complete copies of all of this material should be in the files of the teacher, for her usefulness to the child depends upon her knowledge of his experiences. This confidential material should be provided for the teacher without her request and should be kept in a locked file.

After the teacher becomes acquainted with the child and his case history, she is in a position to talk with the parents in an intelligent manner. She is unable to offer constructive help if part of the child's life is kept secret from her. She needs to know whether the child is an epileptic, whether he is receiving medication, whether he is asthmatic, or whether he must have a special diet.

When the parents come to the school for their first meeting with the teacher they should be aware of the purpose of the conference. She may establish good rapport if she can talk about the child's physical condition and then guide the discussion to the child's mental problems. The teacher should have a definite plan for each conference. Reports, samples of work, texts used, work books, and drawings should be ready to show and be discussed. Make notes of specific questions you would like to ask about the child's habits at home.

Here are some suggested questions for discussion with the parents during an interview.

1. How does he react to coming to school?
2. What are some of his likes and dislikes?
3. Has he had a recent illness or accident?
4. How does he react to a doctor or a nurse?
5. Does he sleep soundly or fitfully?
6. Does he talk about dreams?
7. Does he talk to you about other things?
8. Does he have anything troubling him? Any fears?
9. Does he assume any responsibility at home?
10. How does he spend his time out of school?
11. Does he obey directions?
12. Is he courteous?
13. Does his self-confidence need a boost?
14. What is his response to rules at home?
15. What is his reaction to not having his own way?
16. What discipline works best with him at home?
17. Do you look at his work when he brings it home?
18. Do you comment on it and encourage him?
19. What hobbies, special interests, and abilities has this child shown at home?

Listen to the parents as they talk, consider their remarks carefully for clues to help you work more closely with the pupil. Then have your comments ready: praise the child where possible, and be considerate in expressing concern regarding his misbehavior or seeming inability to perform up to his level of ability. Show the parents that you respect and understand their problems, that you are sympathetic with them, that you are kind with the child but you must also be firm if he is to benefit from being in school.

When parents ask what they can do at home to help the child, suggest materials and activities that are different from those carried out at school. The child should have a chance to change the pace and have a new interest at home.

Many of the children are able to participate in Scout groups. There are special manuals with instructions for assisting boy or girl Scout groups. Such an activity has many advantages for the retarded child. There are many educational toys on the market for parents to use to good advantage.

Suggest the child be allowed to participate in home activities, be allowed to learn to care for his person, to care for his room, to help with the yard or general housekeeping. Suggest that discipline be maintained, that rewards be given for tasks well performed, and that these children be consciously taught the many things their siblings learn by observation.

The rewards system has been tried in many schools and found satisfactory in reducing inattention and thereby aiding in retention. It appears to be helpful in securing better discipline. Mr. Killian, Director of the Denton State School, explained their method, which seems typical of several other schools' approach.

At Denton, the profoundly retarded are rewarded immediately with m & ms. The trainable group use large washers which they place on hooks on a board by each child's name. For misbehaving, a washer is removed from the board. The washers are exchangable for privileges. The educable group use a card and a chart. The names are listed and records are kept daily of merits and demerits. The merits are exchangable for money to go shopping to buy anything they wish.

Keep the conference on a professional level by avoiding personal questions or by criticizing the parents methods. Accept the parents as they are and proceed from that point to try to make helpful, realistic suggestions for the child's future. Most parents respond to genuine interest. Questions should be answered truthfully and carefully, so that parents will develop confidence in the teacher.

If the parent makes a suggestion give it thoughtful consideration. Some part of the idea may be useful. The parent will be pleased, and you may discover that the child will perform better for knowing the idea came from his parents.

When a pupil is present at a conference, he should be allowed to express himself regarding the situation that caused the meeting to be held. Try to discover what the child would like to do about the matter. What would he like to have you do. If the parent's are questioning the child's placement, or you desire to emphasize improvement, or lack of it, the pupil should demonstrate his ability in the area being discussed.

The teacher finds frequently that the parents have not been told or have not been convinced that the child is mentally retarded. They are worried and disturbed over his condition. The teacher is often the one who has the responsibility for counseling with the distracted parents and helping them adjust to the idea that the child will never be able to become the doctor or lawyer of their dreams. The teacher must guide them to accept the child and to love him for himself alone, rather than to reject him because of his disabilities.

Counseling with the parents may also help to win acceptance for the mentally retarded child in the family circle. Siblings frequently cause as much difficulty as parents in the emotional life of the mentally retarded child. The teacher should be able to direct the family to a mental health clinic where trained guidance can be given to prevent the disruption of a family.

Conferences with the parents should be arranged once each semester. If the school approves or requests home visits, these should be made in the early fall. Later the parents should come to the school for conferences. At that time the matters of health, regular attendance, discipline, plan of reporting progress, and room procedures and regulations should be explained by the teacher.

Much of the need for discipline will be eliminated if the teacher has established a cordial and sound relationship with the parents. After the teacher understands the parents' feelings, she can help them to understand their child. Most parents want to follow the plan that is best for the child.

Try to impress upon the parent the value of consistent daily discipline. If the child pouts, ignore it, but stay with the child until that task is complete. Each day, some task must be accomplished correctly, until habit takes over.

The alternative is not appealing, a pouting, grumbling adult, making demands upon everyone in the family. This individual could become a helpful, partially or wholly self-supporting adult with proper training. The retarded child needs love, but also firmness, not indulgence. Make life interesting for the retarded, expand his horizons, give him self-confidence through good habits, and by leading from one small success to another.

The teacher might ditto a few suggestions to give to the parents at the close of the conference.

SUGGESTIONS TO HELP YOUR CHILD

1. Give one direction or command at a time. Follow through.
2. Give deserved praise, but do not praise slipshod work or performance.
3. Do not laugh at mistakes or silliness.
4. Insist on doing each task correctly.
5. Insist upon repetition to secure accuracy.
6. Do not allow the child be a tyrant or the "boss."
7. Do not be unreasonable, but stick to basic rules.
8. It is the parents' responsibility to initiate and carry out proper instruction and discipline.
9. Your child's respect is won by insisting on work being completed, messes being cleaned up, and belongings being kept in an orderly manner.
10. Love your child and appreciate all the things he CAN do.

Reporting Child's Progress. Reports on progress for the educable mentally retarded usually do not follow the same form as those used by the regular grades. There is no group competition for grades among the mentally retarded, for every child proceeds at his own rate of progress.

To satisfy the child and his parents, the teacher may send out a statement at regular intervals to coincide with the other reports from the school system. This is usually a summary of work done as a group, an evaluation of progress according to ability in the basic skills, a health report, and an attendance report.

Near the close of school the teacher may hold a second conference with the parents. If they are seen at meetings or other times, or if problems have been discussed over the telephone, the spring conference may be cancelled. At the close of school she sends a letter to the parents, which gives them detailed information concerning the child's progress and makes recommendations for the following term of school.

A Report to Parents

School ....

Report for .... *Date* ....

Attendance: Days present .... Days Absent ....

Reading	Social Studies	Physical Education
Writing	Science	Library
Spelling	Music	Industrial Arts for Boys
Arithmetic	Art	Homemaking for Girls

....

Teacher

WORK HABITS

1. Accepts responsibility ....

2. Is neat and orderly ....

3. Uses time, energy, and materials well ....

4. Listens and follows directions ....

5. Completes work started ....

6. Works independently ....

7. Works only under direct supervision ....

8. Works alone with some supervision ....

SOCIAL HABITS

1. Is self-reliant ....

2. Is courteous ....

3. Is dependable ....

4. Accepts criticism ....

5. Respects the rights and property of others ....

6. Respects authority and obeys ....

7. Is thoughtful of others comfort and safety ....
8. Gets along with his peers ....
9. Shares spontaneously ....
10. Uses appropriate language at school ....
11. Tattles ....
12. Practices good health habits ....
13. Is fearful or withdrawn ....
14. Practices self-control ....

Reading, Writing, Spelling and Arithmetic are taught to your child on an individual basis or to small groups of children having comparable ability.
(In the actual report card sufficient space is reserved after the name of each subject for a brief summary of the skills and facts presented the past term. This may also include a statement regarding the child's progress and attitude in each subject.)

Staffing, an Evaluation. When a problem develops concerning a child that is of concern to more than one person who has contact with him, this may be a valid reason for calling together all of the personnel concerned in any capacity with this child. In some instances a second staffing may be called to include the parents.

Each person concerned should be notified of the time, the purpose of the conference, and be reminded to bring any pertinent information with him for easy reference. Those present should include the school principal, psychologist, teachers in various areas, in some instances the social or welfare worker, school nurse, and the home room teacher. They should be able to present a cross section report of the physical, emotional, social, and intellectual activities of the pupil.

The reports should be discussed and recommendations made for a solution of the problem or to help alleviate the difficulty that caused the original problem.

SUMMARY

Teachers should have patience, persistence, enthusiasm, and creativity. They must have academic ability and proficiency in many areas of teaching to work efficiently with these children who are handicapped with a poorly functioning brain. Teachers of the educable mentally retarded must be able to counsel and work with the parents, as well as the children, in order that these children will achieve ultimate permanent vocational placement.

REFERENCES

1. Auerbach, Aline B.: *Parents Learn Through Discussion: Principles and Practices of Parent Group Education.* New York, Wiley, 1968.
2. Ausubel, David P.: *Readings in School Learning.* New York, Holt, Rinehart, Winston, 1969.
3. Bailard, Virginia, and Strang, Ruth: *Parent-Teacher Conferences.* New York, McGraw-Hill, 1964.
4. Barsch, Ray: *The Parents of the Handicapped Child: The Study of Child Rearing Practices.* Springfield, Thomas, 1968.
5. Beck, Helen L.: *Social Services to the Mentally Retarded.* Springfield, Thomas, 1968.
6. Bender, Lauretta: *Agression, Hostility, and Anxiety in Children.* Springfield, Thomas, 1954.
7. Bijou, S. W.: Research in the application of the modern behavior theory to the education and training of the retarded, In *Community Day Centers for the Mentally Retarded in Illinois.* Springfield, Ill., Dept. of Mental Health, 1966.
8. Bernhardt, Karl L.: *Discipline and Child Guidance.* New York, McGraw-Hill, 1964.
9. Bruner, Jerome S.: *Toward a Theory of Instruction.* Cambridge, Mass., Harvard Univ., 1960.
10. DeLeon, Shirley: *Montessori for Adolescents.* Children's House. Jan./Feb., 1967.
11. Donahue, George T., and Nichtern, Sol: *Teaching the Troubled Child.* New York, Free Press, 1965.
12. Elmer, Elizabeth: *Children in Jeopardy.* Pittsburgh, Univ. of Pittsburgh, 1967.
13. *Focus on Exceptional Children.* Denver, Newsletter Publication.
14. Garton, Malinda D.: *Productive Citizens or Dependents?* In *The Crescent* of Gamma Phi Beta, p. 6, Dec. 1965.
15. Garrison, Karen: *Let's Learn Together.* Children's House, March/April 1967.
16. Gowan, John Curtis, and Demos, George D.: *The Guidance of Exceptional Children.* New York, David McKay, 1965.
17. Haring, Norris C., Hayden, Alice H., and Nolen, Patricia A.: Accelerating appropriate behaviors of children in a head start program. *Exceptional Child, 35*(10):773, 1969.
18. Haring, Norris G., and Phillips, E. Larkin: *Educating Emotionally Disturbed Children.* New York, McGraw-Hill, 1962.
19. Harris, Irving D.: *Emotional Blocks to Learning.* New York, Free Press, 1961.

20. Helfer, Ray E., and Kempe, C. Henry: *The Battered Child.* Chicago, Univ. of Chicago, 1968.
21. Hillson, Maurie: *Change and Innovation in Elementary School Organization.* New York, Holt, Rinehart, Winston, 1967.
22. Jones, Philip R.: Transportation services for the retarded. In Scheerenberger, Richard C., Ed.: *Non-metropolitan Planning for Mentally Retarded.* Springfield, Ill., Dept of Mental Health, 1968.
23. Kanner, L.: *Child Psychiatry. Springfield,* C Thomas, 1960.
24. Kirk, Samuel A., Karnes, Merle B., and Kirk, Winifred D.: *You and Your Retarded Child,* 2nd ed. Palo Alto, Pacific Books, 1968.
25. Landau, Elliott D.: *Creative Parent-Teacher Conferences.* Salt Lake City, Education Association and Utah Congress of Parents and Teachers, 1960.
26. McKensie, H. S., Clark, M., Wolf, M. M., Kothers, R., and Benson, C.: Behavior modification of children with learning disabilities using grades as tokens and allowances as back up reinforcers. *Exceptional Child, 34*(10):745-752, 1968.
27. Montessori, Maria: *Dr. Montessori's Own Handbook.* Cambridge, Mass., Bentley, 1964.
28. National Education Association: *Conference Time for Teachers and Parents.* Washington, D.C., National School Public Relations Association, in cooperation with the Department of Classroom Teachers, 1961.
29. Rasmussen, Margaret, Ed., and Martin, Lucy Prete, Asst. ed.: *Early Childhood, Crucial Years for Learning.* Washington, D.C., ACEI, 1966.
30. Roger, R., Schroeder, W., and Uschold, K.: *Special Education: Children with Learning Problems.* New York, Oxford Univ., 1968.
31. Special Education: *Strategies for Educational Progress.* 44th Annual CEC Convention, Toronto, Canada, April 17-24, 1966. Washington, D.C., CEC, 1966.
32. Stout, Irving W., and Langdon, Grace: *Parent-Teacher Relationships.* Washington, D.C., American Educational Research Association, in cooperation with the Department of Classroom Teachers, N.E.A., September 1958.
33. Storen, Helen F.: *The Disadvantaged: More Effective Teaching.* New York, McGraw-Hill, 1968.

34. Swift, Joan W.: Effects of early group experiences: The nursery school and day nursery. In Hoffman, M.D., and others: *Review of Child Development Research.* New York, Russell Sage Foundation, 1964.
35. Taba, Hilda, and Elkins, Deborah: *Teaching Strategies for the Culturally Disadvantaged.* Chicago, Rand McNally, 1966.
36. Tansley, A., and Gulliford, R.: *The Education of Slow Learning Children,* 2nd ed. London, Routledge and Kegan, Paul, 1965.
37. Tewksbury, John L.: *Non-grading in the Elementary School.* Columbus, Ohio, Merrill, 1967.
38. Thielke, Rosemary: *Montessori in the Home.* Children's House, Nov./Dec. 1966.
39. Wiesen, A. E., and Watson, E.: Elimination of attention seeking behavior in a retarded child. *Amer J Ment Defic,* 72(1):50-52, 1967.
40. Wolinsky, G. F.: Pieget and the psychology of thought: Some implications for teaching the retarded. *Amer J Ment Defic,* 67(2):250-256, 1962.

5

THE CURRICULUM

GROUPS UNDER THE SPECIAL CURRICULUM

The eligibility of children for the special services of a room for the educable mentally retarded is determined by tests and psychological examinations which have been discussed in chapter three. These children are usually separated into five groups according to their chronological age and their physical and social maturity.

The Preschool Group. The preschool group is usually within the chronological age bracket of five or six years to seven years. Like all young children they are restless, and need physical activity for growth and development. They are also very susceptible to distraction and inattention. They are noisy, usually disorderly, wander aimlessly, chatter, and tear things apart. They have no idea of the value or use of any object.

Constructive activities must be planned for the development of physical and mental health, and for intellectual growth which will lead to better social habits. The preschool child should have the advantage of a consistent well planned routine, whether he is at home or attends a nursery school.

The home should begin to train the retarded child for living with others, just as the regular child is trained. This training will take much longer and will be more detailed than with a regular child.

Areas that should be used for training are outlined here with some suggestions for activities and experiences.

Habit Training: Self-help skills:
1. Personal cleanliness—daily inspection.
   a. Wash hands after toileting and before eating.
   b. Comb and brush hair.
   c. Brush teeth.
   d. Control of sneezing, coughing, nose blowing, toilet needs.
2. Clothes
   a. Can dress self—underwear, socks, shirt, pants or dress.
   b. Can put on shoes and tie them.
   c. Can put on wraps and rubbers.
   d. Does hang up clothes and wraps.
3. Mealtime
   a. Wash hands before eating.
   b. Feeds self properly.
   c. Talks politely at the table.
   d. Says, please, thank you.
   e. Cooperates with others by sitting up, keeping feet quiet, and not crowding with the arms.
   f. Helps clean up after school lunch, stacks dishes, silver, carries own tray.
4. Rest and Sleep
   a. Regular bed time and rising time.
   b. Regular rest period.
   c. Bathes with little supervision.
   d. Can put on pajamas.
   e. Can turn back bed covers and get into bed unaided.
5. Is polite and courteous.

Activities to help develop the self-help skills.
1. Large shoe to lace and tie.
2. Board with various fasteners for practice: zipper, hooks and eyes, buttons, snaps, strings to tie, buckles from boots.
3. Playing house.
4. Dressing and undressing dolls.

All of the above activities, and more that each teacher will discover, should be used daily for self-help training.

Physical Training or Motor Coordination. The small muscles are helped to develop coordination through play activities that use the fingers and hands more than other parts of the body. Some of these activities are: string beads, spools, buttons, macaroni; cut out paper (use blunt scissors); tear paper; sew large sewing cards; scribble on large sheets of paper; color with crayons.

The teacher should ascertain that each child knows how to use scissors, before giving general class directions regarding cutting. Those who do not know how to properly manipulate the scissors should be given instruction and practice. There are left-handed scissors for the child who is left-handed. Begin with blunt tipped scissors.

There are some activities recommended to strengthen the wrist, and help the child control and coordinate the fingers. This may be some simple work with clay, such as making clay balls, flattening the balls into forms by using the hands or rolling pins for pressure.

Another activity is dressing and undressing dolls, fastening the clothes; washing the doll clothes and hanging them on a line using spring-type clothes pins. The use of the handles of the scissors to exercise the fingers by opening and closing the blades is a good game to strengthen the fine muscles.

After the child learns how to hold and to manipulate the scissors, he may start to use them by snipping things, such as paper, clay, play dough, or crisp cloth to gradually attain skill.

Sometimes a cardboard guide may be used to assist the child to follow a line. Later he will be able to follow a line on paper or cloth. As he becomes proficient, change his scissors to pointed blades for finer more detailed cutting.

Some activities to help develop the gross muscles are: hammering nails into a block of wood; carrying objects about; tossing bean bags; stacking boxes and blocks; playing in sand; walking on hands and feet playing animal games; walking on knees; crawling; picking things up off the floor; playing house; dusting the furniture; playing teeter-tootter; swinging; climbing on the jungle gym; playing games with dancing or running movements; wading in the pools; climbing stairs; stepping in and out of old tires or ladder rungs; walking on a beam on the floor; manipulating clay; using poster paint on large brushes standing at an easel; finger painting; marching, crawling through a tunnel.

Social Experiences. The preschool pupil should enjoy many social experiences. These may include: talking about a home; visiting a home; making a play house; talking about entertaining guests; having a tea party; acting out the parts of host and guests; serving simple refreshments. At school the children are part of a group. They learn to work together and to take part in school activities.

There are many opportunities for social experiences in the community. Visit recreation areas, parks and museums. Visit the places where the community helpers are working: the post office, the fire station, the police station, a grocery store, a bakery, a dentist, a farm, the school nurse, a bank. Learn about the weather and seasonal changes.

Sensory Training. Train the senses by matching colors, shapes and sizes; by knowing directions; by feeling weights; by listening and recognizing sounds; by touching to determine smooth, rough, hard, soft, and to recognize the shapes of objects not seen as a cup, pencil, spoon, orange, potato, ball; by smelling to identify odors as, vinegar, cocoa, peppermint, vanilla, cloves, coffee, onions, camphor, molasses, perfume; by tasting to become aware of the varied flavors of some foods and condiments as, sugar, salt, lemon, milk, orange, crackers, banana, peanuts, pickle, chocolate, apple, alum, cinnamon.

Train the Speech. Correct baby talk and mispronounced words. If the child has a speech defect or a special problem refer the parents to a speech therapist. Language for the preschool children is usually very limited. They speak in single words, and make many gestures to secure satisfaction for their needs. They must have help to develop a larger speaking vocabulary and to express their meaning vocally by: class discussion, free play time, dramatizations, telling stories, sharing time, keeping the calendar, playing with puzzles, learning the pledge of allegiance, watching and talking about growing things, making observations about coloring, painting, matching objects and pictures, taking excursions and reporting on their experiences, and playing games.

The Primary Group. The primary group of children are usually within the chronological age bracket of six or seven to ten years. They are retained in the primary group three or four years, depending upon their entrance age and maturity.

Since the mental age of these primary children is generally under the age acceptable for academic work, the program here is largely devoted to helping them become socially adjusted and to acquiring academic readiness.

The primary group of children will continue many of these activities until they individually become mature enough to begin some academic training. This training gradually assumes a more important place in each child's program.

Habit training started at the preschool age should be reinforced in all phases of self-help, and courtesy. Emphasize: following directions exactly as given, being reliable, ready to share, punctual, honest, cheerful and friendly. Teach the pupils to be neat about their work, careful not to waste materials, to complete work once started. With good work habits formed in early years, the retarded child has more time to concentrate on other important skillls.

Physical Skills. Some activities for training the small muscles are: color with crayons within limits; follow a line in cutting out; work with clay, poster paint, finger paint, paste, papier mache; cut out finger plays; weave on small hand loop type looms; weave mats on cardboard or wooden frames; and knit on spools or round frames.

Some activities for training the gross muscles are: run, jump, skip, hop, climb, swing, teeter, stoop, squat, stand on one foot and kick; turn forward roll; play hop-scotch; imitate animals and birds to rhythms; play bean bag games; throw a volley ball over a net; throw a soft ball into a low container; ride a bicycle, scooter, tricycle; haul a wagon with a load without tipping it over; walk a balance beam; play action games, folk dances; swim.

Social Experiences. Units of study with field trips and experiences should center around the home, neighborhood, community, and school.

The home—the parents, the siblings, their duties, pleasures, their part in the community life.

The neighborhood— kinds, what makes a good neighborhood?

The community—facilities for work, study, recreation, protection, sanitation; the community helpers.

Safety—to and from school, on the bus, at school, at home, in the community, traffic and its control.

Plant and animal life in the community.

Visit a museum, a zoo, a park.

Plan a party. Dramatize introductions, the use of the telephone, writing notes of acceptance and thank you and regret, how to leave a party, what to say to the host.

Feature special seasons and holidays with films, drawings, and dramatizations. Continue the play house and free play periods, toys, sand box, blocks, jigsaw puzzles, and make use of the calendar with weather and seasonal reports.

Sense Training. Music is used with primary children for many purposes. It is used for listening pleasure, for learning to recognize some songs, and for resting. Brahm's "Lullaby" and Mendelssohn's "Spring Song" may be played softly after a physical activity, while the children rest with their heads on their arms on the desks, or lie on their cots.

Primary educable mentally retarded children learn to sing many songs. They enjoy singing or keeping time to the music by clapping, marching, shuffling their feet, or playing the rhythm instruments. They learn to listen and to move to the sound of music, to identify high and low tones, loud and soft chords, as well as melodies, songs and many kinds of musical instruments.

Another way to help train the senses of the child is to take him for a walk. Point out the things one sees on a walk around the school house: the sky, the clouds, the color of the ground, the plant and animal life, the building and its color and shape. Back in the classroom ask for a description of some thing the child has seen. Ask for a picture to be made of a tree, a bird, a cloud. Ask the child, "What did you see?" This trains visual memory and assists in training for visual discrimination in sizes, shapes, colors and quantities.

Take the class on a short walk in spring and ask them to be very quiet and to listen carefully and to remember the sounds they hear. When they return to the classroom, make a list of the sounds.

Make up little rhymes or jingles to match a sound or word to help increase auditory discrimination. Tell a short story to the class and list the items on the chalkboard that the pupils can recall. Tell a story that contains certain sounds you are trying to establish. Ask for hands to show when they hear the sound.

Speech Training. Special efforts should be made in the primary group to correct slurring, leaving off endings, and omitting syllables. Use choral readings, nursery rhymes, finger plays, or action poems to help the child. The pupil with a special disability should secure the services of a speech therapist.

The Intermediate Group. The intermediate group of mentally retarded children is usually within the chronological age range of nine or ten to thirteen years. These children remain with the same teacher for three or four years, depending upon their entrance age and maturity.

They should be introduced to a curriculum designed to develop academic skills; to continue strengthening abilities in the areas of music, art and health; and to begin new experiences in the areas of homemaking and industrial arts.

Good work habits should have been established in the primary class. There may be pupils new to the program who will require special help in adjusting to different work schedules, to a busy classroom with many activities in progress, to assuming responsibility for completing assignments on time, for cooperating with the group on unit study and other class projects.

Each area of study requires special skills and these must be mastered in sequence if they are to be useful. Slow and patient teaching, step by step, with many repetitions, presented in varied ways, are necessary to establish habits that will help the child develop into a self-sufficient adult.

In the intermediate age group there continues to be present the problem of the wide scatter of academic achievement. The teacher must daily meet the challange of the child who is in the readiness stage for both reading and arithmetic, and satisfy the child who has advanced to the third or fourth grade reading level but has second grade number lessons. Plans must be made to meet all of these differences, to assist all in the mastery of academic skills at their levels of ability, and to present an enriched program through unit work for their general education. They must be prepared to know about and be able to discuss topics of general interest and of common knowledge concerning health, safety, science, music, current events, school events, and social events. The ability to carry on a conversation will cause them to be more widely accepted in the school. They will have more friends as their ability to socialize improves.

Physical Health. The educable mentally retarded profit physically from a well planned physical education program. Activities and experiences should include units of study: *nutrition* —show the good and damaging effects of proper and improper nutrition on the body, posture, disposition, skin, nails, eyes, by film, pictures, talks, and animal experiments—a sample outline is shown in the chapter on Units: *serving foods*—cleanliness of the persons handling food, correct methods of cooking and serving basic foods; *clothing* and *its care;* care of the eyes, ears, nose, teeth, nails, skin, and hair; value of regular rest and sleep; disease prevention.

Physical Exercise. The pupils should have a daily period of physical exercise. These exercises for the intermediate age may include: folk dancing, swimming, musical games, circle games, volley ball, kick ball, soft ball, table tennis, jumping rope, skating, relay races, forward rolls, push-ups, cart wheels. Many of these exercises may be introduced by films, pictures, visits to a class that is able to demonstrate a skill, and then patient detailed teaching of proper procedures.

8. Learning correct balance and posture. Homemaking class participates regularly in Wendy Ward's Charm School, La Grange, Illinois. (Courtesy Montgomery Ward Co.)

Social Experiences. The teaching procedures of the primary group are extended and enriched but many of the same topics are used, new ones are added as the group matures. Some topics useful at this age are: home and family, family and the community; community helpers and services; transportation and communication; holidays; historical characters of early and of present days; conservation of resources; the meaning of an election and the process of voting.

Many of the units should be concluded with a dramatization the children had assisted in arranging, or a field trip to a point of interest.

Sense Training. The training of the senses continues in the intermediate class. The sense of touch is used in tracing letters to gain a tactile impression of their forms. At this age the boys start learning about the kinds of woods, paints, sandpapers, and materials in the industrial arts shop. The girls learn about homemaking, fabrics, textures, and colors.

Speech Training. The training of the retarded in correct speech usage continues in an intensive drive to eradicate lingering baby talk and dropped endings. Some of these pupils may require help for several years.

The Junior High School Group. The junior high school group of educable mentally retarded children is usually within the chronological age range of thirteen to sixteen years. They remain with their teacher for three or four years. The academic and socializing program is continued with this older group. It is augmented by beginning preparation for economic security through pre-vocational training.

The training and guidance for junior high school age pupils should be practical. Guide these young people to know their potential. Show them how to compensate for their disability. Help them to understand the value of each years's training in school, perhaps there will be an increase in attendance.

Stress the importance of good grooming, regular hours for sleep and rest, punctuality, completion of a job on time, an orderly room, desk or locker, proper care of equipment, a pleasant attitude about taking instruction and following directions.

The junior high school age pupils should start to collect information regarding job opportunities in the community. Studies

9. Forming the habit of checking weight regularly. Lyons Township
High School, Special Education Class.

should be made about some jobs that are realistic for future employment. Let the pupils make appointments and secure information about: job requirements, wage scales, transportation costs to and from the proposed job, cost of uniforms if any, laundry expense for uniform upkeep, union membership and dues, lunch facilities, hours required to work, penalty for being late. This type of information will give these young people a feeling of getting ready to go to work, and help them become aware of some of the real problems they will face when they are out of school.

The possibility of being alone and independent should be explored. How would each person manage to live? Where would he live and what would it cost? After the interviews have been made and material collected, the teacher should prepare lessons on the subjects in simple terms. As pupil interest increases the topics will expand and provide opportunity for individual follow-up of jobs. This will be especially helpful to the youth who plans to drop-out at age sixteen.

There should be industrial arts and homemaking classes for both boys and girls. If the school cannot give them two or three periods a week, the home room teacher should be provided with facilities for simple instruction. This usually requires two rooms, with a glass partition, so the teacher can work with some

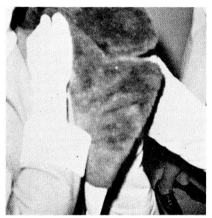

10. Technique for gracefully donning a coat. Homemaking class. Lyons
Township High School.

pupils on an academic basis while others are doing a shop or
homemaking assignment.

The social experiences should include parties, field trips, attend-
ing school events, and visiting each other where possible. The
physical health program should be thoroughly integrated into
the regular classes. These pupils enjoy and can play all kinds of
ball games, kick and throw balls, bat balls, play darts, archery, do
tumbling, push-ups, use horizontal bars, climb ropes, run, jump,
swim, dive, skate, dance—folk and social types. Sometimes an
emotionally disturbed or severely brain injured child may not be
able to participate in group activity. He may be able to assist in
some other way.

Survival Words. This list contains words that each child and
young adult should recognize readily. Some of them may save
a life, others save embarrassment, if understood and acted upon
correctly. Different localities will have a use for some other
words. Each teacher should add to the list or delete as her requirements vary.

Air Raid Shelter	Closed	Down
Bank	C.O.D.	Dynamite
Bell Out of Order	Credit	Electric Rail
Beware	Danger	Elevator
Boy Wanted	Dentist	Employees
Bus Station	Doctor	Employment Agency
City Hall	Do Not	Emergency Exit

Enter
Entrance
Exit
Explosive
Fare
Fire Escape
Fire Extinguisher
First Aid
For Sale
For Rent
Found
Fragile
Fresh Paint
Gasoline
Girl Wanted
Glass
Go
Handle with Care
Hands Off
Help Wanted
Hospital
Hunting Not Allowed
In
Inflammable
Keep Away
Keep Moving
Keep Out
Keep Off

Keep to the Right
Knock before entering
Laborers Wanted
Ladies
Live Wires
Listen
Loitering Not Permitted
Look Out
Lost
Men
Men Wanted
Next Window
No Admittance
No Left Turn
No Parking
No Smoking
No Standing
No Trespassing
Not Responsible
Office
One Way
Open
Out
Out of Order
Pay as you Enter
Poison
Private

Public Telephone
Pull
Push
Quiet
Railroad
Rest Room
Shelter
Stop
Take One
Terms Cash
Ticket Office
Thin Ice
Third Rail
This Way Out
This Side Up
To Let
Toll
Use Other Door
Wanted
Up
Wait
Walk
Watch Your Step
Wet Paint
Women
Women Wanted
Yield

In addition to survival words, Dr. Laura Lehtenin has suggested the retarded will have pleasure and satisfaction from being able to spell names of a few important cities, days of the week, months of the year, the seasons, and for each his own name and address.

The High School Group. The young people in the high school group of educable mentally retarded are usually within the chronological ages of fifteen or sixteen to eighteen or twenty years.

The senior high school presents a great challange to the retarded pupils. At first they are lonesome and lost. The special teacher must guide and support them through this trying period of orientation. The teacher is responsible for finding suitable academic material to sustain enough interest to hold or advance the student's academic accomplishments. The teacher is often responsible for integrating the senior high school student into regular classes in industrial arts, homemaking, and physical education.

11. Helping in the cafeteria. Homemaking Class, Special Education. Lyons Township High School.

The homemaking activities for the junior high or high school pupils should be practical. Many schools are introducing these pupils to simple lessons in nutrition, basic household care, and simple sewing as early as junior high with good results. Certainly by the time they reach high school they should begin to have intensive instruction in these areas.

The boys should have an early opportunity to become acquainted with basic equipment used in industrial arts and crafts. They learn to do precision work and make beautiful objects if properly taught. Boys and girls who have been trained in the proper use and care of equipment, as well as in safety precautions, while in junior high usually meld into the regular classes of high school.

These young people have been observed for many years as they work in the shops, the kitchens, and the craft areas of their various kinds of schools. They enter into the classes with enthusiasm. They do not tire of the repetition of a procedure, so will stay with a job until the product is completed. It is a pleasure to see a youth sanding a piece of wood, and to observe his delight as the wood becomes satin smooth under his care. Or, watch a young woman take a pan of muffins from the oven and test them for texture. Notice her smile as the brown muffin is split open to reveal feathery lightness.

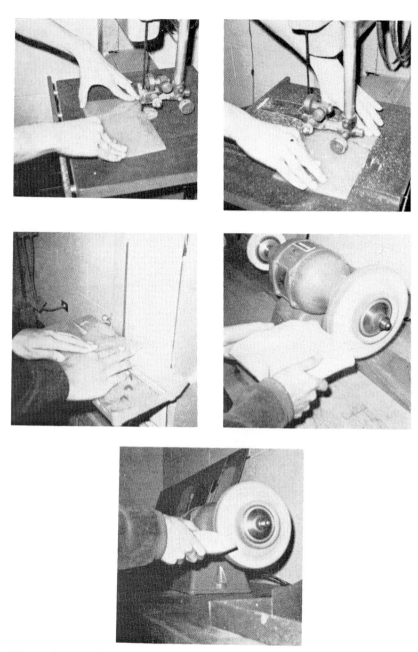

12. Making a plastic tray: a) sawing plastic, b) sawing plastic, c) sanding plastic, d) polishing after shaping, e) final polishing. Industrial Arts, Special Education, Lyons Township High School.

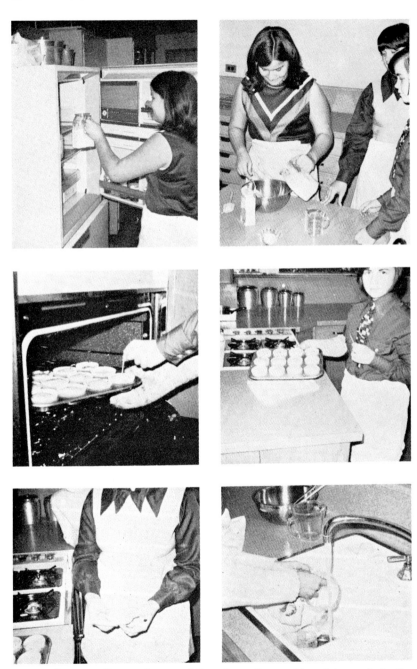

13. Making muffins: a) assembling ingredients, b) mixing, c) testing muffins, d) cooling, e) testing for texture, f) cleaning up after cooking. Homemaking, Special Education, Lyons Township High School.

On a visit to Lyons Township High School, La Grange, Illinois, the young men in Mr. John Russell's class were engaged in many types of crafts. Each worked at his own speed, and each appeared eager to produce a handsome piece of work.

The pupils of Mrs. Helen Stehlik's homemaking class worked efficiently and happily on each visit. One day they made muffins, another day they made fondant for Christmas candy.

These same girls and some of the boys under Mr. Richard Starnes assist in the cafeteria at noon, taking trays, operating the dish washers, transporting food and dishes on trucks, and serving as aides to the ladies in charge. Other pupils of Mr. Starnes were busy assisting Mrs. Pamela Harding in the activity room, operating the ditto machine and collating the pages for later distribution by some teacher to a class.

All of the educable mentally retarded have an academic program geared to their ability. They participate in regular class activity in many areas. They are in regular sections of the school for their academic classes and move from room to room as the others move. They seem to profit from this feeling of "doing as the others do." Their special teacher has no homeroom as such, she follows a rotating schedule from room to room.

As these young people are placed with various high school groups, their experience and maturity, plus the habits they have been carefully taught, result in better cooperation with supervisors and the start of inner control in preparation for community living. These acquired and superimposed habits will carry the individual through favorable and familiar situations. Teachers should realize, however, and prospective employers should be aware of, the probability of relapse under tension and frustration.

Since the retarded have poor judgment, they are often unable to project and deduce the possible results of their actions. Consequently, they are unable to meet the demands of new situations. It is by constant drill on correct habit formation in both action and response that a more secure and responsible individual may be produced.

Social experiences for the senior high school educable mentally retarded pupil are on a functional basis. The field trips, films, visits, parties, luncheons, teas, dramatizations, and job hunting expeditions are definitely pointed to show the teen age pupil how

14.   Making candy: a) preparing ingredients, b) crushing nuts, c) shaping fondant. Homemaking, Special Education, Lyons Township High School.

to take his place in the adult life outside of the home. The teacher is ever alert for on-the-job training situations. He is the contact person for the firm and the pupil. He makes the arrangement for the hours the pupil works, the hours he will be in school, the reports and conferences he will have with the employer and the school.

Larger schools have special teachers to care for the placement of pupils on job training. Some schools do this on-the-job training for the last year of school, on a half time basis, some take it by six week periods full time at work and full time in school, some a semester at a time. The situation varies with the demand for the pupils, the school policy, and the state laws governing such situations.

Transportation and communication units of former years may be taught again with a larger point of view and reviewed as the actual media for arranging interviews for jobs. The field trip that was taken to a hospital or employment office is valuable now. The place does not seem so strange and frightening to the job applicant who must have a physical examination, and fill out an application for a job.

The high school teacher must be thoroughly prepared on many phases of locating jobs. He must be able to teach the young adult how to dress, act, talk, fill out applications, appear at interviews, and how to hold a job once he secures one. He also must teach about budgets, loans, taxes, interest, social security, retirement, savings, insurance, income tax returns, workman's compensation laws, various license bureaus, agencies, and unions. Think of every day living, and there is the field for study for the senior high school mentally retarded youth.

Driver training is important to these young adults, as they definitely will be owning and driving cars. They should have thorough, painstaking training. Those in the range from the middle of the educable group on up, make good drivers if they are properly trained.

As these young people leave the school situation, they should go into work for which they have been partially prepared by their school experiences, which should include on-the-job training.

The teacher must work with the local and state level bureaus of vocational training. At present there are few special residential training centers in the United States for the young adult of educable mental retarded status, who appears to be capable of complete self-support, but for some reason has not been able to secure on-the-job training. This residential training period is from three to six months, then the trainee is placed on a job. Guidance is given to him for a reasonable time so that he feels secure.

The training center program and on-the-job training each has a definite value in the education of the retarded for final complete occupational adjustment. In some high school programs the students work only an hour or two each day and spend the rest of the time in school pursuing academic studies. In other programs the students are on a rotating full time work and then full time school basis.

15.   Cafeteria training: a) receiving trays, b) sorting dishes, c) stacking dishes for the dishwasher. Special educaiton work-study program, Lyons Township High School.

The high school teacher must work out a program tailored to the conditions of the local community. Often there must be preparation for the community to accept on-the-job-training or a training center. Sometimes such a center is first set in motion by an organization of parents and friends of the handicapped. This may include not only the retarded but other handicaps. Such an organization functioned as a Community Workshop and Training Center in Peoria, Illinois. It was sponsored through the cooperative efforts of four community agencies: Peoria Association for Retarded Children, Peoria Area Blind People's Center, Heart of Illinois United Cerebral Palsy Association, and the Crippled Children's Committee, in cooperation with the Illinois Division of Vocational Rehabilitation and the Peoria Junior League.

This center originally started in September, 1960, and had as their motto, "People are our most important product." The small training center and workshop has now been enlarged into The Allied Agencies Center of Peoria where nine agencies work as a team "to provide efficient, economical, thorough service to the physically, mentally, and multiple handicapped through coordinated efforts in therapy, training, education, and research in a centralized facility." The Center was dedicated in the spring of 1969.

Sheltered Workshops and Training Centers. Another development in the program of training and using this retarded segment of our society, is the establishment of Sheltered Workshops. The United States Department of Labor defines them as a non-profit institution designed for rehabilitating activities. In New York, the Sheltered Workshop and training center provides for over one hundred young adults. Zuckerman states, "The facility is in actuality divided into two component parts:—The Sheltered Workshop services for those young adults who are presently doubtful as to their employability and the Training Center which included those young adults who are being directly prepared for employment." This makes a distinction between the Training Center and the Sheltered Workshop that the teacher should remember when approached regarding the establishment of such facilities.

Work-study programs and workshops have been opened in many communities. They offer opportunities for persons who had lost interest in school, or had dropped out to secure more schooling and training for job placement. Some workshops also provide for those unable to meet the stress of work in shops or stores and both train for jobs outside and provide sheltered work areas.

The Opportunity Center, a workshop at Grand Forks, North Dakota, has a well-organized division where training is given in personal care, job opportunity, help with academic subjects, homemaking and industrial arts, and where piece work is done. This Center has a number of agencies involved in its planning and operation; The Grand Forks County Welfare Office, Vocational Rehabilitation Administration, Public School System, Local Chapter of the National Association for Retarded Children, Service Clubs, and many others.

The organization is under a Board of Directors. They have an Executive Committee and an Executive Director. A Personnel Committee and a Fund Raising Committee are under the Executive Committee. The Executive Director has charge of the Bookkeeper-Secretary, Admissions Committee, Clinical Psychologist, Social Worker, Training and Domestic Supervisors.

The Center serves as a training area for students working for a Doctorate degree in Counseling and Guidance at the University of North Dakota. These students are under the direct supervision of a member of the faculty of the University.

A workshop under a similar plan is located in Bloomington, Illinois, The McLean County Sheltered Workshop has students from Illinois State University at Normal working under the supervision of the Head of the Department of Special Education. The

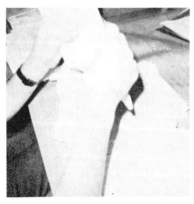

16.   Office work: a) mimeographing, b) collating, c) collating, d) collating. Work-study program, Special Education, Lyons Township High School.

workshop is also open to students of Illinois Wesleyan University, Bloomington.

The McLean County Workshop has a public relations director who carries on the business of the shop, and assists the newly trained workers to secure placement. The workers do small manufacturing jobs and packaging for local companies. This workshop is partially supported by federal, state, and local funds, but the members of the shop produce most of the shop's income from their own labor. Mr. George G. Baird is Executive Director of the workshop.

The Denton State School, Denton, Texas, with a resident population of 1700 has over 500 in classes leading to vocational training. Under the supervision of Mr. E. W. Killian, Director, a sheltered workshop is being prepared on the campus. Many young people have been trained here without such a facility. They have been able to keep jobs and live away from the campus.

This school has the advantage of Halfway houses, where pupils may live while they adjust to their work and an independent life in a community. Some are unable to make the adjustment to the outside world, so they return to the school. There are other Halfway houses established at Austin, Houston, Abilene, Corpus Christi, and Waco. Others are contemplated. This project at Denton is well supported financially and accepted by the people of Denton.

The Arkansas Children's Colony at Conway has a full-time staff of 660 including teachers, nurses, doctors, aides, social workers and others. The many attendants are trained for their work and take additional training on the job.

There are about 900 residents of which 36 per cent are classified as moderately or mildly retarded. For this 36 per cent, a staff of sixty-five, has been provided with thirty-nine classrooms. The program includes academic training, occupational and physical therapy, arts and crafts shops, a speech clinic, a behavior shaping center, a library of over 4500 books, rooms for motor activities and for rhythm and music. The more severely retarded are provided with a good activity program.

The school attempts to train these young people to return to their homes and to adapt to living away from the school. The residents of the Colony are slowly being accepted in the community and are being given opportunities to work as they are trained. These workers continue to return to the Colony each night for there is no other place for them to go.

The Dixon State School and the Lincoln State School in Illinois have programs with similar goals. The Dixon State School has used the Halfway House System for a number of years. Lincoln School operates a large farm and many shops in addition to being used as a research center by the University of Illinois. Both schools give academic and vocational training to residents who qualify, as funds, staff, and facilities are available.

These items are discussed in this chapter to point out the fact that many retarded children are not in public school, many are drop outs, and many are never given any training. With the new concept of practical training for the retarded from infancy to adulthood, parents and youth will become motivated to allow this training to take place. The dedicated teachers in the state schools for the mentally retarded are restoring many lives to happiness and independence, which is the goal of all who work in the area of the retarded. Those who work in other schools often have the added daily help and encouragement of loving parents.

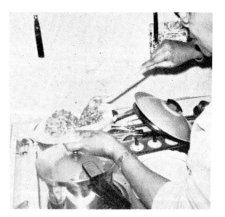

17. Class is instructed in how to apportion lunch servings by Mrs. Mary M. Lockhart, homemaking instructor, La Grange Area Department of Special Education.

Dr. Norman Niesen, Director of the program for the slow learner in the Cincinnati Schools for ten years has rated parental influence as one of the most important factors in the child's success. The parent who cooperates with the school and is interested in the pupil's work, is able to control this child and influence him, and accepts the child's limitations, is the one most likely to have a successful child.

Dr. Niesen explained in a lecture before the Hamilton (Ohio) County Association for Retarded, the value of a work-study program. When he started to institute the program in the Cincinnati schools in junior high and in the secondary schools, people thought it would not work. At that time all of the retarded pupils left school as soon as they were sixteen. Ten years later 85 per cent were completing the courses and graduating. He followed up their work and found that 65 per cent of the graduates had full time jobs and 11 per cent had part time jobs. Most of them had no police records and slight contact with relief agencies.

The La Grange Area Department of Special Education, or LADSE, as it is referred to locally, is an organization of sixteen school districts from DuPage and Cook Counties, for a comprehensive training program for retardates. This is under Public Law 89-10, Title III. The Elementary and Secondary Education Act of 1965, by the La Grange Department of Special Education, is under the sponsorship of Cook County School District No. 204, La Grange, Illinois, Donald R. Reber, Ed.D., Superintendent. Mr. C. Lewis Martin is the Project Director.

The objective of the school is to "give trainable mentally handicapped and lower educable mentally handicapped young adults a training experience that will lead toward a more productive and independent life."

The program is a type of work-study plan. The pupils spend four hours in studies, then four on the job. There are required pre-vocational courses; as: English, history, math, and consumer education. Parental involvement and community cooperation are an essential part of the LADSE program. A twenty-four hour plan is designed for each child through the parents' assistance. The total program places the young adult in a realistic work-world experience with supervision.

18. LADSE trainees in actual shop work: a) assembling spring loading hinge. (Note box of hinge parts and pan of small springs. These must be positioned correctly and a bolt inserted, binding the three parts together.) b) The completed hinge is tested before acceptance.

Care is taken to break down all of the skills into sequential steps to assist in easier pupil understanding and greater achievement. The work shop was a busy place with several operations proceeding at the same time. The project director, Mr. Roland Piller, explained that the group was doing such good work, they were kept busy. Boxes of materials assembled and ready for delivery were stored about the room and other boxes contained materials to be assembled. The day of my visit they were assembling spring hinges at one table, testing them at another table, and preparing them for shipping.

19. LADSE trainee assembling eye droppers.

A second group of young men were assembling eye droppers. A third group were repairing printing press clips for R. R. Donnely Co. This is an exacting procedure of several steps. The young men appeared to have mastered the necessary skills and worked with confidence and precision.

A group of girls under the supervision of Mrs. Mary Lockhart worked in the kitchen preparing lunch. Mrs. Lockhart had taken the girls grocery shopping, where they compared prices, purchased supplies, and were preparing the food to serve at noon. The girls also learned sewing and crafts on other days.

This is the second year for LADSE and this demonstrates how well such a project can be organized when the administrators work together and think of the benefit to the child, to the youth.

The need to develop good attitudes toward daily tasks is an important ingredient of success. The pupil must develop the skills to handle assignments. These things are ever present pressures upon the instructor. Many persons in lectures and articles have emphasized the importance of the pupil learning to accept directions, to be on time, to have tolerance for others, to stay with a job until it is completed, to be present every day unless actually ill.

20.   Craft work of LADSE trainees.

Work-study, or on the job training, emphasizes these factors and helps condition the trainee for a real job. The prospective employee by this time must have accepted his liability, but conversely should have been made fully aware of his abilities. He should realize he is being hired for his abilities. He has an obligation to deliver work on that ability for which he has been hired.

The graduation time is critical for the retarded youth. If he does not have a job ready to start right in working he should be lined up for a workshop before school is out. This, of course, assumes he is capable of being trained for an outside place, if not, a sheltered workshop sould be considered.

Some high school graduates desire to attend a trade school, and some have the ability to be successful. This should be considered. Some trade schools are excellent, and some are not good. Warnings have been issued by several states for teachers to talk with parents and urge them to get the facts concerning any trade school before signing a contract, or paying any money as tuition. Emphasize to the youth and to the parents that a contract is very difficult to break, and a person should take time and study the value to be received. Some salesman may try to rush the prospect into signing as "the opportunity will be gone the next day." Ask the parent to talk with a member of that trade union, or check the school's Federal and State license.

If your school does not have a work-study program for the retarded pupils talk to everyone about it. Sell the program to the administration and to the patrons. Use your influence to secure others to help institute such a program in your area. There the mentally retarded pupils may be trained to develop an initiative for learning basic skills and adjusting to the practical world of work.

As has been previously suggested there should be strong community support for such a venture. Adequately trained personnel should be secured as well as federal, state, and local grants to finance the operation. This is an important part of the work in educating the retarded.

MULTIPLE HANDICAPS

The teacher of any group of mentally retarded children should be alert for the child in the room who is not responding to the program. The child may not be conforming to the expected pattern of the educable mentally retarded because of some physical or emotional disturbance. His non-conformity calls for a careful survey of his case history. A consultation or staffing may be necessary between the teacher, the parent, the school nurse, the child's doctor, the principal, the psychologist, and any other person closely associated with the child's life. The child may need special medication, therapy, or even surgery. He may be a child with a multiple handicap.

Experiences Unfavorable for the child with a learning disability. The child with a special learning disability is frequently placed in a room for the educable mentally retarded. This is not conducive to his academic or emotional improvement, for his requirements are the opposite of the group in which he has been placed. The stimulation that is so necessary for success with the retarded is confusing, mentally and emotionally, to this child. He requires a quiet room with special materials and techniques devised individually to meet his needs.

Strauss and Lehtenin list three areas of disorder of the neurologically impaired: (1) perceptual; (2) thinking, (3) behavior. The child seems able to attend to only one task at a time. The lessons must be centered around one topic, be sequential and well planned. The varied components of the letter and numeral symbols are bewildering to these children. Some methods of differentiating are to use various colors and textures in printing the letters. Many of these same ideas are used with the mentally retarded. Conversely many ideas that are used with the retarded are effective with the neurologically impaired. Cues, colors and markers are used freely.

One method of teaching the form of a symbol is to outline it in about a six inch tall size with a white glue. Let the glue dry. Then fill in between the outlines with a thin coat of the glue and quickly spread over this small smooth glass beads, wheat or other small grains, or mosaic material. This material will offer resistance to the finger tips as the child traces over it, pronouncing the name of the symbol.

The letters or numerals may also be cut out of material of different textures, as felt, burlap, velvet, fine sand paper, rough textured papers, plywood, nylon screen or cotton netting. The letters are mounted on cards of uniform size for ease in handling. Different colors may be used to outline and fill in the letter and numeral symbols. Different colors may be used for the separate parts of a symbol, as in the numeral four, make the straight stem of blue and the "L" shaped part red or orange.

Trace the symbols in clay with a stylus and let the child trace over and over the form, repeating the name or sound you are trying to establish. This must be supervised or the child will aimlessly trace and forget what he is tracing. Unless he repeats and sounds or pronounces there is no value in doing the tracing. Cursive writing is best for this form of tracing as he sees the word as a complete form.

Care must be taken to prevent preseveration in the activities. This is the continuation of an activity once begun, until the child must be compelled to cease. The attention to small details is another obstacle to establishing good work habits, as is the tendency to make irrelevant remarks.

The behavior pattern is erratic and unreliable. The child may be friendly one moment and then perpetrate some uninhibited or even cruel act. There is little attempt at self control. There is much physical activity, talking at random, aimless wandering, and opening and closing of desks.

The neurologically impaired child has a difficult time socially. He does not understand how to be a friend. He irritates people with his actions, repetitive remarks, which are often crude and rude. He will slyly kick or punch someone without a reason, tattle, and will present a general inability to share or to control his emotions.

Usually the real reason for an act is unknown to the child. He may take a devious path to solve a problem. Tom was always following Bill around on the playground and punching him without apparent provocation, tearing up his cap or throwing away his gloves.

Nothing seemed to stop his unexplained feud with Bill. One day as I brought him into the school room after he had kicked Bill, I remarked, "You hurt Bill. You are not able to play with Bill without hurting him, so next recess you wait in here with me, and after they come in from play, you go out and play alone."

Tom looked up, his eyes brimmed with tears, "I want him for my friend. He won't play with me." I finally discovered Tom's chief playmate had always been a much older brother who boxed and wrestled with him. Tom did not know how to be with children his own age or younger. He was too rough. It took about two years help for Tom to become calm enough socially so his peers were not afraid of him physically. He learned to "hold his punches."

It is a challenging task to find something that this child can and will be able to accomplish now. Whatever is found that he will accept and use and be secure in using, should be the foundation for building socializing experiences and for helping him to acquire self-control. Bolster his self-confidence and self-esteem by praise and love for his efforts. A kind word, a smile, a pat on the back are the best rewards a teacher or a parent can give. Try to get the child to say, "I'll try."

Prepare readiness lessons with the idea of eliminating distracting materials. Try to establish good work habits, by presenting one part of the lesson at a time. When that part is completed, try to determine if he understands what he has done. If not satisfied, give him some more work of the same kind but in a different form.

After the child, with a special learning disability, has learned how to study and has overcome some of his perceptual and thinking difficulties, the skills of the basic subjects may be taught. Be certain that each step in the development of any concept is presented and understood.

Concrete devices should be used extensively in teaching arithmetic. This may be in the form of an abacus or other counters. The retention of a concept is reinforced by writing the fact or word and speaking it aloud as it is being written. This technique gives training to the auditory, visual, and kinesthetic senses.

The classroom teacher who has a child with a special learning difficulty should be understanding when he becomes excited and talkative during regular class activities. She may provide him with the seclusion he requires by having a screen placed around his desk, or by excusing him from certain projects and allowing him to rest in another room.

GENERAL CURRICULUM

Scope and Content. The curriculum for the educable mentally retarded must be practical. It should be constructed to suit the child's present and future needs. The scope and content of the curriculum should be determined by his interests and his ability to assimilate it and use it in everyday life.

The curriculum, which includes activities in academic and non-academic fields, should be considered as all of the child's experiences during his day at school. All of these activities should be so arranged and simplified that the educable mentally retarded child will be able to benefit from them. Many of the activities may be integrated within a unit of study; however, the basic skills should have special emphasis.

The teacher, the parent, the welfare worker, the school nurse, and the special area teachers need to work closely together to assist the child in maintaining good mental and physical health.

The teacher must first win the respect of the child and gain his confidence by always being fair and keeping promises. *The mentally retarded child does not take disappointments lightly.*

Areas for Lesson Material. The areas for academic lesson materials should be social situations, social science problems, and health and safety problems. Social experiences help the mentally retarded pupils to appreciate the contributions that others make to our society and to understand that they in turn have individual responsibilities toward others.

REFERENCES

1. Abraham, Willard: *The Slow Learner.* New York, The Library of Education. Center for Applied Research in Education, 1964.
2. Allen, Amy A.: Teaching the social studies for social living: Comprehensive program for the educable mentally retarded. *ETMR, CEC,* 2(3):91, 1967.

3. Allen, Amy A., and Cross, Jacque, Eds.: *Suggested Basic Materials for Slow Learning Children*. Columbus, Ohio, State Superintendent of Public Instruction.

4. Allen, Amy A., and Cross, Jacque L.: Work-study for the retarded. *ETMR, CEC, 2(7)*, 1967.

5. Anderson, Robert M.: Hemenway, Robert E., and Anderson, Janet W.: *Instructional Resources for Teachers of the Culturally Disadvantaged and Exceptional*. Springfield, Thomas, 1969.

6. Barbe, Walter B.: *The Exceptional Child*. New York, Center for Applied Research in Education, 1963.

7. Bitter, James A.: *Work Experience Center: Habilitation of the Retarded*. St. Louis, Jewish Employment Vocational Service.

8. Bluhm, Donna L.: *Teaching the Retarded Visually Handicapped: Indeed They are Children*. Philadelphia, Saunders, 1968.

9. Brown, James W., Lewis, Richard B., and Hardroad, Fred F.: *A-V Instruction Materials and Methods*, 2nd ed. New York, McGraw-Hill, 1964.

10. Button, William H.: *Wage Levels in Sheltered Employment*. Ithaca, N.Y., Cornell Rehabilitation Research Institute, 1967.

11. *Career Opportunities: In the Field of Mental Retardation*. Washington, D.C., U.S. Dept. of Health, Education and Welfare, 1969.

12. Chaffin, Jerry D.: Production rate as a variable in the job success or failure of educable mentally retarded adolescents. *Exceptional Child, 35(7):533*, 1969.

13. Cincinnati Public Schools: *The Slow Learning Program in the Primary and Secondary Schools*. C.B.119, Board of Education, 1964.

14. Clements, Sam D., Lehtinen, Laura E., and Lukens, Jean E.: *Children with Minimal Brain Damage*. Chicago, National Society for Crippled Children and Adults, 1964.

15. Connor, Frances F., and Talbot, Mabel: *An Experimental Curriculum for Young Mentally Retarded Children*. New York, T.C., Bureau of Publication, Columbia Univ., 1964.

16. Coon, Beulah, I.: *Home Economics Instruction in the Secondary Schools*. New York, Center for Applied Research in Education, 1965.

17. Cruickshank, William M., Bentzen, F. A., Ratzenburg, F. H., and Tannhauser, M. T.: *Teaching Methodology for Brain Injured and Hyperactive Children*. Syracuse, Syracuse Univ., 1961.

18. Cruickshank, William M., and Johnson, G. Orville: *Education of Exceptional Children and Youth*, 2nd ed. Englewood Cliffs, N.J., Prentice-Hall, 1967.
19. Drew, Clifford J., and Espesth, Vernon K.: Transfer of training in the mentally retarded: a review. *Exceptional Child, 35(2)*: 129, 1968.
20. Ebersole, Mary Lou, Kephart, Newell C., and Ebersole, James B.: *Steps for Achievement for the Slow Learner*. Columbus, Ohio, Merrill, 1968.
21. *Experiental Development Program: New Readiness for Four- to Six-Year-Old Child*. Westchester, Ill., Benefic Press.
22. Feirer, John L., and Lindbeck, John R.: *Industrial Arts Education*. Washington, D.C., Center for Applied Research for Education, 1964.
23. Frankel, William A.: *How to Get a Job*. Washington, D.C., U.S. Dept. of Health, Education and Welfare, 1967.
24. Fuchigami, Robert: Emerging curricula for the elementary level educable mentally retarded. *Amer J Ment Defic, 7(3)*, 1969.
25. *Functional Basic Reading Series: Pre-primer Through Grades Six*. Pittsburgh, Stanwix House, 1962-69. (Each book on two levels of reading ability, with workbooks and a functional vocabulary. Simple illustrations that appeal to children.)
26. Garton, Malinda D.: How to develop a unit of instruction for educable mentally retarded children. *Ment Retard*, Sept. 1964, pp. 14-16.
27. Garton, Malinda Dean: *Making Friends*. Pittsburgh, Stanwix House, 1965. (Stories for eight- to 12-year-old children.)
28. Gall, Joe: The new adult activity centers. *Motive*, March/April, 1967.
29. Gill, Roy C.: Individualizing the curriculum for the educable mentally retarded high school students through prevocational evaluations. *ETMR, CEC, 3*:169, 1968.
30. Goldin, G. J., and others: Factors in the rehabilitation facility. *Rehab Lit, 29(3)*:66-72, 83, 1968.
31. Headley, Neith: *The Kindergarten: Its Place in the Program of Education*. New York, Center for Applied Research in Education, 1965.
32. Hershenson, David B., Roth, Robert M., and Hilliard, Thomas O.: *Psychology of Vocational Development: Readings in Theory and Research*. Rockleigh, N.J., Allyn and Bacon.
33. Hudson, Margaret W., and Weaver, Ann A.: *To Be A Good American*. Palo Alto, Fearon, 1965.

34. Instructional Materials Center Network for Handicapped Children and Youth. Coordinator: Instructional Center, 1507 M Street N.W., Washington, D.C. 20005.
35. Johnson, G. Orville: *Education for the Slow Learners.* Englewood Cliffs, N.J., Prentice-Hall, 1963.
36. Jolles, I., and Southwick, Selma: *A Clinical Approach to Training the Educable Mentally Retarded.* Los Angeles, Western Psychological Services, 1969.
37. Jordan, Laura: Effective seat work for retarded. *ETME, CEC,* 3:90, 1968.
38. Kephart, Newell C.: *Learning Disability, an Educational Adventure.* West Lafayette, Ind., Kappa Delta Pi Press, 1968.
39. Kephart, Newell C.: *The Slow Learner in the Classroom.* Columbus, Ohio, Merrill, 1960.
40. Killian, E. W.: *Denton State School Report,* Denton, Texas, 1969.
41. Kimberly, John R.: *Professional Staffing in Sheltered Workshops.* Ithaca, N.Y., Cornell Univ. R.R. Institute, 1968.
42. Kimberly, John R.: *The Financial Structure of Sheltered Workshops.* Ithaca, N.Y., Cornell Univ. R.R. Institute, 1968.
43. Kingsley, Ronald F.: Associative learning ability in educable mentally retarded children. *Amer J Ment Defic,* 73(1):5-8, 1968.
44. Kokaska, Charles J.: *The Vocational Preparation of the Educable Mentally Retarded.* Ypsilanti, University Printing, 1968.
45. Kolstoe, Oliver P., and Frey, Roger M.: *A High School Work-Study Program for Mentally Subnormal Students.* Carbondale, Ill., SIU Press, 1965.
46. Kolstoe, Oliver P.: Teaching Educable Retarded Children. Boston, Allyn and Bacon, 1970.
47. Lazarus, Phoebe W.: Cutting, a kinesthetic tool for learning. *Exceptional Child, 31*:361, 1965.
48. Lewis, Patricia F.: A cooperative education/rehabilitation work-study program for educable mentally retarded. *The Essex Plan.* East Orange, N.J., Board of Education, 1967.
49. Litterest, Milton R., and Smiley, Barbara: Interagency coordinating unit. *MR in Illinois, 2*(1):8, 1968.
50. Molloy, Julia S.: *Teaching the Retarded Child to Talk: A Guide for Parents and Teachers.* New York, John Day, 1961.
51. Molloy, Julia S.: *Trainable Children: Curriculum and Procedures.* New York, John Day, 1963.
52. *Mental Retardation in Arkansas: Studies in Selected Services, 1964-1966.* Little Rock, State Board of Health, 1966.

53. McCarthy, James J.: An Overflow of the IMC Network. *Exceptional Child,* 35(4):263, 1968.
54. Montessori, Maria: *The Montessori Elementary School,* translated by Arthur Livingston. Cambridge, Mass., Bentley, 1964.
55. Murphy, William K., and Scheerenberger, R. C.: *Etablishing Day Care Centers for the Mentally Retarded: Guidelines and Procedures.* Springfield, Ill., Dept. of Mental Health, 1967.
56. Neuhaus, Edmund C.: Training the Mentally Retarded for Competitive Employment. *Exceptional Child,* 44(9):625, 1966.
57. Niesen, Norman J.: Organizing for the development of effective curricula for the educable mentally retarded. *ETMR, CEC,* 2:517, 1967.
58. *On-the-job Training Program: Educable Mentally Retarded.* Pocatello, Idaho, School District Number 25, Jan. 1968.
59. Parker, Walter E.: Workships. *MR in Illinois,* 2(2), 1968.
60. Rimmele, Polly Ann Woods: *Step by Step.* LaSalle, Ill., United Cerebral Palsy Association of LaSalle, Bureau and Putnam Counties. Seaton and Sons, Printers, 1967.
61. Rothberg, Jay M.: *Satellite Programs: A Status Report. Exceptional Child,* 35(4):279, 1968.
62. Rucker, Chauncey N., Howe, Clifford E., and Snider, Bill: The participation of retarded children in junior high academic and nonacademic classes. *Exceptional Child,* 35(8):617, 1969.
63. Samoff, Zelda: *Curriculum for Slow Learners, grades K-12,* edited by Morton Alpren. Columbus, Ohio, Merrill, 1967.
64. Scagotte, Edward G.: Tinker Boards—A tactile, kinesthetic approach to learning. *Exceptional Child,* 34(2):129-131, 1967.
65. *Secondary-Vocational Education of the Mentally Retarded.* New York, NARC, 1968.
66. Simpson, Dorothy M.: *Learning to Learn,* edited by N. C. Kephart. Columbus, Ohio, Merrill, 1968.
67. Sharp, Evelyn: *Thinking is Child's Play.* New York, Dutton, 1969.
68. Shores, Lois: *Instructional Materials.* New York, Ronald, 1960.
69. Soforenko, Albert Z., and Stevens, Harvey A.: The diffusion process: A model for understanding community program development in mental retardation. *Ment Retard,* 6(3):25, 1968.
70. Song, A. Y., and Song, R. H.: Prediction of job efficiency of institutionalized retardates in the community. *Amer J Ment Defic,* 73(4):567, 1969.
71. Sparks, Howard L., and Younie, William J.: Adult adjustment of the mentally retarded: Implications for teacher education. *Exceptional Child,* 36(1):3, 1969.

72. Strickland, Conwell G., and Arrell, Vernon M.: Employment of the mentally retarded. *Exceptional Child, 34*(1):24, 1967.
73. Strom, Robert D.: *Teaching in the Slum School.* Columbus, Ohio, Merrill, 1965.
74. Tansley, A. E., and Gulliford, R.: *The Education of Slow Learning Children.* London, Routledge and Kegan Paul, 1961.
75. Turner, Betty: The educable mentally retarded and the junior high school. *School and Community, 54*(3):34, 1967.
76. Turner-Livingston Reading Series: *The Job You Get; The Money You Spend; The Town You Live In; The Person You Are.* Chicago, Follett, 1962.
77. Tudyman, Al, and Grolle, N.C.: *A Functional Basic Word List for Special Pupils.* Pittsburgh, Stanwix House.
78. Tyson, Kenneth L.: *Resource Guide to Selected Materials for the Vocational Guidance of Slow Learners.* Gettysburg, Adams County Public Schools, 1968.
79. U.S. Civil Service Commission: *A Second Look.* Washington, D.C., 1968.
80. U.S. Dept. of Health, Education and Welfare: *Mental Retardation Activities of the U.S. Dept. of Health, Education and Welfare.* Washington, D.C., 1968.
81. Viscardi, Henry Jr.: *The Abilities Story.* New York, Eriksson, 1967.
82. Webster, John D.: *How to Get a Job.* Washington, D.C., U.S. Dept. of Health, Education and Welfare, 1968.
83. Wolfensberger, Wolf, and Kurtz, Richard A.: *Management of the Family of the Retarded.* Chicago, Follet.
84. Zuckerman, George: Helping the older retarded children. *Child Guidance,* April 1962.

6

THE UNIT

METHODS OF TEACHING THROUGH
A UNIT OF STUDY

A unit should provide a complete experience for the child educationally and emotionally. Some of the expected outcomes are learning basic skills, acquiring useful information, and achieving individual success and satisfaction.

As progress is achieved in a study, certain techniques for presentation will facilitate the retention of information.

The teacher will introduce materials and content to the group. This may be followed by a period of discussion. As the subject develops, the pupils will mention pertinent facts which should be listed on the chalk board. The result of such a list should be a story which the teacher writes as the pupils tell it. The story should be read by the pupils. Then it is copied for their booklets.

The next day new or useful words are presented on flash cards. The words may also be written on the chalk board and pronounced by the class.

The pupils may read the story from their copies. The teacher should check the papers to see if the copying is legible and accurate.

The story, which has been written on strips of paper, may then be cut into short phrases and individual words. As the words are shown to the class, the children choose the ones they recognize and build sentences in the wall chart. Many games may be played with the words to ensure retention. *It takes many, many exposures for the retention of a word.*

There must be visual, auditory, and kinesthetic knowledge of the word to make it useful in oral and written language. As the teacher of the educable mentally retarded listens to a child relate a story he has seen on television or heard on the radio, she gains immeasurable satisfaction in recalling that he liked the story because he had learned about one of the characters in school.

AUDIO-VISUAL AIDS IN THE UNIT

Audio-visual aids should be used wherever possible in presenting materials to mentally retarded children. The bulletin board is an important interest center. Proper displays have been discussed in another section, as have the audio-visual, writing and spelling methods and materials.

EXPERIENCE CHARTS

Experience charts are simple stories dictated by the children or prepared by the teacher. These charts, which are printed on lined chart paper, cards, or on the chalk board, are made day by day as the lessons progress. They are excellent for reviewing for content, increasing speed in reading, and assisting in vocabulary retention.

FLASH CARDS FOR WORD DRILL

Flash cards to match the experience charts must be made daily to aid in quick recognition of vocabulary. Health and safety words should also be displayed frequently to keep the child acquainted with words necessary for self-preservation, such as *danger, exit, stop, walk, go, enter, poison, one way, do not enter.* This task may be speeded by proper equipment consisting of lined chart paper, lined sentence strips for flash cards, and felt-tipped pens for lettering. These materials also aid in securing legible uniform lettering in a minimum of time.

THE MODIFIED CORE CURRICULUM

The modified core curriculum as described in this chapter refers to studies dealing with human relationships structured around centers of interest in which the basic subjects are integrated. This plan allows for an overall understanding of some topic, with successful practice on many basic skills. As the areas are explored, the study assumes a lifelike aspect which provides motivation to the pupil for acquiring greater proficiency academically, manually, socially, and economically.

Purpose of the Modified Core Curriculum. The core unit of study provides a practical plan for teaching the educable mentally retarded children. This plan has proved successful in holding interest throughout a series of experiences and activities. It is also useful for motivating the retention of information and basic skills and for teaching other concepts and attitudes which lead to the final objective of producing a self-sufficient adult.

Place of the Core Unit in the Curriculum of the Educable Mentally Retarded. The core unit may be planned for the group by selecting a topic of interest in the area of human relationships as represented in the social studies or science fields, and by grouping materials, activities, and experiences around it from many areas, thus producing a coherent and cohesive unit of study. Such a study could be confined to one segment of a school day or enlarged to occupy all of the school day.

This type of integration should have some place on the daily schedule, even if it is only in a limited segment of time. The children are able to appreciate and understand lessons integrating reading, spelling, writing, social studies, arithmetic, nutrition, health, and safety. The chronological and mental ages, intelligence quotient, maturity, environment, and interests, as well as the ability to profit from activities and experiences, should be considered in planning all units of work for educable mentally retarded children.

Since each group of mentally retarded children will usually have a wide spread of ability in all areas, the teacher will find it expedient to plan work at more than one level. The youngest and the most immature pupils should have some special activities that are interesting and at which they may be successful; conversely, the older children and those with greater ability should have more challenging materials. Although the group may work together on many parts of the unit, they may be separated into small groups for the presentation of basic skills or explanations suited to their requirements.

Sources of Subjects for Units. Educators seem agreed that materials for the educable mentally retarded should spring from realistic situations. After deciding upon the situation and subject, the teacher should look for materials now available in many areas for use with the retarded. Other materials may be adapted. All materials should be screened by the teacher before assignment for class study. If workbooks in a particular subject at the required level are not available, they are easily made by preparing pages equal to the ability of the pupils on ditto sheets, and allowing the pupils to assemble their own books. These books may include the pupils own diagrams, drawings, and stories about the lessons they have been studying.

The teacher must provide the content or subject matter and the background material. She must prepare the details for presentation and for the integration of other areas of study or work. She must plan for all of the activities and experiences in connection with the unit. She must prepare worksheets at several levels of ability to reinforce oral and demonstration teaching. The teacher must coordinate the preparation and presentation of all of these items and carry them through to completion.

As the teacher plans and develops the unit, she must keep in mind the necessity for intensive drill on basic skills and for adequate time to explain every detail. She must remember that the usual child picks up by observation many of the correct social behaviors of our culture, but the educable mentally retarded child does not observe these behaviors unless they are specifically pointed out to him. He will not know the common rules of courtesy and decency unless they are especially taught to him.

The teacher is responsible for building into the units materials and activities that will train the child to have attitudes and habits that are socially acceptable. These should include cleanliness, neatness, courtesy, promptness, honesty, and a respect for property both public and private.

DEFINITION OF A UNIT OF STUDY

Building a unit of work for the educable mentally retarded is an absorbing task that holds interest and rewards for the teacher, as well as for the pupils.

A unit is an organization of experiences and information around some topic of study.

The unit may be one simple, well-rounded endeavor to present a single problem, or it may outline a subject that covers a topic presenting many facets and requiring months of study to complete. Other interesting units may develop spontaneously from either the simple or the complex topics, some of which lend themselves more favorably to broad integration than do others. In adapting the use of the core curriculum to the requirements of the educable mentally retarded, it is not necessary to cover the entire range of civic and human activities or to include every possible opportunity to introduce a basic skill in reading, writing, or arithmetic. If the work is made too complex, the knowledge and the skills may be lost to these children. However, by keeping the structure of the unit simple, the overlapping of the learning areas has a decided advantage, since it helps to fix the information and skills for future use.

Types of Units. There are many types of units among which are the following:

1. *A Resource Unit* contains well-developed ideas covering extensive areas of a general theme. It includes ways to initiate, develop and present material relative to a topic.
2. *A Drill or Topic Unit* is used for the purpose of teaching certain items, skills, or subject matter.
3. *An Experience Unit* is a group of planned life experiences to help the child develop in a social and cultural way according to his needs, utilizing the social, cultural, and physical environment of the school and community
4. *A Project* has a special purpose. This could be a part of a resource or experience unit, as to paint a mural for a play.
5. *An Activity Unit* has a definite goal. The activities are from the interests and needs, and within the.abilities of the group of children participating.
6. *A Block of Time or Core Unit* provides a center of interest for experiences, activities, and learnings, within the topic which is being studied.
7. *The Teaching Unit* is prepared from the resource unit. The topic of the unit is used as the subject of the core unit to be taught. Integrate all reading, spelling, writing, and oral and

written language around the core topic. Other areas may be integrated where feasible, as arithmetic, science, social science, socialization, conservation, and aspects of vocational life.

The teacher is responsible for all materials and content. The retarded do not have the ability to evaluate materials, or to find them unaided for use by the class. With help and supervision the retarded will be able to give back information to the teacher for experience charts, and as descriptive sentences for pictures they will draw about the unit topic. The retarded will learn many new words both orally and by sight. They will learn the meanings of these words, and will be able to add them to their permanent vocabularies. They will retain much of the information taught through the varied activities and experiences.

Selection of a Subject for a Unit. The selection of a topic for study, as well as the wording of the title, is important. If the title of the unit has appeal to the eye and ear, the children will be more interested. The subject should be introduced tentatively by questioning the children. The teacher should list the suggestions as they are made. She should be flexible and ready to consider a new topic if one is listed that has possibilities for development along the lines of the children's needs. If the children feel that they have selected the topic, they may have better motivation to pursue it.

In working with the educable mentally retarded, the teacher must encourage them to believe in themselves and in their suggestions. However, she must have an overall plan for them. When time permits, they should be included in the unit planning, which must be firmly directed, or the original purpose of the unit will never be attained. Later, after they have learned some of the background material about a subject, they often have good ideas for activities, especially for dramatizations.

If the teacher has a definite unit in view, she may introduce the problem by reading or telling a story; by asking questions; by showing pictures, films, film-strips, and materials that may be discussed; or by taking a field trip to make a preliminary survey to arouse interest.

The children's interest may be maintained throughout the development of the unit by keeping the content and the materials simple, direct, interesting, and dynamic. It is literally true that

21.   The Post Office.

the teacher is competing with the movies and with television for the groups' attention and interest. Therefore, she should take a lesson from their methods of approach. She must resort to dramatization.

There are many heroes and incidents in our country's history that may be taught with as vivid dramatization as any fictional incident of the video screen. These true incidents provide excellent material for units of study to assist in character and attitude development.

The educable mentally retarded children enjoy the stories of Washington's boyhood on a farm and his struggles in the wilderness fighting the French and Indians. In the same way, they never seem to tire of stories about Lincoln. They understand and appreciate his hardships and mishaps.

Other sources for subject matter are space and the elements.

Lessons concerning health and safety should be consistently taught throughout the year. These topics may be integrated into almost any unit of study.

OUTLINE FOR A UNIT

A unit should have some form or outline so that everything pertinent to the topic may be included. These are various forms that may be modified to suit a particular topic or condition. The one given here is a suggestion.

Plan for a Unit.

TOPIC

    I. General statement of purpose of the unit
    II. Objectives
    III. Content—should be detailed and well organized
    IV. Procedure
        A. Initiating
        B. Developing and integrating
        C. Culminating
    V. Materials
    VI. Bibliography
    VII. Evaluation—at close of teaching the unit

The Daily Lesson Plan. A special plan must be made for each day's lesson. This must be thoroughly prepared if the lesson is to accomplish any purpose. The topic of the units, as well as the purpose and general objectives, should always be kept in mind. In each lesson as much integration of the basic skills should be used as is possible without creating absurd and unnatural situations.

Lesson Plan

    I. Objectives for this lesson
    II. Materials for this lesson
    III. Procedure for this lesson
        A. Initiating
        B. Developing
        C. Culminating
    IV. Record of outcomes and suggestions for the next lesson
    V. Evaluation

EXPLANATION OF UNIT OUTLINE

Unit Topic. The unit topic is the title of the study which will probe into, and combine, several areas of subject matter and integrate some of the basic skills.

Purpose of the Unit. The purpose or aim of the unit should be stated in one or two specific sentences. These statements should answer the question: Why is this unit being taught?

Objectives. The objectives for teaching the unit should be listed in detail so that they may be used as the source for the experiences and activities carried on throughout the development of the unit.

The Content. The content of the unit must be practical and demonstrable. The educable mentally retarded learn by seeing, handling, and doing. Reading, writing, and spelling are based on the subject of the unit. The material is prepared by the teacher to avoid wasted effort, frustration, and loss of interest on the part of the pupils.

The materials should be within the pupils' comprehension and ability to use with security and satisfaction. Each experience should be followed by a class discussion. A story of some kind should be developed in the same manner that experience charts are created in the primary room. The teacher should use the story as a basis for preparing worksheets for the next day's lesson.

These worksheets may be made in somewhat the same form as the lessons in workbooks that accompany commercially prepared reading, science, or social study books. However, the worksheets for the educable mentally retarded are prepared on levels commensurate with the pupils' abilities. These questions, exercises in matching or filling in blanks, should provide for the determining of comprehension, sight vocabulary recognition, sequence of ideas, and word meanings.

This worksheet form has been found most practical when it has been made at three levels of ability, because usually the children in the educable mentally retarded room can be separated into three groups. Worksheets for the readiness and primer group should have some simple matching exercises, a few words to trace or copy, and a picture or the space to draw a picture. The second group may have sentences to copy or sentences with blanks to fill in from a choice of two words. The third group may have a space

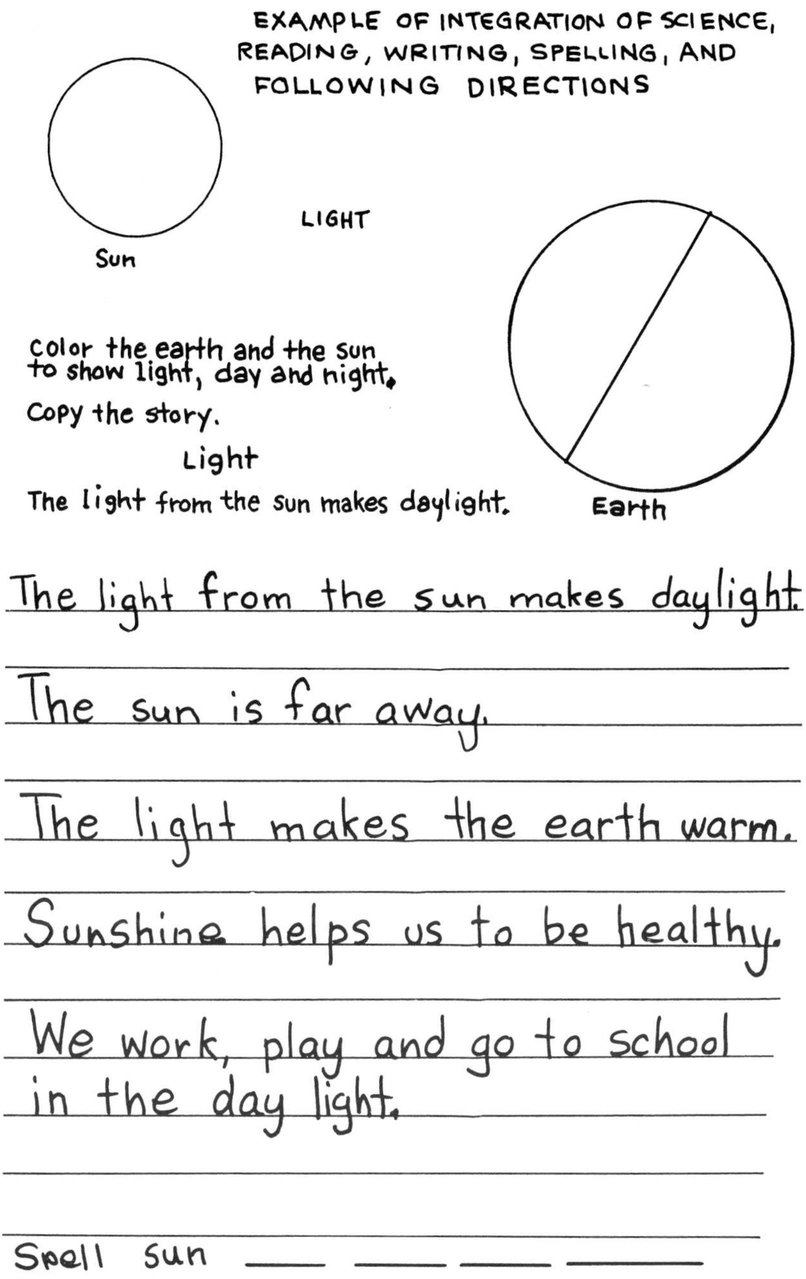

EXAMPLE OF INTEGRATION OF SCIENCE,
READING, WRITING, SPELLING, AND
FOLLOWING DIRECTIONS

LIGHT

Sun

Color the earth and the sun
to show light, day and night.
Copy the story.

Light

The light from the sun makes daylight.   Earth

The light from the sun makes daylight.

The sun is far away.

The light makes the earth warm.

Sunshine helps us to be healthy.

We work, play and go to school
in the day light.

Spell sun ____ ____ ____ ____

22.   Worksheet—an example of integration of basic skills.

EXAMPLE OF COMPREHENSIVE AND VOCABULARY TEST WITH SPELLING AND WRITING.

THE EARTH

FILL IN THE BLANKS WITH THESE WORDS:
WE, LIVE, ON, EARTH, ROUND

THE EARTH IS _____.

WE _____ ON THE EARTH.

THE_____IS ROUND.

WE LIVE____THE EARTH.

FILL IN THE BLANKS WITH THESE WORDS: SHINES, MAKES, PLANTS, GROW, SUNSHINE, WARM

THE SUN_____ON THE EARTH.

THE SUN _____THE PLANTS GROW.

THE SUNSHINE IS _____.

THE SUN MAKES THE_____GROW.

THE_____IS WARM.

THE SUN MAKES THE PLANTS_____.

WRITE AND LEARN TO SPELL THESE WORDS:
SUN, SUNSHINE, SHINE, GROW, WARM, MAKES, PLANTS

_____

_____

_____

_____

23. Worksheet—for second grade reading level.

to write a sentence or two about the topic, some matching words and pictures, or blanks to fill in from a choice of not more than three words. There should also be some words to spell and to use in sentences.

The junior high school and the high school pupils should have this same type of unit work, only on more specific topics selected for more mature interests and related in a large measure to the subjects their peers are studying. Lessons prepared for the older group will be on an interest level corresponding to their chrono-logical age, but still commensurate with their mental age and ability level. Many interesting stories are being rewritten and published especially for the junior and high school retarded or slow learner groups. The stories are often shortened, stripped of extraneous matter and made understandable, yet kept interesting.

Procedure. The outline for the procedure should include an account of the manner in which the unit will be initiated and suggestions for initiating the studies of various areas. To insure enthusiastic reception and retention of the material provided in the unit, the instructor must provide a sound motivation to create spontaneous interest. Motivation means to incite, to induce, to stimulate through appeal to associated interests or by special devices. It is of prime importance that the teacher stimulate a desire to read so that she can take advantage of the child's com-plete potential ability in all of the other learning processes.

The motivation for the unit as a whole must be directed toward the pupils' interests or greatest needs. For the older pupils, a unit on communication might develop out of the pupils' need to know how to use the telephone, how to fill out an application for a job, or how to write the answers to the questions on tests for their drivers' licenses.

Other ways to motivate enthusiam are through personal con-ferences and interest inventories. Topics for units of study may also arise out of such interests as hobbies, pets, future plans, a part-time job, wages, fishing, airplanes, space travel, a trip to the museum, dolls, a play house, or a game.

The procedure should include the methods by which the unit will be developed through activities, experiences, and the inte-gration of all of the areas involved in the study. The objectives for each area to be included in the entire unit should be stated under this part of the outline.

The procedure finally should include the culminating activities of the unit.

Materials. A complete list of materials to be presented throughout the unit will save time and confusion as lesson plans are made and presented to the class. Such a list assists the teacher to evaluate the materials and makes the daily planning simple and pleasant.

Evaluation. The teacher should carefully evaluate each lesson and, at the close of the unit, evaluate the entire study. This should be done while the responses and discussions are fresh in mind. She should note the strength, the weakness, the high and low point of interest, and the parts needed to be reviewed or enlarged upon.

This evaluation will influence the lesson plan for the following day. Some changes may be required, since each lesson plan must be based on the knowledge, skills, attitudes, and concepts that have been established.

The Bibliography. The bibliography should include complete information on the sources of everything used in connection with the unit. An annotated bibliography will be the most useful to the teacher for future reference.

INTEGRATION WITH OTHER AREAS

After the teacher has decided upon the general objectives for her study, she must survey all of the areas of learning and decide which ones would contribute helpful material for the attainment of these objectives. In building a unit she should avoid overlooking some potent possibility; yet she should not be a slave to form and attempt to include everything. There must be a specific reason or list of objectives directly connected with the study for each area that is included.

The Language Arts and the Social Science must be woven into a pattern of functional value to the children. Practical problems must be developed for arithmetic from the arts and crafts, homemaking and shop areas, as well as from the social science area.

TYPE OF WORK SHEET TO PREPARE
FOR THE PRIMARY LEVEL READER. HE
MAY TRACE THE WORDS, FILL IN THE BLANKS,
AND COLOR THE PICTURES.

clouds

See the clouds.

See the _ _ _ _ _ _ _.

Sun

See the sun.

See the _ _ _ _.

24. Worksheet—for primary level.

Language Arts in the Modified Core Curriculum. The Language Arts are usually considered to include reading, oral and written language, spelling, and writing. These provide the medium in a core unit for the children to learn to use the basic skills as they are imbedded in a body of other useful knowledge.

Oral Language in the Core Curriculum Unit. Greater fluency in using oral language may be developed by means of experience stories or sharing periods. Sometimes it is wise to overlook grammatical errors if a child is doing well with his story. However, correct usage of the English language should be emphasized constantly in all work throughout the day.

Correct oral language may also be taught by simple dramatization that appears spontaneous. The use of a few props and the unit materials will achieve the effect desired. Such dramatizations could include practice in using the telephone, welcoming visitors to the room or to the home, entertaining visitors, making introductions, saying good-by to host or guests, or shopping at the school store. The teacher should instruct the children carefully so that there is no loss of self-confidence through corrections during these dramatizations.

Written Language in the Core Curriculum. Correct usage in writing is best learned by practice. Experience charts provide an opportunity for the teacher to show the use of capital letters, periods, commas, quotation marks, question marks, titles, and paragraphs.

The teacher makes use of every opportunity for the children to write letters of inquiry, invitation, and thanks. These activities provide excellent motivation for experience in using new vocabulary, as well as new skills.

The children should write or be helped to write stories of their own experiences. They must be taught how to make a sentence and a paragraph and when and where to punctuate and use capital letters. These stories furnish reading materials which may later be illustrated by drawings or paintings by the children.

The educable mentally retarded children should acquire enough experience and ability to enable them to take down information over the telephone, to make out a receipt, to prepare a shopping list, or to write a friendly letter.

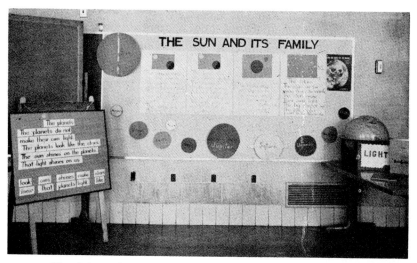

25. Materials used in a study of the sun and its satellites.

Sometimes the teacher is able to locate published materials that will sustain interest until a basic vocabulary can be established; however, usually the teacher must prepare these materials. Although the interest level may be that of a ten or thirteen-year-old child, the content of the reading material could be as low as a readiness stage necessitating much oral language and practice on pre-primer material. This material is easily adapted from the unit being studied.

As long as the child is in the reading readiness stage, he should not be forced to recall words. However, as soon as he has sufficient muscle coordination to trace, he may begin tracing letter and word forms. He can *draw* the letter or word forms, and, as he does this, he begins to realize that these forms have different shapes.

Thus, it is possible the child may learn to write his name without knowing the letters in the name or being able to write other words. Learning to write his name is very important to the mentally retarded child.

Eventually the child will learn a basic sight vocabulary and the names of the letters of the alphabet. As he learns to read and as he matures, he should learn the alphabet in sequence. This will enable him to learn to locate words in lists and directories.

While the child is emerging from the readiness stage, he is able to make good progress in oral language. Through the unit study he is acquiring knowledge that enables him to enter into discussions with his classmates and with friends of his own chronological age. This gives him status with his peers.

TOPICS FOR UNITS

Each year, units should include such topics as health care, nutrition, safety, and seasonal or holiday materials. For the fall months of September, October, November, the weather changes provide interesting topics about fog, frost, harvest, the insects and animals getting ready for winter, the migration of some species, the reptiles hibernation, the plants rest period, the Pilgrims, the Puritans, the Indians, harvest, Halloween, Thanksgiving, the shorter daylight hours and how these things have affected our lives.

For the winter months of December, January, February, (and part of March) use the forces of nature. Talk about the sea-

26.   Posters for Social Studies.

sonal changes, the snow, the wind, the ice, the sleet, the holidays, Christmas, New Years, Valentines, Patriotic Days of February, the lenthening daylight hours.

With March comes the first of spring and April with showers. The weather is an ever present source of wonder to children once their curiosity has been aroused. Again the fog, the frost and the rain march across the land. There are floods from melting snow and ice accumulations and the heavy spring rains. The plants begin to put forth leaves and flowers. The sections of the country not experiencing this rejuvenation will hear about it in the papers and on the radio and TV. What is happening to the plant and animal life at this time of the year? What holidays are being observed?

May and June have an abundance of plant and animal life for discussion. Units may consider safety in summer camps, on holiday trips, at cook-outs, while swimming, hiking, and playing games.

A UNIT FOR A PRIMARY GROUP

A unit for a primary group should usually be limited to a specific topic and be adjusted to pupils' mental age, maturity and attention span. Most primary age pupils are only able to work or listen for brief periods. They will not understand how to look or to listen at first and must be taught to do this, before a class project can be undertaken. If some of the pupils are mature enough to look and listen, they may have some unit experience while the younger group rests.

The unit should use the teaching unit type for the plan. The lessons should be brief and feature actual activity. Safety to and from school is a topic that seems to offer a type of physical activity that is meaningful to the very young child, and may even interest some of the more immature children in the class. This topic should be taught and be reinforced in many ways throughout the pupils' school years.

The unit may be limited in scope to crossing the street, and observing the traffic signal lights. The time spread of the unit would depend on the children's interest. It could be taught over a period of two or three weeks.

OBEY THE TRAFFIC SIGNALS

Purpose: To teach primary age educable mentally retarded children the meaning of traffic signals, and the importance of obeying the signals.

Preparation: Prepare a bulletin board with material about traffic signals. Make the red, amber and green disks large enough to be easily seen and manipulated by the children. On another portion of the bulletin board post colorful pictures showing traffic signals, traffic policemen, and patrol boys.

Presentation: Discuss the bulletin board. Tell a story or show a film about traffic safety. Try to stimulate the children to respond with their ideas and knowledge of traffic safety. Teach some songs about traffc and safety. Consult your own school library for available material. Motor clubs usually supply new posters and teaching materials each month.

Activities: Make small sets of traffic signals from construction paper for each child. The youngest pupils may be able to paste the disks in place, some of the more mature pupils may be able to cut out the disks for the signals. Set up some form of traffic signals in the room and all practice obeying them. Teach the simple rules for crossing a street. Stress the importance of stopping and looking both ways before stepping off the curb to cross the street. Go to a street crossing and observe the lights and the traffic and practice looking both ways before crossing.

MODIFIED CORE CURRICULUM UNITS

Examples of units using the modified core curriculum plan are given in this chapter to show how the basic skills are incorporated with the other areas of learning. These plans also present an adaptation of the outline for preparing units.

The first unit, "Summer Fun," illustrates the integration of the areas of learning and skills common to most elementary schools. The unit outline is adapted or modified to meet the needs of the educable mentally retarded of intermediate age. The teacher should plan to take from two or four months' time to complete this unit.

The second unit, "The Weather," has a definite plan for fifteen days. It is developed from a list of questions the children asked during the study of "Summer Fun." This simple unit could be used by teachers who do not care for long units or for the core plan. Detailed lesson plans are included with the unit about the weather.

The third small unit was developed for the children whose interests in clouds went further than the unit about weather. The five lesson plans in this area show how to present a topic in a brief time. The elements for motivation are included in all of these plans in the presentation of the materials.

SUMMER FUN

I. Purpose

To enrich the lives of the educable mentally retarded children, whose chronological ages are from ten through thirteen years, and whose mental ages are from five through eight years.

II. Objectives

A. To foster an appreciation of simple, orderly, pleasure in summer.

B. To learn how everyday living can be enjoyable.

C. To learn some healthful exercises for social skills and for recreation.

D. To learn to sing and to participate in games and dancing.

E. To learn to make useful articles that may be used in group situations such as picnics.

F. To learn to eat wisely in the summer and to prepare the right kind of food and drinks for lunches, picnics, and snacks.

G. To learn good grooming and correct costuming for summer outings and for home wear.

H. To learn how to make a simple costume for summer, a beach bag, beach pillow, place mats, coasters for drinks, hot dish mats, and some pottery for candy dishes or snacks.

I. To learn health and safety rules for outdoor play in summer.

J. To learn simple first aid.

K. To learn the skills of the basic subjects needed to carry out these objectives.

L. To achieve knowledge and skills as they relate to everyday living.

M. To assist in achieving self-realization, economic competency, good human relationships, and civic responsibility.

27.   A display of some materials developed for the unit "Summer Fun."

III. Integration with Other Areas

A. Social Studies.
   1. Specific objectives.
      a. To appreciate the help we receive from the people who take care of the city parks, picnic grounds, play areas, and public transportation.
      b. To realize that we cannot live without the help of many other people and that we must help others too.
      c. To learn about available places for good summer fun and the way to get there.
      d. To recognize the rights of others.
      e. To have respect for public and private property.
   2. Development.
      a. Discussions concerning information gained through reading, viewing films, excursions, games, recordings, songs, etc. Pupils by groups or individually write stories about these things for experience charts and for review.

b. Dramatizations using situations as they might be seen on a picnic ground or at the beach. Titles might be— "The Show-Off in the Swimming Pool" or "Careless Picnic Group at the Beach."

c. Excursions to park, zoo, aquarium, or museum.

d. Maps and pictures pertaining to the study.

e. Films relating to the workers who help us and to places suitable for recreation, such as fishing, boating, or ball games.

f. New songs relating to the unit.

B. Nutrition, Personal Health and Safety.

1. Objectives.

a. To learn how to have an enjoyable summer with simple preparation.

b. To learn to eat wisely in the summer; to prepare the right kinds of food for lunches and picnics.

c. To learn social skills for summer happiness.

d. To learn good grooming and correct costuming for summer outings and for home wear.

e. To learn how to make some simple articles for summer use.

f. To be familiar with the basic groups of foods.

g. To learn simple safety rules for travel, picnics, and games.

h. To learn simple first aid for insect bites, cuts, burns, and poison ivy.

i. To prepare a picnic lunch.

2. Development.

a. Reading for information on the topics. Give talks on manners, clothing, behavior, sanitation, grooming, health, safety, and table decorations.

b. Dramatizing and actually practicing the following activities:

(1) Prepare lunches using basic foods.

(2) Set a picnic or luncheon table.

(3) Learn how to serve and to be served at a picnic or luncheon.

(4) Learn how to care for the skin, hair, nails, and teeth.

      (5) Learn how to care for clothes.

      (6) Learn how to avoid contagion at the beaches, swimming pools, and parks.

      (7) Learn what to do if stung by an insect, if cut, burned, or if brought in contact with poison ivy.

      (8) Learn how to be safe at a wiener roast.

      (9) Learn how to be safe when fishing or boating.

      (10) Know how to choose suitable games and how to play them.

      (11) Be able to join in group singing or conversation.

      (12) Make luncheon cloths, napkins, pottery.

      (13) Make charts, posters, booklets about foods, health and safety.

   c. Viewing films related to safety, personal health, and nutrition.

C. Language Arts.

  1. Objectives.

    a. To learn skills in the tool subjects.

    b. To learn how to communicate with people through spoken and written language.

    c. To learn how to write simple letters, notes of thanks, and invitations.

    d. To locate and read the different sections of the newspaper for information about foods, clothing, and types of recreation.

    e. To develop desirable attitudes toward rewarding entertainment.

    f. To learn how to locate places in the community through the use of the newspapers, telephone directory, and in answer to inquiry.

    g. To read for information about community health, safety, transportation, and the use of public facilities.

    h. To listen to a story and be able to relate it to others for their entertainment.

  2. Development.

    a. Use newspapers, telephone directory, books, catalog, library, experience charts, and all of the materials collected to gain information for the social studies area, and in other areas in the group's daily experiences. Direct the reading toward objectives listed under the areas of activity. Teach a sight vocabulary of words pertaining to safety. Present recordings of stories. Give individual help in mastering the ability to read. Discussion, conversations, and sharing experiences will develop the oral language ability.

b. Teach writing as it is needed in such activities as the completion of menus, experience stories in the areas studied, stories of activities, letters of inquiry, notes of invitation and thanks. Give individual help in mastering the ability to write legibly.

c. Limit spelling to words needed to carry on friendly correspondence and to make grocery or other lists. Select words from the pupils' daily work in the class. Give individual help to assist in learning to spell functional words.

d. Develop Activities.

   (1) Discuss the following:

      (a) The places we are to visit.

      (b) The places other people have visited.

      (c) The people who work to provide the equipment or materials we use for travel or play.

      (d) The plans for the trip; when we go, how to get there, how to act on the trip, what to wear on the trip, where to eat, how much the trip will cost, and when to return home.

      (e) The use of the telephone.

   (2) Draw or paint pictures of the places we wish to visit or that we have visited.

      (a) Writing stories of experiences we had during the summer.

      (b) Making a booklet and a cover for the stories and the drawings.

   (3) Dramatize experiences.

D. Arithmetic.

  1. Objectives.

    a. To assist in developing independence in solving problems.

    b. To learn how to make change.

    c. To learn to tell time.

    d. To learn measurements of time, quantity, and distance.

    e. To become conscious of the time needed to go to different places and to return home.

    f. To develop the skills needed to solve simple problems encountered everyday in buying groceries, clothes, or in recreation.

  2. Development.

    a. Use functional problems prepared by the teacher in connection with foods, shop, science, nature study, and recreation.

    b. Drill on the needed skills in addition, subtraction, multiplication, and simple division.

    c. Use a sequential developmental pattern for presenting the needed skills.

    d. Use films teaching the number concepts, number flash-cards, flannel board, rocks, buttons, spools or other objects for counters. Use the pegboard, abacus, scales, ruler, thermometer, measuring containers for liquids and bulky foods, play money, real money, and the telephone.

E. Music.

  1. Objectives.

    a. To learn songs and dances for recreation.

    b. To attain social skills.

    c. To learn how to be socially acceptable.

    d. To learn good manners in a social situation.

    e. To learn to participate.

    f. To learn the rights of others.

    g. To learn to listen to music, to follow directions, and to take turns.

  2. Development.

    a. Through songs.

    b. Through listening to recordings and other music.

    c. Through participation in many kinds of rhythm activities.

F. Science and Nature Study.
  1. Objectives.
     a. To appreciate the beauty of summer time.
     b. To appreciate the value of sunshine to plant and animal life.
     c. To learn to care for the natural beauty of parks and recreation areas.
     d. To develop a feeling of responsibility and a desire to conserve the natural beauty and resources of our country.
     e. To learn about the insects, birds, and animals around the neighborhood and community in the summer.
     f. To learn about the different plants and flowers seen on picnics and excursions.
     g. To learn to look for the evening star, the Big Dipper, the North star, and the different phases of the moon.
     h. To learn to ask questions about things seen so that they may become meaningful to the observer.
  2. Development.
     a. Excursions, picnics, walks.
     b. Science books, story books, magazines, newspapers.
     c. Specimens.
     d. Stories written by children and read to the class.
     e. Drawings, modelings.
     f. Reports from observations or reading.
     g. Films and film-strips.
     h. Experiments.
G. Physical Education.
  1. Objectives.
     a. To learn to enjoy healthful exercise for recreation.
     b. To appreciate sports for entertainment.
     c. To learn how to participate in some games for social acceptance as well as enjoyment.
     d. To learn fair play.
     e. To learn to respect the rights of others.
     f. To learn to take turns.
     g. To learn to appreciate the equipment and facilities used for recreation.

     h. To acquire good behavior patterns for group play.

     i. To learn individual responsibility for the proper use of public and private property and the importance of safety habits.

     j. To learn to make good use of leisure time.

     k. To learn the value of good health before participating in strenuous sports.

  2. Development.

     a. Participate in recreation indoors and outdoors.

     b. Attend competitive games of various sports.

     c. Listen to radio and TV broadcasts of games.

     d. Make a scrapbook of pictures of athletic events.

     e. Read stories or view films about athletic events.

H. Industrial Arts.

  1. Objectives.

     a. To learn the use and care of basic tools and materials.

     b. To acquire habits of safety and consideration for others.

     c. To learn the use of measurements and the value of accuracy.

  2. Development.

     Make small articles, such as wooden coasters, hot-dish pads, small trays, and articles for recreational purposes.

I. Art.

  1. Objectives.

     a. To develop an appreciation of simple, orderly decoration.

     b. To develop behavior patterns suitable for working in groups.

     c. To learn to take turns.

     d. To learn to take measurements.

     e. To learn the use of color in decorating.

     f. To learn the value of accuracy in making an article.

     g. To learn the care of tools and equipment.

     h. To learn the value of materials, such as cloth, yarn, clay, or patterns.

     i. To learn skills connected with making different kinds of articles.

j. To learn how to use textile paint in decorating articles.

k. To learn how to make posters and booklet covers.

l. To learn how to use clay and form small articles from it.

m. To learn how to decorate the fired clay.

n. To learn how to use patterns.

o. To learn how to use the finished products.

2. Development.

a. Present an opportunity to discuss picnics being planned or lunches to be given by the group. Ask for suggestions for table decorations and for the menus. Call for suggestions for making articles that would contribute to a more attractive table.

b. Draw sketches of things that the children would like to make. Display the sketches and discuss their possibilities.

c. Plan for objects that are functional.

d. See that each child will have a satisfying experience.

e. Decide on one type of work, such as clay modeling, for all to use for the first project.

IV. Presentation

A. Discuss with the children the many ways they may have fun during vacation in the summer. List the suggestions given by the children: trips to the beach; fishing; boating; picnics; excursions; visits to the park or zoo; backyard picnics; swimming; traveling; playing games; listening to music; gardening; playing with pets; going to ball games or playing ball.

B. Make charts of the suggestions given by the pupils.

C. Guide the class in deciding on a question for the next lesson and in looking for materials. The teacher makes the experience charts, sentence strips, flash-cards, and worksheets for class reading, writing, and spelling. She should follow through on the class questions, and, as new ideas are expressed, the entire core unit will grow. The watchful teacher will be able to guide the suggestions into useful channels in the different areas of the plan.

V. Evaluation

Benefits derived by the class from the study of the unit included:

A. A more wholesome attitude toward friends and neighbors.
B. A better understanding of what is expected of either a spectator or a participant in various forms of recreation and entainment.
C. A better appreciation of the facilities offered for our pleasure in summer.
D. A feeling of part ownership in community recreation facilities, with attendant feelings of responsibility for their care and proper use.
E. Increased knowledge of plant, animal, and insect life.
F. An increased feeling of self-respect.
G. Development of greater self-reliance and independence.
H. Interest in possible future employment and economic independence.
I. Increased skill in tool subjects and in the functional areas leading toward vocational training.
J. Stimulation of better oral and written language.
K. More legible writing.
L. Improved spelling ability.
M. Increased interest in art and crafts.
N. Increased interest in reading.
O. Increased ability to sing, play games, and use basic skills.
P. Increased understanding of useful words.

REFERENCES

1. Ackley, Edith Flack: *Dolls to Make for Fun and Profit.* New York, Lippincott, 1951. (5-8)
2. Adair, Margaret Weeks: *Do-it-in-a-day Puppets, for Beginners.* New York, John Day, 1964.
3. Allen, Betty: *Mind Your Manners,* rev. ed. Philadelphia, Lippincott, 1964.
4. Anderson, Clarence W.: *Blaze Shows the Way.* New York, Macmillan, 1969. (There are other "Blaze" stories.)
5. Arnold, Oren: *Marvels of the U.S. Mail.* Abelard-Schuman, 1964.
6. Arnold, Wesley F., and Cardy, Wayne C.: *Fun with Next to Nothing.* New York, Harper, 1962. (Handcrafts.)
7. Aulaire, Ingri d' and Aulaire, Edgar Parin: *Animals Everywhere.* Garden City, N.Y., Doubleday, 1954. (k-3) (Animal stories.)
8. Beim, Jerrold: *Tim and the Tool Chest.* New York, Morrow, 1951. (1-3)

9. Beim, Jerrold: *Time for Gym*. New York, Morrow, 1957. (1-3)
10. Blough, Glenn O.: *After the Sun Goes Down*. New York, Whittlesey House, McGraw-Hill, 1956.
11. Blough, Glenn O.: *Wait for the Sunshine*. New York, Whittlesey House, McGraw-Hill, 1954. (2-4) (Seasons and growing things, illustrated.)
12. Blough, Glenn O.: *Who Lives in This House?* New York, Whittlesey House, McGraw-Hill, 1957.
13. Blough, Glen O.: *Who Lives in This Meadow?* New York, McGraw-Hill, 1961.
14. Bradley, Duane, and Lord, Eugene: *Here's How It Works*. Philadelphia, Lippincott, 1962.
15. Branley, Franklyn M.: *Flash, Crash, Rumble, and Roll*. New York, Crowell, 1964.
16. Britannica: *We Learn About Other Children*. Encyclopaedia Britannica, 1954.
17. Bronson, Wilfred S.: *Beetles*. New York, Harcourt, Brace, 1963.
18. Bronson, Wilfred S.: *Polliwoggle's Progress*. New York, Harcourt, Brace, 1949.
19. Brouillette, Jeanne S.: *Insects*. A Follett Beginning Science Book. Chicago, Follette, 1963.
20. Browne, Georgiana K.: *Look and See*. Los Angeles, Melmont, 1958.
21. Buchheimer, Naomi: *Let's Go to the Telephone Company*. New York, Putnam, 1958. (See other *Let's Go* books.)
22. Buck, Margaret Waring: *In Ponds and Streams*. Nashville, Abingdon, 1955.
23. Buck, Margaret Waring: *In Woods and Fields*. New York, Abingdon-Cokesbury, 1950.
24. Buck, Margaret Waring: *In Yards and Gardens*. New York, Abingdon-Cokesbury, 1952.
25. Buck, Margaret Waring: *Pets from the Pond*. Abingdon, 1958.
26. Burnford, Sheila Every: *The Incredible Journey*. Boston, Little, Brown, 1961. (Three pets journey across a wilderness area in Canada to reach their home.)
27. Carlson, Bernice Wells: *Act It Out*. New York, Abingdon, 1956. (Children's plays.)
28. Carlson, Bernice Wells: *Fun for One or Two*. New York, Abingdon-Cokesbury, 1954. (3-6) (Collection of indoor activities.)
29. Carlson, Bernice Wells: *Make It and Use It*. New York, Abingdon, 1958. (Handicrafts for boys and girls.)

30. Cavanna, Betty: *The First Book of Wild Flowers.* New York, F. Watts, 1961.

31. Chapman, Jane A.: *Girl's Book of Sewing.* New York, Greenberg, 1952. (4-9)

32. Chapin, Cynthia: *Wings and Wheels.* Community Helpers Series. Chicago, Whitman, 1967.

33. Clapper Publishing Company: *How to Make Sock Toys, Three Hundred Sixty-Five Easy Scrapcraft Ideas.* Park Ridge, Ill., Clapper, 1959.

34. Clark, Mary E., and Quigley, M. C.: *Etiquette, Jr.,* rev. ed. New York, Doubleday, 1965.

35. Colonius, Lillian, and Schroeder, Glenn W.: *At the Bakery.* Chicago, Melmont, 1954.

36. Combstock, Nan: *McCall's Golden Do-It-Book.* New York, Golden Press, 1964.

37. Conklin, Gladys: *When Insects are Babies.* New York, Holiday House, 1969.

38. Cormack, Maribelle: *First Book of Trees.* F. Watts, 1951. (3-7)

39. Cummings, Richard: *Hand Puppets.* New York, McKay, 1962.

40. Dalgliesh, Alice: *America Travels,* rev. ed. New York, Macmillan, 1961.

41. DeLeeuw, Adele Louise: *It's Fun to Cook.* New York, Macmillan, 1952. (6-9)

42. Derek, Jervis: *The Seasons.* New York, John Day, 1962.

43. Duvoisin, Roger Antoine: *Two Lonely Ducks.* New York, Knopf, 1955. (k-1) (Counting book.)

44. Eastman, P. D.: *Are You My Mother?* New York, Beginners Books, Div. Random House, 1960.

45. Eastman, P. D.: *Go, Dog Go!* New York, Random House, 1961.

46. Elting, Mary: *First Books of Firemen.* (Benjamin Brewster, pseud.) New York, F. Watts, 1951. (1-4)

47. Elting, Mary: *Ships at Work.* Garden City, N.Y., Garden City Books, 1953.

48. Encyclopaedia Britannica Picture Story Booklets. Chicago, Encyclopaedia Britannica.

49. Flack, Marjorie: *Walter, the Lazy Mouse.* New York, Doubleday, 1963.

50. Fletcher, Helen Jill: *The Big Book of Things to Do and Make.* New York, Random House, 1969.

51. Garelick, May: *Sounds of a Summer Night.* New York, Scott Books, 1963.

52. Gaul, Albro T.: *The Pond Book.* New York, Coward-McCann, 1955.
53. Gilbert, Miriam: *Starting a Terrarium.* Maplewood, N.J., Hammond, 1961.
54. Green, Arthus S.: *Art and Crafts for Primary Grade Children.* Minneapolis, Dennison, 1962.
55. Greene, Carla: *Railroad Engineers and Airplane Pilots. What Do They Do?* New York, Harper and Row, 1964.
56. Hage, M. K. Jr., and Ryan, Robert H.: *How Schools Help Us.* Chicago, Benefic Press, 1962.
57. Hammond, Winifred G.: *The Riddle of Seeds.* New York, Coward-McCann, 1965.
58. Hanna, Paul Robert, and Kohn, Clyde F.: *Cross Country.* Chicago, Scott, Foresman, 1950.
59. Hawes, Judy: *Bees and Beelines.* New York, Crowell, 1965.
60. Heal, Edith: *First Book of America.* New York, F. Watts, 1952. (3-5) (The story of freedom, of the ideas, and of the men who led the way and shaped our country's growth.)
61. Huntington, Harriet E.: *Let's Go to the Brook.* Garden City, N.Y., Doubleday, 1952. (1-3)
62. Huntington, Harriet E.: *Praying Mantis.* Garden City, N.Y., Doubleday, 1957.
63. Hylander, C. J.: *Out of Doors in Spring.* New York, Macmillan, 1950.
64. Hylander, C. J.: *Out of Doors in Summer.* New York, Macmillan, 1950.
65. Kohn, Bernice: *Telephones.* New York, Coward-McCann, 1967.
66. Kraus, Richard C.: *Square Dances . . . . . and How to Teach Them.* New York, Ronald, 1950.
67. Leaf, Munro: *Being an American Can Be Fun.* Philadelphia, Lippincott, 1964.
68. Lehr, Paul E., and others: *Weather.* New York, Golden Press, 1963.
69. Limbach, Russell T.: *American Trees.* New York, Random House, 1942.
70. Marcher, Marion W.: *Monarch Butterfly.* New York, Holiday, 1954. (1-4) (Life cycle of butterfly.)
71. Matschat, Cecile Hulse: *American Butterflies and Moths.* New York, Random House, 1942.
72. Maxwell, Gavin: *Ring of Bright Water.* New York, Dutton, 1961.
73. McClintock, Marshall: *Let's Learn the Flowers.* New York, Chanticleer, 1948.

74. McClintock, Marshall: *Leaf, Fruit, and Flower*. New York, Chanticleer, 1948. (Nature primer.)
75. McClung, Robert M.: *Green Darner*. New York, Morrow, 1956. (Story of a dragonfly.)
76. McClung, Robert M.: *Stripe*. New York, Morrow, 1951. (Story of a chipmunk.)
77. McClung, Robert M.: *Tiger*. New York, Morrow, 1953. (1-3) (Story of a swallowtail butterfly.)
78. McGregor, Ellen: *Tommy and the Telephone*. Chicago, Whitman, 1950.
79. Meshover, Leonard: *You Visit a Dairy, Clothing Factory*. Chicago, Benefic, 1965.
80. Morrow, Betty: *See Up the Mountain*. New York, Harper and Brothers, 1958.
81. Myers, Carolyn: *Miss Patch's Learn-to-sew Book*. New York, Harcourt, Brace and World, 1969.
82. Norling, Josephine (Stearns), and Norling, Earnest Ralph: *First Book of Water*. New York, F. Watts, 1952. (2-4) (The many roles of water.)
83. North, Sterling: *Rascal. A Pet Raccoon*. New York, Dutton, 1963.
84. Parish, Peggy: *Let's Be Early Settlers with Daniel Boone*. New York, Harper and Row, 1967.
85. Parish, Peggy: *Little Indians: Handcrafts*. New York, Simon and Schuster, 1968.
86. Pfadt, Robert E.: *Insects Series: Grasshoppers*. Chicago, Follett, 1966.
87. Phillips, Mary Geisler: *Dragonflies and Damselflies*. New York, Crowell, 1960.
88. Pistorius, Anna: *What Dog Is It?* Chicago, Wilcox and Follett, 1951.
89. Pondendorf, Illa: *True Book of Animal Babies*, 1955; *True Book of Animal Homes*, 1960; *True Book of Spiders*, 1962. Chicago, Children's Press.
90. Pondendorf, Illa: *True Book of Pets*, 1954; *True Book of Science Experiments*, 1954; *True Book of Weeds and Wild Flowers*. Chicago, Children's Press, 1955. (1-4)
91. Reed, William Maxwell: *Patterns in the Sky*. New York, Morrow, 1951. (5-8) (Maps, and the story of the constellations)
92. Rogers, Frances and Beard, Alice: *The Birthday of a Nation*. Philadelphia, Lippincott, 1945.
93. Rogers, Frances: *Lens Magic*. Philadelphia, Lippincott, 1957.

94. Ronan, Colin A.: *The Stars*. New York, Macmillan, 1966.
95. Schlein, Miriam; *How Do You Travel?* Nashville, Tennessee, Abingdon, 1954.
96. Schneider, Herman, and Schneider, Nina: *You Among the Stars*. New York, W. R. Scott, 1951. (3-5)
97. Schwalbach, James: *Fun Time Crafts*. Chicago, Children's Press.
98. Schwartz, Julius: *It's Fun to Know Why*. New York, (Whittlesey House) McGraw-Hill, 1952. (4-7) (Experiments with things around us.)
99. Seignobosc, Francoise: *Springtime for Jeanne-Marie*. New York, Scribner's Sons, 1955. (k-1)
100. Selsam, Millicent E.: *Plenty of Fish*. A Science I Read Book. New York, Harper and Row, 1960.
101. Selsam, Millicent E.: *Nature Detective*. New York, W. R. Scott, 1958.
102. Selsam, Millicent E.: *Seeds and More Seeds*. New York, Harper and Brothers, 1959.
103. Schultz, Charles M.: *A Charlie Brown Christmas*. New York, Parents Magazine, 1965.
104. Shannon, Terry: *Where Animals Live*. Chicago, Whitman, 1958.
105. Smith, J. Russell, and others: *Our Neighbors at Home*. Philadelphia, Winston, 1952.
106. Smith, Marie Elizabeth: *Social Learning Readers*. Westchester, Illinois, Benefic Press.
107. Tibbets, Albert B.: *First Book of Bees*. New York, F. Watts, 1952. (3-5) (Story of how bees live in communities.)
108. Tresselt, Alvin: *Johnny Mapleleaf*. New York, Lothrop, Lee and Shephard, 1948.
109. Tresselt, Alvin: *I Saw the Sea Come In*. New York, Lothrop, Lee and Shephard, 1954. (k-1) (A boy explores the beach on foggy morning and finds children's kind of treasures. He saw the tide come in while he was alone. When the sun came out, other people came to the beach.)
110. Tresselt, Alvin: *The Rabbit Story*. New York, Lothrop, Lee and Shephard, 1957.
111. Warner, Gertrude Chandler: *The Box Car Children*. Chicago, Scott, Foresman, 1942. (3-4) (Four children who are orphans run away from an imaginary evil grandfather. They live in a box car and have many adventures. They get to know the grandfather and love him before they discover he is the man they ran away from.)

112. Watson, Jane Werner: *Wonders of Nature*. New York, Golden Press, 1958.
113. Watts, Mabel: *The Narrow Escape of Solomon Smart*. New York, Parents Magazine, 1966.
114. Wilcox, Charlotte E., McCall, Edith S., and Bolton, William, M. D.: Health Action Series. *Come On* (Grade 1), *Here We Go* (Grade 2), *Step Lively* (Grade 3). Chicago, Beckley-Cardy, 1962.
115. Williams, Jay: *The Cookie Tree*. New York, Parents Magazine, 1967.
116. Williamson, Margaret: *First Book of Birds*. New York, F. Watts, 1951. (2-6)
117. Withers, Carl: *Ready or Not, Here I Come*. New York, Grosset and Dunlap, 1964.
118. Wyler, Rose: *The First Book of Weather*. New York, F. Watts, 1956.
119. Young, Miriam: *Miss Suzy*. Parents Magazine, 1964.
120. Zarchy, Harry: *Creative Hobbies*. New York, Knopf, 1953.
121. Zarchy, Harry: *Leathercraft*. New York, Knopf, 1953.
122. Zarchy, Harry: *Let's Make More Things*. New York, Knopf, 1953.
123. Zarchy, Harry: *Model Railroading*. New York, Knopf, 1955.
124. Zarchy, Harry: *Stamp Collector's Guide*. New York, Knopf, 1956.
125. Zarchy, Harry: *Woodworking*. New York, Knopf, 1952. (3-5) (A father and son activity book.)
126. Zaeitz, Barbara: *Easy-to-do Book, Make A Sweet*. Cookbook. New York, Grosset and Dunlap, 1969.
127. Zeitz, Barbara, and Paul, Edith: *Easy-to-do Book. Simple Sewing*. New York, Grosset and Dunlap, 1969.
128. Zim, Herbert S.: *Comets*. New York, Morrow, 1957.
129. Zim, Herbert, S.: *Fishes*. New York, Simon and Schuster, 1956.
130. Zim, Herbert S.: *Frogs and Toads*. New York, Morrow, 1950.
131. Zim, Herbert S.: *Lightning and Thunder*. New York, Morrow, 1952. (4-7)
132. Zim, Herbert S., and Baker, Robert Horace: *Stars*. New York, Simon and Schuster, 1951. (3-5)
133. Zim, Herbert S.: *The Sun*. New York, Morrow, 1953. (3-6)
134. Zim, Herbert S.: *Reptiles and Amphibians*. New York, Golden Press, 1957.
135. Zim, Herbert S.: *What's Inside of Plants?* 1952; (2-5) *What's Inside of Animals?* 1953; (2-4) *What's Inside of Me?* 1952; (2-5) New York, Morrow.

THE WEATHER

I. Purpose

To assist the children in developing an awareness and understanding of some facts about the weather; to be able to discuss the weather with others regarding the natural phenomena of clouds, rain, and thunder storms; and to be able, by referring to forecasts, to dress properly and to stay well and healthy.

II. Objectives

A. To understand what clouds are and how they are formed.
B. To understand the cause of rain and its importance to us.
C. To know what to wear in the rain.
D. To know where to seek protection during thunder storms and tornadoes.
E. To know how to read the thermometer.

III. Integration

A. Arithmetic.
  1. Learn to read the thermometer.
  2. Keep a chart of daily weather and temperature.
  3. Make thermometers of paper for recording and practicing reading of temperatures.
  4. Use measuring and numbering for thermometers.
B. Health and Safety.
  1. Discuss lightning, thunder, and tornadoes.
    a. Causes
    b. Proper precautions for safety and health.
  2. Discuss protection of the body when out in severe weather.
C. Language Arts.
  1. Listen to weather reports on the radio or TV.
  2. Read weather reports.
  3. Read stories about the weather.
  4. Discuss these reports in class.
  5. Write stories about personal experiences in various kinds of weather.

28.   Materials for a unit, "The Weather."

6. Read these stories to the group.
7. Learn new words.
8. Discuss effects of weather on customs and culture of people.

IV. Materials and Methods

A. Present experiments that help explain the phenomena of rain, snow, fog, wind, and storms.
B. Keep daily weather and temperature charts.
C. Show different kinds of thermometers, such as weather, candy, fever, and oven.
D. Present experiment showing how the thermometer works.
E. Make replicas of thermometers for daily seat work. Read the real thermometer several times daily and change the replicas to match. Make a large replica of the thermometer for the bulletin board.
F. Make scrap books or booklets.

V. Presentation

A. The daily lesson plans.

1. Lesson one.

   Prepare a large thermometer of lightweight cardboard. Mark the degrees for temperature plainly. Thread a narrow red ribbon through a slot at the lower end and fasten it to a white ribbon coming down from the slot at the top. After an explanation to the class place it on the bulletin board. Show other kinds of thermometers to the children and explain their uses.

2. Lesson two.

   The teacher should help the children make small thermometers similar to the large one on the bulletin board. Keep these in the scrap books or with the stories about the weather for a special booklet.

3. Lesson three.

   a. Provide a calendar form for the children to keep a daily record of the weather and temperature. Show them how to use the form and write the record for that day. Keep these with the other weather stories and materials.

   b. Change the temperature daily on the children's play thermometers so that they will become aware of the changing weather.

   c. Appoint a helper to have charge of the real thermometer and adjust the one on the bulletin board daily.

   d. Write a short story on the chalkboard about the weather to be copied by the children for their story booklets.

   e. Write a list of new words on the chalkboard for the children to copy and learn.

   f. Assign these words according to ability for spelling words.

4. Lesson four.

   a. Take the group to the library. Look for information about the weather.

   b. Check out books and materials for further study and for reports.

5. Lesson five.
   a. Children make oral reports on materials they found at the library.
   b. Make a list of words from the reports for spelling and for sight recognition.
   c. Use a flash-card drill for words on the previous list.
6. Lesson six.
   a. Show a film about the weather.
   b. Hear reports from the class about the film.
   c. Add new words to the spelling list.
   d. Hear spelling of words on previous list.
7. Lesson seven.
   a. Write on the chalkboard the story that the group dictates, listing things they have learned about the weather.
   b. Read this story to the class and have the pupils read it.
   c. Select words for spelling list.

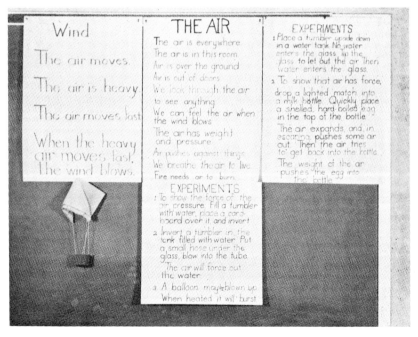

29.   Experience charts about the air.

    d. Have pupils copy this story for their booklets.

    e. Spell the words from lesson six.

8. Lesson eight.

    a. Tell stories about the weather.

    b. Write stories about the weather.

    c. Help the pupils with spelling words needed for their stories.

    d. Put stories into booklets.

    e. Add new words to spelling list.

9. Lesson nine .

    a. Read or tell an interesting story to the group about some true or fictitious event caused by weather conditions.

    b. Write on the chalkboard a story as it is dictated by the class.

    c. List new words for spelling.

    d. Review all flash cards for new vocabulary from lesson one through the present lesson.

10. Lesson ten.

    a. Present an experiment showing how the thermometer works.

    b. Make a chart showing the steps in the experiment and the way the thermometer works.

    c. Have the pupils copy this chart.

    d. Add new words to spelling list.

    e. Spell the words from the previous list.

11. Lesson eleven.

    a. Discuss the causes of rain, fog, snow, wind, and storms.

    b. Show a film demonstrating these things, or have pictures available to illustrate the discussion.

    c. Add new words to the spelling and vocabulary list.

    d. Spell the words from the previous list.

12. Lesson twelve.

    a. Read stories about rain, thunder, lightning, and other storms.

    b. Discuss safety and health precautions.

    c. Have the class give stories about things they have learned concerning the weather.

d. Have the class write the stories for their booklets.

e. Add new spelling words to the list.

f. Spell the words from lesson eleven.

13. Lesson thirteen.

   a. Present experiment showing how rain is caused by warm, moist air meeting cool air.

   b. Make a chart showing the steps in the experiment.

   c. Present simple water barometer and explain how it works.

   d. Copy this chart for the scrapbooks or booklets.

   e. Add new words to spelling and vocabulary lists.

   f. Spell the words from the previous lesson.

14. Lesson fourteen.

   a. Discuss proper clothing to wear in various kinds of weather.

   b. Discuss other care of the body for health at different times of the year.

   c. Review safety and health rules for weather and storms.

   d. Try to relieve fears about thunder storms.

   e. Copy on the chalkboard, as the class dictates it, a story about health and safety during storms.

   f. Have the class copy the story for their booklets.

15. Lesson fifteen.

   a. Collect all of the drawings and stories from each child.

   b. Use drawings and stories for booklets.

   c. Have the children assist in assembling the booklets.

   d. Have each child select one of his own stories and read it to the group.

   e. Evaluate the unit and list the outcomes.

   f. Note if the class has an interest in some phase of the unit that would warrant further study. For example, if the group is interested in clouds, a short series of lessons about that topic may be beneficial. Use the same general outline—but simplify it.

VI. Bibliography

List the materials that were used in presenting this unit.

CLOUDS

I. Purpose

To learn more about the causes of rain, snow, and other weather conditions.

II. Objectives

To learn what causes different kinds of clouds and what the different kinds of clouds mean to the man on the ground and to the man in the air.

III. Integration

A. Arithmetic.

Present material about distances; height of clouds from the ground; size of clouds; amounts of rainfall and snow; velocity of the wind; how fast storms travel; size of hail stones.

B. Language Arts.

Direct oral and written language exercises; reading for information and pleasure; spelling new words; writing for legibility.

C. Art.

Direct drawing and painting of cloud formation.

IV. Materials

Use films, pictures, and the sky.

V. Activities

A. Locate pictures for the bulletin board.

B. Watch the sky for cloud formations.

C. Read weather reports.

D. Field trip to airport; discuss weather with the manager; the effect of weather on flying; difficulty of landing in a high wind.

E. Make weather vanes.

F. Make experience charts.

G. View films or other audio-visual media.

VI. Presentation

A. The lesson plans.

1. Lesson one.

a. Discuss clouds in general. Get a story from the group showing what they know about clouds.

b. Compile a list of things the pupils want to know about the clouds.

      c. Direct the children to copy the story and the list in their note books.

      d. List new words for spelling.

  2. Lesson two.

      a. Form committees to look for materials about clouds.

      b. Read stories and show pictures about clouds to the group.

      c. Spell words from lesson one list.

      d. Put new spelling words on list.

      e. Make flash cards and have word drill.

  3. Lesson three.

      a. Hear committee reports.

      b. Check the list of questions and assign new questions to the committees.

      c. Write the answers to questions on the chalkboard for the pupils to copy for their writing lesson.

      e. Spell the words on the list and add new words.

  4. Lesson four.

      a. Hear committee reports.

      b. Make a weather vane and a rain gauge.

      c. Spell the words assigned and add new words to the list.

  5. Lesson five.

      a. Take trip to the airport.

      b. Show a film about clouds.

      c. Discuss the trip and film.

      d. Make a class story about the trip and the scenes from the film.

      e. Copy the story for the scrap book.

      f. Spell the words from the list and add new words.

      g. Prepare stories and drawings for the booklet.

VII. Outcomes

Evaluate the results of the study.

VIII. Bibliography

Let the children help prepare their list of source materials.

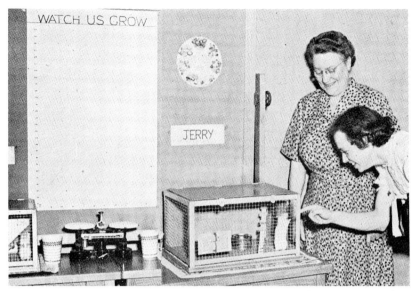

30.   Mrs. Garton explains nutrition experiment, using white rats, to student teacher.

A SHORT UNIT FOR JUNIOR HIGH SCHOOL
A Nutrition Experiment

I. Purpose

To interest pupils of junior high school age in the value of well-balanced meals.

II. Objectives

A. To teach the value of eating good foods in the right proportions every day.

B. To teach the proper care of pets.

C. To teach the value of cleanliness.

D. To teach the costs of food for pets.

E. To teach the pupils how to keep records.

F. To teach the pupils how to use the balance scales.

G. To teach the pupils how to use measuring spoons, cups, scales, rulers.

H. To increase the vocabulary.

I. To improve oral and written communication.

J. To teach the importance of legibility in writing and in making numerals.

III. Materials
   A. 2 wire cages.
   B. 2 white rats, a few days old.
   C. 1 balance scale measuring grams.
   D. Supply of clean cottage cheese cups, pint size (to hold the rats while being weighed).
   E. Supply of small drinking cups for measuring out the rats' daily food portions.
   F. Large wall chart showing the starting date of the experiment and the weight of the rats.
   G. Supply of basic foods.
   H. Fresh supply daily of cake, fresh foods, and coffee.
   I. Newspapers.
   J. Cotton.
   K. Soap or detergent powder.
   L. Sawdust.
   M. Measuring equipment: spoons, cups, ruler.
   N. Jars for storing dry food.
   O. Record book and pencil.
   P. Scrub brush and old cloths.

IV. Content
   A. Forms for letters requesting the various supplies to be used in the experiment.
   B. Material from the library, books, magazines, texts, on: basic foods for human needs; care of pets; care of food for pets; how to feed pet rats; how to handle them; proper care of the cages; how to use balance scales.
   C. Studies on how to evaluate the material that was recorded about the rats.
   D. Collecting bulletin board material about nutrition.
   E. Studies comparing the rats' nutrition to that of the pupils.

V. Presentation
   A. Motivation.
      1. Writing letters of request for materials.
      2. Setting up the cages.
      3. Seeing the white rats for the first time.
   B. Development.
      1. Studying foods for good nutrition.
      2. Studying about proper care of pets.

3. Preparing the foods, weighing, measuring, storing.
4. Feeding the white rats.
5. Weighing and measuring the rats.
6. Watching the rats play and noting growth.
7. Cleaning the cages on Monday and Thursday.
8. Keeping records.
9. Deciding to share knowledge with other classes.
10. Making bulletin board attractive.

C. Evaluation.
1. Comparing the development of the rats.
2. Comparing the value of the rats food to that of the pupils.

VI. Concluding Activity

A program was prepared from daily lesson charts and from stories and records kept by the pupils. The pupils decided to include some of their other activities in the program. The chart showing the rats growth was the center of the backdrop, with the rats in their cages on either side of their record. This program was given as an assembly program for the children of the regular fourth, fifth, sixth, and seventh grades. The participants displayed good control, poise and pleasure in presenting the program.

THE PROGRAM

The participants were seated facing the low stage, with the audience back of them. Marjorie stood and announced: We will sing a round for you, Three Blind Mice.

After the round she read:

Our class has two pet white rats.
They are named Tom and Jerry.
We have learned some interesting things about foods from having Tom and Jerry in our room.
We want to share some of these things with you.
We want you also to know that in our room, sometimes we work, sometimes we play.
First we will tell you about our work with our pet rats.
Howard will tell you where we got the rats.

Howard read:

We got our rats from the University.
They were on the train for three days.
They had been fed on the train.
They were newly born rats when they started out.
They were about sick when we got them.
They came on a Saturday.
The caretaker fed them.
Three rats had been sent to us.
One rat died on Sunday.
So we have two rats.

Billy will tell you about when we first got the rats.

Billy read:

We had cages ready for the rats.
We had to feed them a good diet before starting our experiment.
We read in a book what to feed the rats to make them grow.
We bought the supplies:

two pounds, whole wheat flour,	32c
one pound dry skim milk,	39c
one-half pound sugar,	6c
⅔ ounce, salt	1c
	——
Total cost for basic diet	78c

We brought other added foods from home daily, so they would
   be fresh.
We had named the rats Tom and Jerry.
Jerry bit the tip off Tom's tail when they were little.
We fed both of them the basic food and carrots, celery, apple,
   cheese and meat bits, for the two weeks.

Gerald will now tell you about the rats' special diet.

Gerald read:

Some of us have been eating lots of sweets and drinking coffee.
We thought it would be interesting to see what would happen
   to a rat that ate cake and drank coffee instead of basic foods.

We fed Tom a diet of cake and coffee.
We fed Jerry a diet of basic foods.
Jerry had clean, fresh water to drink.
We kept them on this diet for two weeks.

Jerry grew fast. His fur was slick and thick.

Tom did not grow so fast. His fur looked fuzzy.
His eyes were not bright.
He had a bad disposition.
He was not playful like Jerry.

Delores will tell about caring for the white rats.

Delores read:

We take turns caring for the white rats.
They are very tame.
We have to be careful to never hurt them.
We make slow motion when we put our hands in the cage so
    the rats will not be frightened.
They know we are their friends.
They let us pick them up and smooth their fur.

We clean the cages every Monday and Thursday.
We scrub the cages with hot soapy water.
We dry the cages and tray carefully.
We scrub the food boxes and water cans.

We put newspapers and saw dust in the trays under the cages.
This makes the trays easy to clean.

We put in fresh water every day.
We put in clean materials for their nests.
They like cotton and paper.

Mary will tell about the records we kept.

Mary read:

We have kept a record of the white rats' weight every week.
They were so small we had to weigh them on a special scale.
We weigh them on a scale that shows grams and ounces.
A gram is a small part of an ounce.

On April 9, when we started the experiment,
Tom weighed 29.9 grams, Jerry weighed 31.2 grams.
They were both fed the same diet for ten days.
On April 19, Tom weighed 52.4 grams, Jerry, 49.3 grams.
On April 23, Tom weighed 60.9 grams, Jerry, 64.2 grams.
April 26, Tom weighed 65.2 grams, Jerry, 78.5 grams.
April 30, Tom weighed 76.6 grams, Jerry 92.1 grams.

By this time poor Tom looked so sad and fuzzy we asked that
he be put on a good diet too.
On May 4, Tom weighed 83.6 grams, Jerry weighed 102.1 grams.
May 11, Tom weighed 90.0 grams, Jerry weighed 110.7 grams.
May 13, Tom weighed 89.9 grams (he had tipped over his pan
of water during the weekend), Jerry weighed 124.9 grams.
May 17, Tom weighed 103.1 grams, Jerry weighed 130.7 grams.

Bob will tell about our conclusions.

Bob read:

Our experiment ended on May 17th. We had found a good
home for our pets. We could see that eating just sweets and
drinking coffee was a poor diet for a rat. We decided it
would be better for us to eat a good diet too. We need good
food every day.

From our big chart WATCH US GROW, you can see that Tom
was affected greatly during the two weeks he was on the cake
and coffee diet. He has never caught up with Jerry in size. He
was heavier than Jerry when the experiment started.

Good food made the rat's fur shiny and his eyes bright.
Good food should make our hair shiny and our eyes bright.

You have now seen some of our work, we will show you how we
play.
Our last number will be a square dance.

A SHORT UNIT FOR SECONDARY SCHOOL

Units for the older pupils should center about young adult
interests, and be channeled toward the responsibilities of self-
support and of supporting a family. The pupils age range chronologically will be from about 15 or 16 to 18 or 20 years. A sample

of a unit in a simple form with the emphasis upon taking care of your money is given as a guide.

A Budget

I. Purpose

To teach about budgeting one's income.

II. Objectives

A. To attempt to impress upon the pupils the value of money.
B. To attempt to show the money cost of living.
C. To teach why one's expenses must not exceed one's income.
D. To show one can plan to spend one's income wisely.
E. To help learn the value of saving for a purpose.
F. To help pupils understand the need for knowing how to recognize good values in purchases.

III. Content

A. Income.
   1. Salary for regular work.
   2. Salary for part time work.
B. Expenses.
   1. Fixed expenses such as: shelter, food, health, social security, income tax withholding, other taxes, utilities, car payments, car upkeep, insurance.
   2. Flexible expenses such as: recreation, charity, church, clothes.
   3. Luxuries such as: ready-cooked foods, ready-sliced foods, ready-made clothes that will not wear well, toys that are not substantial, frequent meals at the drive-in.

IV. Procedure

A. Motivating Activities.
   1. Film or film-strip on budgeting.
   2. Newspaper advertisements.
   3. Posters.
   4. Discussion in class.
   5. Talks by former classmates who are now economically independent.

6. Bulletin board display of charts on budgeting and related material such as comparison of cost between cash and time payments.

B. Integrated Activities.
1. Arithmetic.
   a. Cost of items needed for a family of four for a week's food.
   b. Compare with expected salary for several jobs.
   c. Determine amount left for shelter, car, TV payments, if any.
   d. Find the savings on items bought for cash over time payments.
   e. Find the savings on groceries if bought at week-end sales over regular prices.
   f. Find out how much interest loan companies charge.
2. Art.
   a. Posters showing real needs and luxuries.
   b. Scrapbooks showing household items of good values.
   c. Charts showing how the dollar is to be spent.
   d. Drawing showing ways to save and how waste occurs.
3. Oral Language.
   a. Discussion in class of the problems involved in making a budget.
   b. Discussion of the costs of possible purchases for a home, why one item is superior over others.
   c. Dramatize shopping experiences: banking, making a loan; renting an apartment; making purchases for a holiday dinner, a picnic, a cook-out; buying a suit, a pair of shoes, a coat.
4. Written Language.
   a. Make a list of items one must buy for one day's food for a family of four, two adults and two children ages 5 and 9.
   b. Make a list of the items one needs to furnish a living room, a bedroom, a kitchen.
   c. Write a letter answering an advertisement in a newspaper.
   d. Write an order for some merchandise.

e. Write a letter to accompany the return of some item you ordered by mail that was not satisfactory.

f. Read labels on merchandise, on garments, on foods.

V. Culminating Activity

A. Field trip to a local bank or savings company and observe how money is deposited and withdrawn, and loans are processed.

B. Dramatization of a family living by a budget, and a family without any plan.

VI. Outcomes

Evaluate the result of each day's lesson. Prepare the lesson plan for the next day to include time to correct or to emphasize any points you feel were not quite understood.

VII. References

Help the pupils prepare a list of the materials that have been used in the study. The teacher should have a complete list of all materials used.

SUMMARY

The teacher of the educable mentally retarded will find that the possibilities for using the framework of a modified core curriculum plan for units of work are varied, interesting, and challenging.

By modifying the unit plan to meet the group's requirements, she is able to introduce realistic situations and activities that are beneficial and stimulating to the children. All of them are able to take part in this kind of unit so that it becomes a real group activity.

Methods for integrating the Language Arts skills with other areas of learning are suggested.

The modified core curriculum units may be based upon social science integrated with the other areas of learning and with additional instruction in the basic skills. This presents an excellent plan whereby the educable mentally retarded may acquire adequate knowledge and skill to become self-sufficient, socially acceptable, appreciative of pleasant human relationships, and able to accept limited responsibility.

7

READING FOR THE RETARDED

Teachers and parents are particularly interested in preparing children for a useful life. Someone has said that a useless life is an early death. It is our business as educators and parents to motivate the lives entrusted to our guidance for a satisfying degree of usefulness.

We must understand the child—his possibilities as well as his liabilities—for effective planning. We must consider his needs and his unconscious innermost feelings. These needs and desires are basic in all persons.

Perhaps the strongest unconscious feeling is the desire for life itself. Entwined with this is a fear of the unknown. Another strong feeling which influences human behavior is the wish to be accepted, to be appreciated. These together with the child's needs of love, security, protection, guidance, and control should direct the planning of all work for the retarded.

Reading is an important and sensitive area to teach. It is a complex activity, and the retarded child is not able to perform all of the necessary elements without intensive preliminary readiness based upon his unconscious feelings and basic needs.

As motivation is slowly developed, the retarded child becomes confident in his own ability to perform. Perhaps giving this child a feeling of security, of being loved and appreciated, has accounted for the amazing success of the "grandparents" plan in effect in so many state schools for the retarded, that I have visited in the last few years.

In public schools, helpers or aides for the teachers allow time to provide the intimate approach to each child. Time is necessary to unlock the child's restraint, the fear of ridicule, and to allow freedom of expression. Growth begins as the child's hostility is overcome with affection, and suspicion is replaced with trust.

The teacher has studied the child's many tests, which all give helpful information for the remediation of the slow learner. A chart should be prepared of the child's strength and weaknesses, as a guide to selecting and preparing materials to his advantage.

Sometimes a child responds quickly to a program. Other times a child is so disorganized the response is very slow. Work with such a child by using many body movements, orienting him to himself and to his environment. Help him to coordinate his movements, to do things for himself, to learn to do things in more than one way. Help him to use more than one kind of toy or manner of playing, of coloring, or other school materials or equipment.

In a speech and language test conducted by the Speech and Language Research Laboratory, University of Chicago, it was found that most people use only 403 words in more than 80 percent of their everyday conversation. The ten nouns most frequently used in order were *man, picture, woman, mother, thing, way, hand, girl, kind,* and *face.* The ten verbs most frequently used, in order of use were *look, think, know, go, seem, see, say, get, try,* and *come.* The ten most frequently used adjectives in order of use were *young, old, good, evidently, little, hard, happy, serious, nice,* and *sad.* This emphasizes the value of thoroughly teaching these few words to each child to improve communication. Also it may help explain the extremely limited vocabulary of most mentally retarded children.

Accustom the children to hearing different terms for objects. They usually have one name for an object. Use games to show a thing may be called more than one name. Language is used to communicate and it is often very complicated. The retarded child uses a simple form, often resorts to signs, or retains baby talk until after he is in school. This is difficult for the teacher and requires much patient work to break the habit of years. Most

31.   Reading readiness lesson following a trip to the zoo. Mrs. Garton with pupils, Whitaker Elementary School, Finneytown School District, Cincinnati, Ohio.

schools now have the help of a speech therapist, but the teacher must continue the program every day in the classroom.

Many things assist in weaning the child from baby talk. One is association with other children, who often fail to pay attention to his baby babbling, and he is left out of activities. Another incentive to speak correctly is listening to his classmates as they give reports in class. He is frequently ignored until he learns to speak so he is understood. This often produces an incentive to try the language and speech games both individually and in groups, working with sequences, rhymes and simple directions.

Many of the pupils will respond with conversation to an atmosphere of ease in the classroom. They will volunteer statements through which the teacher will discover these mentally retarded children have many assorted pieces of information. It is difficult to get them to sort out fact from fiction, to generalize, to make associations or to vary the items. Therefore, the material used to achieve these factors must be very simple, interesting, and be presented in several ways.

The following ways for overcoming inhibition to new materials and arousing interest have been effective with many children.

1. Form letters from thin coils of plastic clay.
2. Draw letters or words with a finger, in heavy clay type finger paint. Pupils enjoy the brightly colored paints.
3. Roll out play dough or plastic clay and draw letters or words on the surface with a stylus.
4. Prepare ditto copies of letters and words for the children to color or outline with color.
5. Illustrate words with simple stick or scribble drawings.
6. Let the children illustrate a special wish and then tell about it.

The child who cannot read will learn facts from the audio-visual materials and the discussion period. The use of these

32. Individual help and encouragement secure results.

media vitalize the lessons and hold the interest. There is new material being produced and evaluated constantly by all of the federal, state, and local educators. In many areas wonderful lessons are broadcast daily. Where these cannot be reached locally, use pictures, films, and other means to keep the lesson meaningful.

The child who is ready to learn to read should be taught to copy material. He can learn to copy neatly and accurately. He can learn to leave a space between the words, to watch for capitals and punctuation. He is gaining a concept of letter forms, of words, and of sentences. As the child learns to read, he is taught to look at the words, to listen to the words, to think about the words. He may need to follow the sentence wih his finger or a marker, but the important thing for him is the reading ability.

Reading Readiness. Language development is the basis of a reading readiness program. The child must be able to speak and to have a knowledge of the meaning of the words he uses before one attempts to present the printed word.

He must be able to see differences and likenesses between objects and pictures and symbols. He must be able to express his thoughts so he can be understood, and to carry out simple directions to show that he understands.

Language is developed through use. The child must be encouraged to talk freely during a discussion period, the "show and tell" or "sharing" periods. Each child must have an opportunity to stand before the class and to tell a story, to hold up an object and say a few words, or to talk for a longer period. Sometimes the teacher must ask questions to get the child started to talking. Gradually the child learns to stand still, to keep both feet on the floor, and to keep the hands quiet.

Lotto type games are good to develop the ability to distinguish between pictures. Use many kinds of things for matching, pictures of objects, names, letters, numerals, and shapes. Label some objects in the room and give a child a matching name to one object, let him hunt for it. Use picture stories for sequence memory training. Use flash cards with pictures and words and plain cards to match with the name and the picture. Teach some of the more commonly used prepositions by acting them out.

33. Student teacher and pupil, Mrs. Garton's group, Illinois State University, Normal, Illinois.

At this stage the child will be starting to write his own name and may be ready for some pre-primer reading. Use several series to be sure he has a firm basis before presenting a first reader. He will usually be about ready for a first reader when he is of an age to enter the intermediate program. One important skill the primary teacher should always develop is the left to right eye movement. If this habit is firmly fixed in the primary class there will be much more pleasure in starting to use the primers and first readers.

READING IN THE CURRICULUM

Mental Age and Readiness. The child of average intelligence is expected to begin reading at the chronological age of six or six and one-half years. To achieve success, he should be well physically and mentally.

The educable mentally retarded child at that chronological age may have a mental age of three to four years. He will not be ready to read until his mental age approaches the chronological age for usual children to begin to read. In the meantime he is in school, and if he is fortunate enough to have been recognized early, he will be in a special room. There he will be having an intensive readiness program. This program will include readiness

34. A reading lesson.

for every area of living, as well as for the basic subjects of the language arts and arithmetic.

If the child is in a regular room and the teacher is aware of his difficulty, she may prepare special materials for him. The teacher in the regular room may not be aware of the child's retardation and think of him as being stubborn or lazy. She will attempt to have him make progress with the group. This will result in frustration and an intense dislike for school.

Educable mentally retarded children are usually eight to ten years of age chronologically before they are ready for formal reading. They may know a few words and have some experience with charts and primers before that age.

The educable mentally retarded child, as well as the normal child, has many problems that complicate his ability to understand and to retain concepts. The normal child, because of his ability to reason and arrive at sound judgments, is able to overcome his problems or to accept them philosophically and to be able to proceed with his education in a satisfactory manner. The mentally retarded child is overpowered by similar obstacles because he is unable to complete a solution to his problem.

The teacher must be understanding of this child's problem and his intense feeling of frustration. She must remember that the educable mentally retarded child cannot be hurried or coerced into learning, and that he will progress at his own rate of speed, depending upon his physical, social, emotional, and intellectual maturity.

Reading Motivation in the Curriculum. The mentally retarded child has usually had several frustrating years of being unsuccessfully exposed to reading. When the period of readiness arrives, the teacher must assume the responsibility for proper motivation.

The child will seldom respond to a re-hash of the primer or first reader he has been using for the past two or three years. Therefore, the teacher must find something that will hold his attention. This may be a thrilling story about the past or the present, or it may be a topic in which the child has indicated an interest. These subjects will fit into the unit plan and provide the proper motivation for the child's reading program.

A science demonstration or a story about animals frequently will hold the interest of the group and provide another subject that may be integrated into the core curriculum unit plan. The manner of introducing the subject is important. *The teacher's interest and enthusiasm cannot be overemphasized.* Without the spark that she alone can provide, the presentation will fail.

Once the child's interest in reading has been aroused, progress is much easier. However, to insure continued progress, the teacher should keep the content of the reading material simple, practical, and geared to the child's level of interest and comprehension.

Methods for the Reading Readiness Program in the Curriculum. The educable mentally retarded child who is not ready to read requires special training in visual and auditory imagery, in coordination and in rhythms, in social situations, and in storytelling. This child needs many new experiences that are carefully arranged from simple walks about the school building to trips to the neighborhood store, a fire station, a farm, or creamery. These activities may be integrated into the core unit to help the child achieve self-sufficiency.

READING READINESS

The children should be encouraged to participate in the following activities to develop a readiness for reading:

1. Take turns in classroom activities and duties.
2. Know own name in a list of names.
3. Begin to be aware of the clock, of the position of the hands of the clock when it is time for recess, noon, dismissal.
4. Locate the signs that read EXIT.
5. Learn to listen to a short story.
6. Learn to relate an incident.
7. Learn to look at a picture and name an object, an action, or a color.
8. Develop the ability to make up a story about a picture.
9. Visit the library and select picture books.
10. Learn to match objects, pictures, numbers, shapes, and colors.
11. Arrange sequence stories in the correct order. Tell the story.
12. Take a walk and recall objects and incidents viewed.

13. Look at a picture and decide what may happen to one of the characters.
14. Make a drawing of a favorite toy, or illustrate a story.
15. Help with a puppet show.
16. Make a peep show box.
17. Learn rhymes and action songs.
18. Guess peers identity from hearing a voice.
19. Identify many kinds of sounds.
20. Help prepare a bulletin board by selecting appropriate materials from an assortment provided by the teacher.

Developing the Ability to Observe Visually. The teacher should show the pupils how to take part in the following activities to develop better visual awareness of their environment.

1. From a description of an object in the room have some child guess what it is.
2. Act out directions.
3. Match colors.
4. Match shapes.
5. Match sizes.
6. Match objects.
7. Name the objects in a box that were exposed briefly. Increase number of objects as the child becomes more proficient. Change the objects frequently.
8. Play games like ring toss or bean bags.
9. Take a walk and list the things seen.
10. Train from left to right in all games.
11. Match a design of blocks.
12. Work simple jigsaw puzzles. Make these with simple pictures cut into two pieces, then gradually increase the number of pieces.
13. Take field trips.
14. Show pictures of familiar objects with a part covered or missing. The child names the missing part.
15. Give the readiness pupils materials and allow them to improvise their own games.
16. Use the television programs, but with discretion.

m	n
n	m

r	r
i	i

VISUAL DISCRIMINATION
OF SIMILAR LETTERS

horse	house
house	horse

who	how
who	how

VISUAL DISCRIMINATION
OF SIMILAR WORDS

35. Visual discrimination.

17. Make up sets of related objects by pasting four or five pictures on each side of cardboard. Punch a hole by each object. Tie a colored string through each hole on one side of the cardboard and let the pupils try to match the related object. The use of heavy colored roving cotton, or shoe strings, makes the stringing easier.
18. A game to improve observation is "Follow the Leader."
19. A marching game with pupils giving directions arouses interest.
20. Place objects about the room and give directions for finding them: over, under, beside, by, between, on top, in, on.
21. Teach word meanings for opposites, show illustrations, ask pupils to illustrate.
22. Play "Simon Says Thumbs Up," with an R and an L on the appropriate mittens.
23. Sort materials.
24. Find pairs of objects.
25. Bounce a ball and a child repeats the number of bounces.
26. Learn to tell differences and likenesses.
27. Describe an object out of doors and have pupils tell what it is.
28. Call a noun or verb, ask a pupil to tell what he thinks when he hears the word.
29. Show a picture and talk about it, then cover it, and have pupils tell what they have seen.

Developing Auditory Perception. The teacher may assist the children to learn about sounds from these activities:

1. Listen to sounds to identify the source.
2. Listen to musical tones to identify high and low notes.
3. Listen to and identify beginning sounds of words.
4. Find pictures of words and make a scrapbook.
5. Listen for rhyming words.
6. Make up little jingles.
7. Listen to sounds and imitate them.
8. Tap with pencil inside desk, pupil taps back same number.
9. Bounce a ball three times as child listens with back to you, he bounces his ball three times.

10. Repeat several objects and have pupil repeat in same order.
11. Play some music and let the class act out the rhythm. The next day repeat the music and have the pupils tell what they did when they heard the tune the day before.
12. Tell a story, show a picture, have pupils retell story using the picture as a cue. Next day tell the story, but do not show the picture.
13. Point to pictures of things that begin with the same sound. Repeat with children pronouncing the words.
14. Use tape recorder for pupils to hear their own voices and compare with correct pronunciation of words.
15. Teacher pronounces three words. One does not begin like the other two words. Pupils raise hands when they can say the odd word.
16. Make up stories to stress ending words as rhymes.

Developing Coordination and Rhythm. The children will be helped in developing coordination and a sense of rhythm through practicing the following activities:

1. Saying nursery rhymes with finger play activity.
2. Choral reading.
3. Echoing.
4. Rhythm band activities with records or piano.
5. Clapping, skipping, hopping to music.
6. Singing alone and in groups.
7. Playing games requiring throwing, running, jumping, and walking.
8. Cutting out pictures.
9. Coloring within lines to become aware of the shapes of objects and that forms have limits.
10. Painting; finger painting.
11. Playing house.

The teacher should have a plan for each lesson, a purpose for the things taught or presented. The slow learner must be taught the skills necessary to read effectively. He must be taught to observe and to draw conclusions, to think what the effect of his action will be on himself, on what he is doing, and as he grows older, to apply this ability to other problems that develop in his life at play and at work.

Some games are helpful in developing this ability: going through a maze, arranging sequence pictures, shadow puppet shows. These games develop the ability to think of cause and effect. The puppet must be held at the correct distance and angle, the timing must be right with the story. These games also assist in motor control and strengthening of coordination.

There are many ways to help the child achieve reading readiness. These few ways are listed to illustrate the types of help the educable mentally retarded need to develop this readiness for reading.

ACTIVITIES FOR DRILL

In a word recognition game the children enjoy raising their hands when they know a word and coming to the teacher to claim it. They like to be allowed to build sentences and, later, to read them to the class.

The sentences on the long strips of paper may be cut apart into words and phrases and the children allowed to build them back a word at a time. There is keen rivalry for the word in the set of cards that has the period on it, for the possessor of that card may be allowed to read the reassembled sentence.

Another way to hold interest in remembering words is to place the words face down in a box. A child selects a card. If he knows the word, he gets to keep it. If he does not know it, he holds it up for someone else to recognize. Every child has a chance to have at least one word. The teacher should prepare picture cards for the children who are in the readiness group, thus assuring personal recognition, which is a big factor in reading success. Sentence strips may be presented to the group for reading. Allow the child time to look at and to consider the word. If he is able to give the correct reply unaided, he becomes more self-confident. Prompt help should be provided if a child falters.

THE SIGHT VOCABULARY

A list of words on the chalk board should be used as a review or as a drill on new words. The class is divided into two groups. Each side chooses a word from the list. The teacher writes the words again on the board and appoints leaders. Each leader chooses someone from his side who plays a version of tic-tac-toe with his opponent. They try to see which side can cancel across first by using the chosen words which must be spelled and pronounced correctly each time. Different words and new leaders are chosen for the next game. These leaders may sometimes be the children who cannot read or write.

The Word Wheel. Mentally retarded children enjoy a version of the word wheel in learning new words. Each child makes a wheel from heavy paper with a paper fastener in the center so that it will turn easily. Under a small window in the top section the words are written so they will show through the window. For the beginner the words may be written consecutively as in a familiar sentence or rhyme. When the child has learned the process and is sure of the words as he turns the wheel, he may play the game with the same words but in a different order. Later a new word may be mixed with familiar words.

The Tachistoscope. The tachistoscope is also a helpful device to use in drill for word retention and quick recognition. This may be easily made from a strip of tag board folded lengthwise with a window cut in one side. The open lengthwise edges of the cardboard are taped together. The words are typed or written on strips of paper. These strips are drawn through the folded cardboard. The child pronounces the word as it appears in the window.

The strip of paper with the word list should be several inches longer than the tachistoscope or the holder for it. A card with a window the size of one line may also be made to fit over a page in a book or over a large chart. This is a help to poor readers, as it enables them to concentrate on a particular line or a part of a line.

Card Games. Card games similar to *Old Maid* are useful in improving visual discrimination and building sight vocabulary. The cards are made in pairs, except the odd card, which may have a different word each time. The cards may be made from lightweight cardboard, such as tag board, or cardboard from the laundry. The words to be learned are typed on the cards. When the set of words has been learned, they may be blacked out and another set of words typed just below that line. The cards may be used many times in this way.

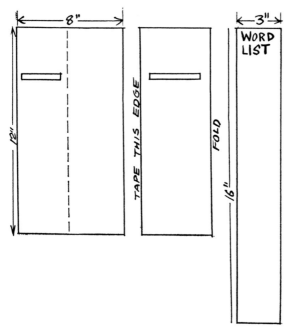

36. The Tachistoscope.

Many different ways may be found to vary the idea of word games, such as "Climbing the Ladder," "The Stepping Stones," or "Climbing the Stairs." These are all helpful aids in holding interest in a word drill.

VISUAL DISCRIMINATION

Sets of words or letters may be arranged in irregular sequence and dittoed for matching, finding similarities, and marking certain words or letters for visual discrimination.

Jigsaw puzzles are also good for this kind of training. The beginner may have a picture or a symbol cut in two parts. When he can match those, the same picture may be cut into three parts and later into four or five parts. Using large, clear, simple objects will eliminate unnecessary confusion.

Similar and Dissimilar Words and Letters. To assist in visual discrimination, the teacher may make sets of flash cards showing similar and dissimilar sets of letters or words. As a spare time project the children may be allowed to make their own sets of cards or other materials.

The teacher shows the children how to use a ruler, a pencil, squared paper, and a printing set. The one-inch squared paper is a good size to use for ruling off four squares into a 2 x 2 inch box. Using the teacher's cards as models, the children print the letters in the squares.

The teacher may also print difficult words in pairs on squares of paper for recognition. She should prepare similar material on the ditto for the children to use.

The teacher may cut words apart for the beginners in reading to reassemble. At first the child needs a pattern, which will be discarded as he improves.

VISUAL AND AUDITORY DISCRIMINATION

Lotto games may be made by the pupils. Pictures from magazines may be pasted onto paper in squares drawn on the paper. These may be used for the recognition of beginning sounds of words, vowels, endings, or other skills that suit the children's need. Disks or small squares of paper may also be used for markers. The one who secures a straight line of words across the page may read the sounds, words, or other correct answers. Words for drill may also be made into a lotto game.

CONFUSION WORDS AND LETTERS

Words and letters of the alphabet that are confusing to children may be used in drills for recognition and comprehension. The confusing words and letters may be printed on cards for proper identification. They may also be placed in squares, and, as the teacher pronounces one and uses it in a sentence, the children circle the correct word or letter.

SPEECH DEFECTS

Children with marked speech defects should have systematic speech training under a speech correctionist. The regular teacher may also help improve speech habits by insisting that words be pronounced correctly.

MARKERS FOR READING

Markers are useful in giving the child confidence in knowing where he is reading. If he does not have to worry about which line he is using, he is able to concentrate on looking at the words and interpreting them into visual concepts.

ORAL READING

The educable mentally retarded child should be allowed to read orally, because he needs this reinforcement of visual and auditory imagery for retention. Oral reading will help the child to gain confidence in his own ability. The teacher will assure him frequently that as long as she does not help him pronounce a word, he is reading correctly. Oral reading provides the teacher with a means of checking the child's reading for fluency, rhythm, and pronunciation.

SHORTER WORDS

Studies have shown that slow learning children learn faster and retain better with the use of short words and sentences. It appears to be helpful to arrange the words in a familiar pattern of speech.

When writing or rewriting stories for children use words commensurate with the ability of the pupils involved. Necessary new words should be used several times before a new word is introduced. The Stanwix Functional Basic Reading Series attempts to introduce a new word nine times before presenting another word. This requires a change of position in the sentence and includes a new thought. This also shows the pupil the importance of proceeding from left to right on the page.

SHADOW BOXES

Children love to make shadow boxes to illustrate their stories. A cigar box is perfect for this purpose, as the lid may serve as an extension of the background and may also be decorated. The lid may be closed and serves to protect the contents as the box is carried about.

A shoe box or similar box is satisfactory. The children will surprise you with their interest and eagerness to find pictures, or make drawings, cut them out, and mount them in the boxes for display.

PUPPET SHOWS

Puppet shows are simple to make when the pupils participate. A method found practical with a primary and an intermediate group was to read a story to the group. One with a dramatic idea about animals and children usually caught the children's imagination and interest. The pupils were allowed to choose the character to represent and find a picture about, or to construct some kind of costume for a finger or hand puppet. Old magazines are a source of pictures to be cut out and mounted on sticks for ease of maneuvering above a platform. Pupils may tell the story and act out the events, or the story may be reread.

A TV SHOW

Read a story to the class. Let the pupils plan the scenes and select the ones each would like to draw or paint, or find pictures to represent. Pass out uniform sheets of drawing paper.

When the drawings are completed, assemble them in sequence with strips of masking tape into one long strip. The pictures may be attached to the rollers of the TV box. A pupil turns the rollers as another pupil narrates the story. The children enjoy seeing their pictures over many times. They may ask to see it months later.

The TV box is easily made from a stout corregated cardboard box: Cut out one side leaving a frame. Bind the edges of the frame with tape and cover with wall paper on the front and sides or paint it. Cut holes on the top, at the rear of the box, for two poles of suitable length to pass through. The poles serve as the rollers for the pictures. They are turned from the top. The picture strip turns more easily if rolled inward for winding.

COMPREHENSION

After the child has read a story, he should be urged to tell the story to someone in the class, or to the teacher. The teacher should ask questions about the story for comprehension. This also assists in retention of the facts of the story.

Exercises relating to stories or class work should be prepared by the teacher. These may consist of short sentences with blanks for inserting words from a list; words to use in sentences with

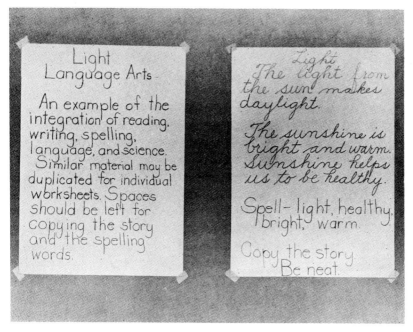

37. Worksheet—for language arts.

the missing word indicated by dots corresponding to the number of letters in the correct word; simple questions to be answered with a sentence including a word from a given list; questions to be answered with a complete sentence with no list of words given; and directions to be followed. This material should be prepared at several levels of difficulty from beginning reading to the highest level in the class.

EXERCISES FOR COMPREHENSION

Examples of exercises for comprehension and retention are given here as suggestions for work that the teacher should use in developing the unit for integration in all areas.

Directions to Follow

1. Draw a cloud.
2. Draw the sun. Color the sun yellow.
3. Draw a tree. Color the tree green.
4. Draw a tree in the wind.
5. Draw a tree in summer.
6. Draw a tree in winter.

Sentences for Comprehension

1. Where is a safe place when lightning is near?
2. What two kinds of lightning do you usually see?
3. Is the North Star always in the North?
4. In what direction do you look to see the sun of a morning?
5. What are some of the uses for water?

Individual Reading Assignment

Read this story and fill in the blanks.

SPRING

The class went for a walk to the school farm.
We saw a tractor and a plow.
We saw baby chickens, a cow, and a calf.
We knew that spring had come.
We saw a tractor and a ....
We saw ...., a cow and ....
We knew that .... had come.
Learn to spell baby, chickens, calf, spring, plow.

Flash Cards. The teacher should prepare flash cards illustrating opposites and words that are difficult to understand. These cards, which are used in the presentation of all new words in the stories and for review of other vocabulary, should have large print.

Labels as an Aid to Word Recognition. Labels on objects used in presenting the unit are an aid to word recognition. The lettering should be simple manuscript writing that corresponds to the regular letter forms which are taught the children. Doors, windows, chairs and other objects about the room may have signs on them. The teacher should be cautious about putting up too many labels at one time, for they may lose their effectiveness.

Daily Record Sheet. Mimeographed record sheets for each child's individual work make a uniform, convenient way to keep track of each child's progress, difficulties, evaluation of methods tried, anecdotal notes, suggestions and assignments.

Daily Record for ....
Date .... Hour ....
Work of the Day   Learning Activities, Materials
Assignment
Work completed
Work to be completed
Relationship of learning activities to child's needs
Notes for anecdotal records, or comments
Suggestions, evaluation

SUMMARY

Reading is a complex activity for the educable mentally retarded to learn. The skilled teacher should have a good rapport with the pupil. The skilled teacher should also be able to provide incentive and inspiration, well-structured lessons at the correct ability level, spiced with imagination, tempered with patience, and combined with judicious repetition for retention.

MATERIALS FOR TEACHER AND STUDENT

1. Armed Forces Institute: *Servicemen Learn to Read; Stories for Today; Stories Worth Knowing; Use Your Language Tools; New Flights in Reading.* Madison, Wis.
2. Bauer, William W., and others: *The Basic Health and Safety Program.* Grades 1, 2, 3. Glenview, Ill., Scott Foresman.
3. *Beckley Cardy Stories: Buttons Stories; Cowboy Sam.* Chicago, Beckley Cardy.
4. Bell and Howell Language Equipment.
5. Betts, Emmitt A.: *The American Adventure Series.* Chicago, Wheeler.
6. Bobbs Merrill Stories: *The Childhood of Famous Americans Series.* Indianapolis, Bobbs Merrill.
7. Bode, Dwight G.: *Ideas: For Teaching Special Education Students.* Washington, Iowa, County Superintendent Special Education Department, Washington County School System, 1967.
8. *Bright and Early Beginners Books,* Beginning Readers Program. New York, Division of Grolier Enterprises.
9. Bush, Wilma Jo, and Giles, Marian Taylor: *Aids to Psycholinguistic Teaching.* Columbus, Ohio, Merrill, 1969.
10. Carson, Esther O., and Daly, Flora M.: *Teen Agers Prepare for Work.* Books I and II. Castro Valley, Calif., Carson.
11. *Conceptual Learning Program Knowledge Aid.* Morton Grove, Illinois, Division of Ridedut Corp.
12. Correlated Language Arts Program. LaSalle, Ill., Open Court.
13. Disney Story Books: *Our Animal Story Books.* Chicago, Heath.
14. Dolch, Edward W.: *Reading Readiness Games.* Champaign, Ill., Garrard.
15. Eastman, P. D.: *Go, Dog Go!* New York, Random House, 1960.
16. Fearon Materials for Special Education and Pacemaker Books. Palo Alto, Fearon.
17. Feldman and Merrill: *Ways to Read Words, More Ways to Read Words.* New York, Teacher College, Columbia Univ.

18. Ferron Publishers: Titles including reading and phonics. Palo Alto.

19. Frostig, Marianne: The Frostig Program for the Development of Visual Perception. Chicago, Follett, 1964.

20. Frostig, Marianne: Frostig Training Perceptual Program (Ditto Masters). Elizabethtown, Pa., Continental.

21. Frostig, Marianne: Frostig Readiness Skills (Ditto Masters). Elizabethtown, Pa., Continental.

22. Garton, Malinda Dean: *Making Friends*. I-2, with workbook, Functional Basic Reading Series. Pittsburgh, Stanwix, House, 1965.

23. Garton, Malinda Dean: *Making Friends*. I-1, with workbook, adapted for junior high interest and age. Functional Basic Reading Series, Pittsburgh, Stanwix House, 1967.

24. Goldberg, Herman R., and Brumber, Winefred T.: *Rochester Occupational Reading Series*. Supermarkets, Restaurants and Cafeterias, Bakeries, Gas Stations, each on three levels. Chicago, S.R.A.

25. Goldstein, Herbert, and Levitt, Edith: *Reading Readiness Program for the Mentally Retarded, Primary Level*. Urbana, Ill., R. W. Parkinson.

26. Gray, William, and others: *Basic Reading Skills for Junior High Schools*. Glenview, Ill., Scott Foresman.

27. Greet, W. Cabell, and others: *In Other Words*. Glenview, Ill., Scott Foresman, 1968.

28. Hartley, E. Twyla: *Snip, Clip and Stitch*. A Clothing Construction Program, Teachers Manual. Urbana, Ill., R. W. Parkinson, 1965.

29. Harr Wagner Books: *Jim Forest Readers, Morgan Bay Readers, Deep Sea Series*. San Francisco, Harr Wagner.

30. Haugen, T. J., and MacDonald, R. L.: *Programmed Instruction and the Education of the Slow Learning Child*. Van Nuys, Calif., Media Educational Materials, 1965.

31. Hurst, John, and Tom, Judith: ". . . . and therby hangs a tale." Chicago, Children's Press.

32. Johnson, Marjorie S., and others: *The Read Series*. Cincinnati, American.

33. Kaluger, George, and Kolson, Clifford J.: *Reading and Learning Disabilities*. Columbus, Ohio, Merrill, 1969.

34. Landmark Books, *The "All About" Series*. New York, Random House.

35. Lang, Phil G., Ed.: *Programmed Instruction.* Chicago. The Sixty-sixth Yearbook of the National Society for the Study of Education, Part II. Univ. of Chicago, 1967.

36. LaValli, Alice, and Runge, Lillian: *Doorways to Employment: Want Ads, Application Forms, Street and Highway Signs, Industrial Safety Signs,* Detroit, The L-R Learning Aids.

37. Lawson Series, Workbooks for the Slow Learner: *Color Me American; Safe and Sound; Better Living; Everyday Business; Newspaper Reading,* ELK Grove, Calif., Lawson.

38. Let's Learn Sequence. Philadelphia, Instructo.

39. Lewis, Shari, and Oppenheimer, Lillian: *Folding Paper Masks.* New York, Button Books.

40. Macmillan: *Aviation Readers; Vocabulary Readers; Gates Series; Cross Country Trucker; State Trooper.* New York, Macmillan.

41. Merrill Little Wonder Books—Easy Readers: (1) *Keep Your Eyes Open,* by Michael Folsom; (2) *Question and Answer Book,* by Mary Elting. Columbus, Ohio, Merrill.

42. Messner Books: *Everyday Science Stories; The Treasury of Greenbar Island; A Chimp in the Family.* New York, Julian Messner.

43. Metropolitan Life Insurance Company, New York, N.Y. Write for list of aids.

44. McKee, Paul, and others: *Reading for Meaning Series.* Readiness, primary and grades 1-6, with workbooks, rev. ed. Boston, Houghton Mifflin.

45. Monroe, Marion, and Greet, W. Caball: *My Second Dictionary.* Glenview, Ill., Scott Foresman, 1964.

46. National Association for Mental Health: *What Every Child Needs.* New York, NAMH.

47. *New Alice and Jerry Basic Series.* Evanston, Ill., Row Peterson.

48. New Reading Books: *Dan Frontier Series; Tommy O'Toole Series; Sailor Jack Series.* Chicago, Benefic Press.

49. *New Rochester Occupational Reading Series.* Chicago, SRA.

50. Operation Alphabet: *TV Home Study Book,* with four workbooks. Philadelphia, Adult Education Project.

51. *Peabody Language Development Kits.* Circle Pines, Minn., American Guidance Service.

52. *Pleasure Reading Series.* Champaign, Ill., Garrard.

53. *Programmed Instruction: Reading in High Gear.* Accelerated Basic Reading Program for Culturally Disadvantaged Student. Chicago, SRA.

54. Reader's Digest: *Step One; Step Three;* Stories and work sheets, paper back. Pleasantville, N.Y.

55. *Reading Laboratory Series*: Work-text to study occupations. Chicago, SRA.
56. *Reading Skill Builders*: Grades 1-6. Pleasantville, N. Y., Readers Digest.
57. Remedial Education Center: *Go Fish, Vowel Dominoes*. Washington, D.C.
58. Robinson, H. Alan, and Rauch, Sidney J.: *Guiding the Reading Program*. Chicago, SRA, 1965.
59. Robinson, Helen M., and others: *The Open Highway Readers*. Glenview, Ill., Scott Foresman, 1969.
60. *Royalty*, a card game-scrabble type.
61. Samford, Clarence, and others: *You and Your Community*. Chicago, Benefic Press, 1967.
62. *See and Read Biographies*. New York, Putnam.
63. Scott Foresman: *Box Car Children; Surprise Island*. Glenview, Ill.
64. Scott Foresman: *First Talking Machine*. Glenview, Ill.
65. Scott, Louise Binder: *Tell Again Story Cards*, Level I and II. Manchester, Mo., Webster, Division of McGraw-Hill, 1967.
66. Scott, Louise Binder: *Paper Bag Puppet Patterns*, Grades K-2. Manchester, Mo., Webster, Division of McGraw-Hill.
67. Shawn, Bernard: *Foundations of Citizenship*. Book I. Phoenix, New York, Frank E. Richards, 1963.
68. Smith, Nila Blanton: *Be A Better Reader*, Books I through VI. Englewood Cliffs, N.J., Prentice-Hall.
69. Smith, Nila Blanton: *Reading Instruction for Today's Children*. Englewood Cliffs, N.J., Prentice-Hall, 1963, 1964.
70. Stanwix House, ed.: *Functional Basic Reading Series*. Pittsburgh, Stanwix House.
71. Steck-Vaughn Materials. Austin, Texas.
72. Stern, Catherine, and others: *Structured Reading Series*. Syracuse, N.Y., Singer.
73. Stone, Clarence R.: *Eye and Ear Fun*: For developing independence in word recognition, grades 1-6. Manchester, Mo., Webster, Division of McGraw-Hill.
74. Sullivan, M. W.: *Programmed Reading*. A Sullivan Associates Program, rev. ed. Manchester, Mo., Webster, Division of McGraw-Hill.
75. Sullivan, M. W., and others: *Sullivan Story Books*. Manchester, Mo., Webster, Division of McGraw-Hill.
76. *Teaching Resources*: Boston, New York Times Services.
77. Titus, Nicholas, and Gebremariam, Negash: *Trouble and the Police*. Syracuse, N.Y. New Readers Press.

78. Turner, Richard H.: *The Turner-Livingston Reading Series: The Money You Spend, The Person You Are, The Family You Belong To, The Jobs You Get, The Friends You Make, The Town You Live In.* New York, Washington Square, New York Univ.

79. Viking Junior Books: *Teen Age Stories.* New York, Viking.

80. Vivian, Charles: *Science Games for Children.* New York, Dover, 1963.

81. Wilson, John A. R., and Roebeck, Mildred C.: *Kindergarten Evaluation of Learning Potential.* Manchester, Mo., Webster, Division of McGraw-Hill, 1967.

82. Women's Division of the Institute of Life Insurance: *How Budgets Work and What They Do, the Family Money Management.*

83. Zimmerman, Irla Lee, Steiner, Violette G., and Evatt, Roberta L.: *Preschool Language Manual; Preschool Language Picture Book; Preschool Language Scale.* Columbus, Ohio, Merrill, 1969.

REFERENCES

1. Allen, Robert M., and Wallach, Edward S.: Word recognition and definition by educable retardates. *Amer J Ment Defic,* 73(6):881, 1969.

2. Altonen, Anita Louise: Language training for the mentally retarded. *ETMR, CEC,* 2(2):70, 1967.

3. Barbe, Walter B.: *Educator's Guide to Personalized Reading Instruction.* New York, Prentice-Hall, 1961.

4. Bearnall, E.: *Making a Start with Marionetts.* London, G. Bell, 1960.

5. Billingsley, James F., and Boyd, Susan: Teacher planning and programmed instruction for the adolescent mentally retarded. *ETMR, CEC,* 3(3):117, 1968.

6. Carlson, Bernice W., and Gingland, D. R.: *Play Activities for the Retarded Child.* Nashville, Abingdon, 1961.

7. Chalfant, James, Kirk, Girvin, and Jensen, Kathleen: Systematic language instruction: An approach to teaching receptive language to young children. *Teaching Exceptional Children,* 1(1):1, 1968.

8. Christiansen, Ted: Visual imagery as a factor in teaching elaborative language to mentally retarded children. *Exceptional Child,* 35(7):539, 1969.

9. Clawson, William B., and Schlanger, Bernard B.: Oral vocabulary responses of educable mentally retarded adolescent boys in a dyadic situation. *Exceptional Child, 34*(10):761, 1968.

10. Cruickshank, W. M., and Johnson, C. Orville: *Education of Exceptional Children and Youth,* 2nd ed. Englewood Cliffs, 1967.

11. Descoeudres, Alice: *The Education of Mentally Defective Children,* translated from the Second French Edition by E. F. Ross. New York, Heath, 1928.

12. Dunn, Lloyd M., Ed.: *Exceptional Children in the Schools.* New York, Holt, Rinehart, Winston, 1963.

13. Durrell, Donald D.: *Improvement of Basic Reading Abilities.* Yonkers-on-Hudson, N. York, World Book, 1956.

14. Fernald, Grace: *Remedial Techniques in Basic School Subjects.* New York, McGraw-Hill, 1943.

15. Goldstein, Herbert, and Seigle, Dorothy: *Illinois Guide for Teachers of the Educable Mentally Handicapped.* Illinois Council for Mentally Retarded Children. Danville, Ill., Interstate Printers.

16. Haring, Norris G., and Hauck, Mary Ann: Improved learning conditions in the establishment of reading skills with disabled readers. *Exceptional Child, 35*(5):341, 1969.

17. Haring, Norris G., and Phillips, E. Lakin: *Educating the Emotionally Disturbed Child.* New York, McGraw-Hill, 1962.

18. Hutt, Max L., and Cibby, Robert C.: *The Mentally Retarded Child,* 2nd ed. Rockleigh, N. J., Allyn and Bacon, 1965.

19. Ingram, Christine P.: *Education of the Slow Learning Child,* rev. ed. New York, Ronald, 1960.

20. Johnson, G. Orville: *Education for the Slow Learners.* Englewood Cliffs, N. J., Prentice-Hall, 1963.

21. Kingsley, Ronald F.: Associative learning ability in educable mentally retarded children. *Amer J Ment Defic, 73*(1):5, 1968.

22. Kephart, Newell C.: *The Slow Learner in the Classroom.* Columbus, Ohio, Merrill, 1960.

23. Kirk, Samuel A.: *Early Education of the Mentally Retarded.* Urbana, Univ. of Illinois, 1961.

24. Kirk, Samuel A.: *Educating Exceptional Children.* Boston, Houghton Mifflin, 1962.

25. Kraus, Richard: *Play Activities for Boys and Girls.* New York, McGraw-Hill, 1957.

26. Linsmeier, Mary T.: *Montessori in the Home.* Brookfield, Wisc., Mary Linsmeier Schools.

27. Mazurkiewiez, Albert J.: *New Perspectives in Reading Instruction.* New York, Pitman, 1964.

28. McConnell, Freeman, Horton, Kathryn B., and Smith, Bertha R.: Language development and cultural disadvantagement. *Exceptional Child*, 35(8):597, 1969.

29. McLeod, Pierce H.: *The Undeveloped Learner: A Developmental Corrective Reading Program for Classroom Teachers.* Springfield, Thomas, 1968.

30. Mooring, Ivy P., and Currie, Robert J.: A conceptualized model for community services for the mentally retarded. *Exceptional Child*, 30:5, 1964.

31. Mykleburst, H. R.: *Development and Disorders of the Written Language.* New York, Grune and Stratton, 1965.

32. Myklebust, Helmer R., and Johnson, Doris: Dyslexia in children. *Exceptional Child*, September 1962.

33. Nugent, Marion A.: *Home Training Manual.* Boston, Dept. of Mental Health.

34. Pollock, Morris, and Pollock, Miriam: *New Hope for the Retarded.* Boston, Porter Sargent, 1953.

35. Reich, Rosalyn: Out of the classroom: Puppetry—A language tool. *Exceptional Child*, 34(8):621, 1968.

36. Rosenzweig, Louis E., and Long, Julia: *Understanding and Teaching the Dependent Retarded Child.* Darien, Conn., Educational Pub. Corp., 1960.

37. Rothstein, Jerome H.: *Mental Retardation.* New York, Holt, Rinehart, Winston, 1961.

38. Roswell, Florence, and Natchez, Gladys: *Reading Disability: Diagnosis and Treatment.* New York, Basic Books, 1964.

39. Russell, David H., and Elizabeth F.: *Listening Aids Through the Grades.* New York, Teachers College, Columbia Univ., 1964.

40. Russell, David H., and Karp, Etta E.: *Reading Aids Through the Grades.* New York, Teachers College, Columbia Univ., 1964.

41. Salvin, Sophia Tichnor, and Light, Beulah: *Curricula, Methodology and Habitation of the Multiply Handicapped.* Los Angeles, Univ. of Southern California, 1963.

42. Smith, Nila Blanton: *Reading Instruction for Today's Children.* Englewood Cliffs, N.J., Prentice-Hall, 1963.

43. Smith, Nila Blanton: Reading Instruction in the Elementary School. *Today's Education*, 59(2):42, 1970.

44. Strang, Ruth: *Diagnostic Teaching of Reading.* New York, McGraw-Hill, 1964.

45. Strauss, Alfred A., and Lehtinen, Laura E.: *Psychopathology and the Education of the Brain-Injured Child; Volume I, Fundamentals and Treatment.* New York, Grune and Stratton, 1947.

46. Tansley, Albert Edward, and Gulliford R.: *Education of Slow-Learning Children.* New York, Humanities, 1961.
47. Theodore, Sister Mary, O.S.F.: *The Challenge of the Retarded Child.* Milwaukee, Bruce, 1968.
48. Weber, Elmer W.: *Educable and Trainable Mentally Retarded Children.* Springfield, Thomas, 1963.

8

WRITING

THE OBJECTIVES IN TEACHING WRITING

T̲HE objective in teaching the mentally retarded child to write is to help him achieve legibility for communication. This involves neatness, attention to letter size, spacing, smooth forms, and, in cursive writing, the proper joining of the letters to form words.

IMPORTANCE OF ESTABLISHING CORRECT HABITS

Writing is one subject that depends largely upon habit for its efficient use. Writing, a sensori-motor skill, is learned by repetition. The movements of the arms and fingers are stimulated by visual, auditory, or mental images. Children should write with large movements until they are able to control and integrate their muscular coordination.

Frequent opportunities to practice at the chalkboard assist in familiarizing the child with the arm movements necessary for writing. The large and small muscles must be trained to respond to demand. In using the chalkboard, only the chalk touches the board. The child must learn to hold the hand away from the surface of the board, and use the chalk to make the letters. Some authorities recommend as much as fifteen minutes a day at the board for each child, which should be in several "lessons" for the retarded, not all at one time. Here, it is easy to watch for careless

175

letter forms, spacing, and size. Also the children learn to stand on both feet, pay attention to their work, and listen for new directions.

To assist in achieving better motor control and developing coordination and rhythm which are necessary for neat writing, some exercises and games may be useful. These should be adapted to the needs of the particular child.

1. Make objects from clay or play dough. Form balls, pat, roll, punch and pull the clay into various shapes.
2. Use large sheets of newsprint and draw scribbles with soft lead pencils or crayons.
3. Use heavy finger paint on smooth paper.
4. Do finger plays.
5. String beads of various sizes.
6. Use finger puppets.
7. Use building blocks for free time play.
8. Use large sewing cards with simple outlines. These are available in masonite and in heavy cardboard. Use the colored, tipped strings.
9. Practice walking on a crack or a beam on the floor.
10. Practice walking up and down stairs.
11. Use music to practice hop, skip, and jump skills.
12. Practice stretching, squatting, marching, and dancing.
13. Kinesthetic development may be assisted by moving the fingers over smooth, rough, cold, or wet surfaces.
14. Learn to use scissors.
15. Learn to color neatly within an outline.
16. Learn to drop small objects in a hole in a box top.
17. Learn to work puzzles.
18. Learn how to fold paper.

MOTIVATION

One of the best ways to arouse interest in learning to write is to begin presenting the child's name for sight recognition, and for writing by tracing, or holding the child's hand at first, until he is able to hold a pencil.

The child who can write his name legibly has a socially acceptable skill that will be a source of satisfaction to him now and throughout his life. This ability will increase his confidence, his social status with his peers and with adults, and prepare him for signing legal documents.

Once the child has mastered writing his name, he begins to see the value of writing it to label his drawings, and his other belongings. The incentive to write notes, to write his friends' names, addresses and phone numbers, helps him to continue improving his skill.

As needs appear, the child's interest is stimulated and motivation is accelerated. These needs increase with age and advancement through the school. They will include writing practical lists of materials for class work, simple records, letters of inquiry and thanks, invitations and applications for jobs and for licenses.

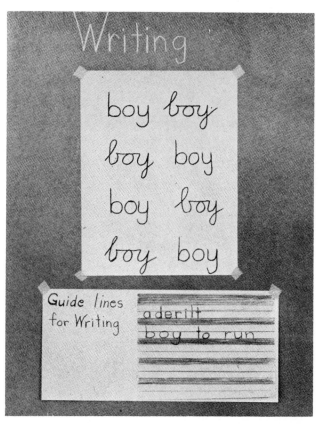

38. Illustration for teaching spacing in writing and a practice sheet for the transition to cursive writing.

CURSIVE WRITING

In most schools the child is introduced first to manuscript writing and later is taught to change over to the cursive letter forms. The educable mentally retarded child could profit by being taught cursive instead of manuscript writing, as this would help him to visualize the word as a unit. The child who uses the manuscript form has a strong tendency to write the words together without spacing.

Some of the group may be from schools where manuscript writing was taught first. Special work at their ability level must be prepared in manuscript writing until they can master cursive writing. The children should all be able to easily read manuscript writing as it is much like printing.

Cursive writing should be started with large arm exercises in the air and at the chalk board. Then later when they have some control they are started at the desks. Use first the large arm exercise in the air, then large circles on the paper with crayon or primary type pencil. Up and down movements, and movements to the right and out and away from the body come next. These exercises may be supplemented by more chalk board writing.

The exercises that are made with the arm in the air to imitate letter forms need positive direction and close supervision. The children may stand or sit or alternate as they do arm exercises. Direct them to point the fore finger and to make the arm go out and around, or up and down in front of the body.

When the children are at the chalk board they should be shown how to stand, in front of it and away from it, not touching the board. The left hand should be at the side or back. The chalk held within the hand by thumb and four fingers. Ask the children to try to make the same movements on the chalk board with the chalk they have been making in the air.

They will need help for many weeks, with practice in the air and again at the chalk board before they gain sufficient control of the large arm and shoulder muscles to form anything but scribbles. Begin giving them materials for following the lines and for using colors to trace over outlines to get the idea of form.

The teacher should be proficient in writing techniques. The movements she demonstrates should be rhythmic and easy for the child to imitate. The movements used in cursive writing and in manuscript are similar. The round letters should start and proceed anti-clockwise. The stem letters and beginning lines of most letters are made by up and down movements, and by movements out and away from the body.

When the teacher feels that a group of the children are ready, show them how to sit at their desks, to sit straight and tall, with both feet on the floor. Place a piece of primary type writing paper on each desk. Show each child how to hold the paper with his left hand to keep it steady, and how to keep moving the paper as he writes on it, and how to keep the paper's edge parallel with his writing arm. Show him how to hold the pencil between the thumb and two fingers. Hold his hand while you trace an "0." Let him try alone as you help another child.

This is slow tedious teaching. Just a little may be accomplished each day before the children become restless. At certain stages in the instruction the teacher may feel that one child needs added help, and some may not be given help in writing that period. Later they may be taken care of individually during a readiness period for numbers or reading.

There are several good systems of cursive writing on the market that may be studied by the teacher. A system that is simple will be followed with more ease by the pupils.

The left-handed pupils should be taught all of the same procedures as the right-handed pupil, but from a left-handed angle. Turn the paper to the right so the edge of the paper is parallel to the left arm when it is on the desk in writing position. The pencil then moves across the page from left to right toward the writer's body.

In cursive writing present the lower case letters first, and the round letters first. The only capital letters that might be presented first would be the initial letters of the child's names.

It is well to note that some children who have been taught the manuscript form seem unable to learn to use script. Many teachers feel that, as long as the educable mentally retarded are proficient in manuscript writing, there is no need to change. Even those who are able to change from manuscript to the cursive form are seldom ready for it before they are twelve years of age or have achieved third grade academic ability. One method to help the child gain dexterity in making the letters correctly is to prepare complete sheets of each letter in small and in capital forms for tracing. The use of different colors for each repetition of a word or letter compels the child to observe when a form is completed.

Tracing paper may be clipped to the cards or pages and the child shown how to trace over the copy. He may be given five or six sheets of tracing paper so that he can change the used sheet for a fresh one. The teacher should check him frequently to see if he is making the letter forms correctly. As the letters are taught, combine them and show how each letter is carried on to the next to form a word or a part of a word. It may be necessary to hold his hand and to help him trace until he gains confidence enough to work alone. He should return all of the practice sheets to the teacher to be checked.

MANUSCRIPT WRITING

Some teachers may be required or prefer to teach manuscript writing to beginners. Whether cursive or manuscript is being presented, good posture is important for success. It should be noted, however, the posture for manuscript writing is slightly different from that for script. The child should sit straight at the desk with feet flat on the floor. His arms should rest on the desk. The paper should be vertical to the body. The soft lead pencil should be held comfortably between thumb and fingers. Since almost any child has a tendency to slump in his seat, special

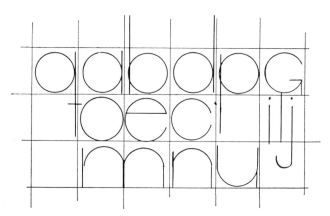

39.   Presenting manuscript writing to the children.

attention must be given to retaining good writing posture. The teacher should walk about the room and lightly touch the slouched child on the back to remind him to sit properly.

The half-inch squared paper will be a helpful aid to the child if he has difficulty in spacing, or in keeping the letters within a good range of size.

Letters like *l, i,* and *j,* that are narrow, take up half a space. When they are used together in a word, as in *lilt,* at least a third of a space should be left around each letter.

There are two wide letters, *M* and *W.* In the capital forms, they take up as much space as a round letter, but the small case forms of these same letters take one and one-half to two spaces, depending upon the system being taught. Most systems of manuscript writing use the *M* with the straight sides and the *W* with the flared sides. This device also assists the child to remember which is an *M* or a *W.*

In teaching the tall letters, leave plenty of space between the lines so that the letters do not overlap. All of the letters should be formed simply and precisely, without curls or decorations which confuse the children.

The teacher should explain to the child that he must keep the letters tall and straight above the line or long below the line so that they are easily distinguished from the short letters. It is better to skip a line on the paper in order that all of the letters will be formed perfectly.

The round letters are made close together as in the words *soon, see* and *bead.* The spacing is important for neat writing. Watchfulness at the early stage will prevent bad letter formation and sloppy writing.

MANUSCRIPT WRITING LESSON

Use of the Chalkboard. The teacher may find the following directions helpful:

1. Use a music liner to draw lines on the chalkboard. Omit the chalk from the clamps numbered two and four. Have the lines drawn before the class assembles. Use soft chalk to form the letters, because it makes a broad stroke that is easy to read.

2. Present all of the lower case forms first. These forms are based on a circle and a straight line.

Chalkboard Practice. Children who have never written will make faster progress by regular practice at the chalkboard than by starting with pencil and paper at their seats. This type of practice uses the large arm and shoulder muscles and produces a kinesthetic feeling for the form of the letters. Refer to cursive writing for chalkboard directions.

Desk Practice. After the child has practiced at the chalkboard for a time, the teacher should show him how to practice with paper and pencil at his desk. One method of helping the child achieve success is described below. Here are directions for the teacher to follow.

1. Prepare the chalkboard with lines before the class assembles.

2. Prepare a cardboard disk that will fit between the lines on the board. Have a foot ruler and chalk at the chalkboard.

3. Have a supply of writing paper and medium-soft lead pencils ready to distribute. The practice paper should have wide-spaced lines with light guide lines between the heavy base lines. These base lines may be emphasized with a heavy line of crayon.

40.   Spacing for tall letters.

4. For each child, have a six-inch ruler and disk the right size to fit between the lines of the writing paper.

5. Stand in front of the group and see that every child has his desk cleared and is paying attention. Talk to the children about what they are going to see you do and what they will be doing themselves very soon.

Use simple directions like these: "Keep watching me. See this circle. See this chalk. I am going to draw an *O*. Watch me. I will make another *O*. Draw around the disk from the top down on the left side and then up on the right. See, I draw around this way."

6. Pass the practice paper, pencils, rulers, and disks. Play money of the nickel or dime size is excellent for disks. Say "Now you may try to make an *O*. Place the paper straight in front of you. Put both feet on the floor. Sit up straight. Raise your arms and let them drop on the desk beside the paper. Pick up the pencil in the hand you use for drawing pictures. Pick up the disk in the other hand. Lay the disk on the paper *between* the heavy blue lines."

"Now you may try. Some of you know how to do this, but since it is fun to do, we will all draw *O* at the same time."

7. Walk about the group, checking and showing how to place the disks. See that the children all understand what is meant by *between*. Continue directing the children: "All together, draw around the disk." Hold the children's hands and guide them to form the letter correctly. Repeat many times, "go down and around and up."

8. Try to make a rhythm of the exercise as you repeat, "*O*. Go down on the left side, around and up to the top. *O*. Pick up the disk. Lay it down. Draw around the disk. Go down on the left side. *O*. Pick up the disk. *O*. Lay down the disk. Look to see if the disk is between the lines."

Remind the children to keep a nice space between the letters. Unless they have guidance on spacing, all of the letters will be too close together.

After several rows have been made by specific direction, go about, guiding hands and offering praise as the next row of *O*'s is being made without direction. Those who are able to do so may now make a row of *O's*, using the narrower space and no disks for guides. The other children continue using the disks.

When a row is completed, each pupil should lay down the disk and pencil and sit straight to indicate that he is ready to have his work checked.

Let those children whose letters are neat and well shaped and who have had writing experience proceed with copying words from a chart which you have prepared. These should be simple words beginning with *O* or having *O* in them. The other children continue to draw the *O*. Let them whisper, "O, O," as they form the letters.

Repeat the procedure for many, many lessons. There are some children who will need other reinforcements to help the memory process.

TRACING IN CLAY

Use tracing in clay as another method to aid the child to learn the letters' forms. Since this substance offers resistance to the muscles, it slows down the writing process so that the child can remember what he is doing.

Directions for Making a Clay Plan for Tracing. Select an ordinary tin or aluminum cookie pan, about 12 x 18 inches, with very low sides or rims. Two pounds of an oil base plastic clay is a good medium for the writing mixture. Smooth this evenly over the bottom of the pan.

Use an orange stick or large wooden skewer to trace a word or letter lightly on the clay. Give the stylus to a child and show him how to trace while he repeats the letter or word. Most children enjoy this type of repetition. After the child has made a deep mark to the bottom of the pan, allow him to smooth out the clay and start a new copy.

Presentation of *a*. Use the chalkboard, the liner, and the disk for the letter form of *a* the same as in presenting *O*. Direct the children: "Today we will learn to make the letter that says *a*, given the short sound. First we will make an *o*. Then take the ruler in your left hand and put it on the right side of the *o*. Draw a little line from the line on your writing paper at the top of the *o*, right against the *o*. Draw down to the bottom line on the paper that the *o* sits on. Lift the ruler. That is an *a*."

41. The clay pan.

Proceed with the same instructions as for teaching O. Practice an a and o for several days; then follow with the round lower case letters, c and e.

Presentation of the Tall Letter d. To introduce the letter d, proceed in the same manner as for a, but explain and show that d has a tall line on the right side. The tall line must reach away up to the next line on the writing paper above the top of the a.

If possible, give some distinguishing characteristic to each letter so that the child will have a peg upon which to hang the letter in his memory. Proceed with the presentation of the rest of the letters of the alphabet using the disk and ruler to demonstrate their correct forms.

KINESTHETIC TRAINING

As another means of helping the child remember the letters, paste cutouts of the letters on small cards made from various materials. Since a rough surface will be remembered more easily than a very smooth one, fine sandpaper is excellent for this purpose. Let the child lightly trace over the outline with his forefinger. Use small glass seed beads to outline the letters—they may be obtained at hobby shops. They are available in colors. The beads are smooth to the finger tips, yet offer resistance. On cardboard make another set of letters. Cut out the letter to form a stencil on the cardboard which the child may block out with his pencil. When he lifts the card, the heavy black letter remains in a true form.

There are many commercial materials available, such as stencils, plastic letters, letters for flannel boards, and magnetic letters for steel boards.

Give the child with a muscular involvement a large, very soft pencil. Wrap the center of the pencil with tape, or push a soft rubber ball onto the pencil to aid in grasping it more efficiently.

As the children attempt to write the letters, go about the group and help them. Show them how to hold the pencil and how to place the ruler vertically across the lines on the writing paper to make the stems of the letters. Explain the directions by showing them again with their rulers and disks what is meant by "Draw straight up and down," or "Draw around the disk."

Be patient! *Repeat* and *show,* and *help* the child *to do.*

Regardless of the order in which you decide to present the letters, be consistent in presenting their formation. Use the circle and the straight line in teaching manuscript letter forms; watch both the spacing of the letters and the spacing between the words to avoid crowding on the lines.

Demonstrate on the chalkboard each day the lesson that is to be taught. The children learn much from watching the writing process on the board.

CONSONANTS

Follow the basic reading series being used by the group in presenting the initial consonants in sequence. In teaching writing, always use the name of the consonant instead of its sound. Introduce the beginning consonant sound by using the words that are prepared for practice writing. In teaching the letter *d*, pronounce words from the list, such as dog, do, and day.

A child who is having trouble remembering where to start a new row of writing may use heavily blocked out areas above and below the lines to show the space in which he is to write.

After the pupils complete the small letters, start the capital letters. Proceed in the same manner as in presenting the lower case letters. Start with the round letters and the vowels and then follow later with the consonants.

If the children are not producing good letter formation, slow down the procedure and review until neat legible copy is obtained. Begin to emphasize the names of the letters and to try for rapid recognition.

Continue with the short lists of words, beginning with the letter being taught for practice writing. Add a short sentence for the better pupils to use for practice.

PRACTICE ON ENDINGS, s, ed, ing

The child, in the meantime, is beginning to recognize a few words. As his vocabulary slowly expands, present words to which the common endings of *s, ed,* and *ing* may be added. Let the child practice writing the endings independently many times before adding them to the root words.

Some children will learn to write neatly and accurately within a reasonable time. Other children will learn so slowly that they will require two or three years time to learn to make all of the small letters. They may not even be ready to try to write before they are nine or ten years old.

LENGTH OF WRITING PERIOD

Ten minutes a day is usually enough for an intensive writing practice. It is the persistent daily repetition that results in good writing.

USE OF ALPHABET CHARTS

Alphabet charts should be displayed in the Primary and Intermediate Rooms, where the children may easily refer to them. If the children in the group are using both manuscript and cursive forms these charts should be permanently shown. By looking at the charts when they are undecided about the form of a letter, they may see how to make the correct shape of that letter.

SUMMARY

The teacher should be proficient in cursive and manuscript techniques; make careful preparation for each writing lesson; set up a definite routine for all directions; assist the children constantly to gain confidence and produce legible copy.

REFERENCES

1. Enstrom, E. A.: The left-handed child. *Today's Education*, April 1969, p. 43-44.
2. Freeman, Frank N.: How to deal with left-handedness. *NEA Journal*, Jan. 1960.
3. Freeman, Frank N.: *Guiding Growth in Handwriting, Manuscript to Cursive.* Columbus, Ohio, Zaner-Bloser.
4. Gray, William S.: *The Teaching of Reading and Writing: An International Survey.* Chicago, UNESCO and Scott Foresman, 1956.
5. Green, Fred J.: Guide lines: writing—cum—discipline. *Clearing House Journal*, 7:21-24, 1967.
6. Kephart, Newell C.: *The Slow Learner in the Classroom.* Columbus, Ohio, 1960.
7. *Kittle's Penmanship, Worktexts, Grades 1-6.* Cincinnati, American Book.
8. Osterhaut, Edna Davison: *Teaching the Retarded Child at Home.* Durham, N. C., Seaman's, 1950.
9. Nugent, Marion A.: *Home Training Manual.* Boston, Dept. of Mental Health, 1957.
10. Patton, David H., and Johnson, Eleanor M.: *Spelling and Writing, Teacher's Manual.* Spelling for World Mastery Series, Columbus, Ohio, 1958.
11. Pollock, Morris, and Pollock, Miriam: *New Hope for the Retarded.* Boston, Porter Sargent, 1953.
12. Strauss, Alfred A., and Lehtinen, Laura E.: *Psychopathology and the Education of the Brain-Injured Child; Volume I, Fundamentals and Treatment.* New York, Grune and Stratton, 1947.

9

SPELLING

The object of teaching children to spell is to provide them with a means of communication where oral language cannot be used. The children must be made to realize that there are many everyday events requiring a note or a letter, such as the thank-you note, the letter to a friend or relative, or a note to the teacher.

MOTIVATION

Once the child is ready to communicate by writing, he should be allowed to learn to spell some useful words. He may want to give his mother a present and to add his own message. He may ask for help in spelling words or even ask for help in writing the words. That is the time to give him the assistance he wants and to encourage him to complete the message. From such a small beginning, the child may acquire an interest in learning to spell.

Spelling is taught in all areas of school work. The child should be made aware that the words in all of his books, the work on the chalkboard, the worksheets, and workbooks are there to read, to understand, and to use.

METHODS FOR TEACHING SPELLING

The words that the child will be using most frequently in writing messages should be taught first in spelling. He should be trained through writing letters or stories to recognize, spell, pronounce, and use them.

Lists of the most frequently used words have been prepared by specialists in this field of study. The teacher should go over several of these lists and prepare one suitable for the children in her room. About one-fourth of the total words used in most oral and written language includes such words as *the, and, is, that, it, to, a, I, in, of, for, you, be, we,* and five or six more common words.

In a test conducted by the Speech and Language Research Laboratory, University of Chicago, it was found that most people use only 403 words in more than 80 percent of their everyday conversation. The first thirty-three words in order of use were: is, the, and, a, to, I, that, it, he, of, she, not, be, in, this, look, or, like, do, her, there, that, on, well, has, his, they, think, know, but, have, just, very. Of these thirty-three words only four words made up one-sixth of the total: the, and, a, to. Therefore, the teacher can see the importance of preparing a short functional list of words and of teaching these words to the children as soon as it is practical.

Presentation of the Alphabet. Before the child can spell, he must know the names of the letters of the alphabet. Authors differ on the order of presentation but agree they should not be taught in alphabetical order, which is learned later.

When the teacher feels that the child has acquired an adequate basic sight vocabulary, she may present the consonant sounds in lessons that are separate from other activities. The sounds should not be presented in isolation, but in combination with a vowel or a word.

The vowels seem best understood when the short sound is presented first. The mentally retarded children remember the sound better if it is presented alone and later put into a word. Games similar to dominoes for matching pictures and vowels, and to Old Maid for matching sets of pictures and words, are useful in arousing interest in learning the short vowel sounds.

The teacher may have the pupils watch the shape of her lips as she makes the sound of the letter, or she may have them look into a mirror and try to imitate the shape of her lips.

As the training in the sounds of the vowels proceeds, the children become aware that the letters *a, e, i, o,* and *u* do not always say the same thing. They learn that the vowel says its name in some words, that it has a short sound in others, and that it takes on yet another sound with some consonants. The different sounds of some of the consonants and the blends which are confusing require much drill and explanation before they are understood.

Keep the spelling rules simple for the retarded. One rule to stress is that consonants only make voiced sounds when they are accompanied by a vowel. Also teach that our language has many service, or sight words, that do not fit into any rule, such as "on" and "of."

Children with Speech Difficulties. Good methods of teaching speech should be used for visual and auditory training. In working with the educable mentally retarded, the teacher should be careful that the child is observing her and understands what she is trying to show him. Refer those pupils to a speech clinic for therapy, when there is a special difficulty.

Introduction to Formal Spelling. When the child has a sight vocabulary of about fifty words and knows the names and some of the sounds of the letters of the alphabet, he is ready for formal spelling. The approach should be through the tactile, as well as through the kinesthetic, auditory, and visual senses.

Stimulation of the Tactile Sense. The tactile sense may be stimulated by *feeling* the shapes of plastic letters, letters cut from felt or cardboard, or letters cut from fine emery paper and glued to cards. The child passes the finger tips over these surfaces, as well as around the outlines of the letters. As the child traces over the letters or words, he repeats the name or sound he is to learn.

Stimulation of the Kinesthetic Sense. The kinesthetic, or muscular sense may be developed by tracing the letters or words on stencils, around plastic letters, over the letters through tracing paper, over the letter forms on the chalkboard, and, with a stick, in the sand box, or in plastic clay that has been smoothed into a shallow pan. The clay, which offers more resistance than the other media, is reserved for helping those with more difficulty in retaining the letter or word forms. As the word is traced in the clay, it is spoken audibly. The child's arm and hand is getting a stimulus, the vocal chords and the ear are also being stimulated, and finally the word is his. The child has assimilated the word! He has confidence in his ability and can spell the word. After this word has been written several times, the clay should be smoothed out and the child should try to write the word or letter from memory. This procedure should be varied with other sense training techniques which are described in this chapter.

Introduction of the Tracing Technique. The teacher should prepare an entire set of the letters of the alphabet and a set of the words the children are learning. The letters or words written on typing or drawing paper with various colored crayons should be several inches tall in either manuscript or cursive. These master sheets should have about eight repetitions to a page, and every other word should be written in a different color crayon. For a suggestion as to the form to use, the teacher should refer to the illustration accompanying this section.

The children use tracing paper over the worksheets, both of which should be arranged where the pupils have easy access to them. As each child traces or copies the words, he must stop at the end of each word and pick up a different colored crayon to resume the copying task. By this act he is made to realize that the word has been completed. He gradually forms a mental picture of the configuration of the word. From this image he begins to see the component parts and finally to realize that the words are composed of individual letters which he must learn to use in order to be able to spell.

Importance of Spelling. Spelling should be taught throughout the school day in connection with every area of learning. The spelling words must be used by the children in oral and written exercises. This continued use will make the words a permanent part of their language.

The teacher should not rely on one series of spelling workbooks for help and inspiration; instead, she should use every resource to provide the educable mentally retarded with adequate spelling materials.

Repetition Needed for Retention. Since these children need much drill on every sound and word, they must have specially prepared worksheets. Only the teacher can provide for the repetition and the practice necessary for the retention of a usable vocabulary. The mastery of even a few simple spelling words is a long and a difficult process. For this reason, the child should have a mental age of about 7-0 years before he is ready to learn to spell. His progress will be very slow. The teacher must not try to hurry him; yet she must keep him moving along. She will find that some children retain the vocabulary very well, while others build up to a plateau and then seem to forget every word. For the latter children there is only one course open, and that is to start over.

When necessary to "start over," try something new with this child. He may not be hearing or understanding, or may be afraid he is unable to perform the task. If he is not hearing the sound correctly, he cannot respond correctly. He may not be able to hear within a certain range of sounds. Teach him to listen for the beginning sounds, for rhyming sounds, and to attempt to imitate them.

Patterns of speech and regional pronunciation may be the block to his understanding. Have the child talk to you. Find out if he has a language problem. Listen to him. Try to put yourself in his place. If the child will respond to you and relate any word, and attempt to communicate with you, there has been progress.

Keep talking and give him plenty of time to respond. Look pleased when he does volunteer a word, a sentence. The correct sounds will come later, they should not be the principal concern at this time. If the child has a speech problem the speech therapist should be contacted. The child will learn to spell only after he becomes familiar with correct speech sounds.

SUMMARY

The educable mentally retarded child should acquire a useful written language ability. The spelling words should be selected with care to suit his present and his adult requirements. The words should be presented to him in a slow but continuous process to assure their retention.

REFERENCES

1. Ayer, Fred C., and Townsend, Rebecca M.: *My Imaginary Line, Spelling Book, Primary.* Austin, Texas, Steck-Vaughn.
2. Bell and Howell Electronic Programmed Equipment.
3. Billington, Lillian E.: *Spelling and Using Words.* Morristown, N.J., Silver Burdett.
4. Collins, Marianne: Auditory Training and Language Development in Infants. *Eye, Ear, Nose and Throat Monthly,* 47(9):408-411, 1968. (Methods for the hearing impaired child, good techniques for the retarded.)

5. Continental Press: *Visual Motor Skills.* Elgin, Ill., Continental.
6. Dolch, Edward W.: *Phonic Lotto, Sight Word Cards, Games.* Champaign, Ill., Gerrard.
7. The Economy Company. Oklahoma City: Workbooks, Supplies.
8. Electronic Futures, Inc., North Haven, Conn.: Machines, cards, tapes.
9. Engleman, Siegfried: Teaching reading to children with low mental ages. *ETMR, CEC, 2(4)*:193-201, 1967.
10. *Eye and Ear Fun Books,* C. R. Stone. Webster.
11. Eye Gate House, Inc., Jamaica, N.Y.
12. Heilman, Arthur W.: *Phonics in Proper Perspective.* Columbus, Ohio, Merrill.
13. The King Company: Phonic Lingo, Readograph, other teaching aids. Chicago.
14. Meighen, Mary, Pratt, Marjorie, and Halvorsen, Mabel: *Phonics We Use, A, B, C, D, E.* Chicago, Lyons and Carnahan.
15. O'Donnall, Mabel, Towens, Willmina, and Brown, Carl F.: *The Reading Road to Spelling Books.* Evanston, Ill., Row, Peterson.
16. Patton, David H., and Johnson, Eleanor M.: *Spelling and Writing, Teacher's Manual.* Spelling for Word Mastery Series. Columbus, Ohio, Merrill.
17. *Peabody Language Development Kits.* Circle Pines, Minn., American Guidance Service, 1968. (Authors and Ed.: Lloyd M. Dunn, James O. Smith and Kathryn B. Horton.)
18. Phonetic Games. Washington, D. C., Remedial Education Center.
19. Pollock, Morris, and Pollock, Miriam: *The Clown Family Speech Book* (Teacher's Manual for *We Want Toto!*). Springfield, Thomas.
20. Pollock, Morris, and Pollock, Miriam: *We Want Toto!, Speech Workbook,* Springfield, Thomas.
21. Rogers, Don C., Ort, Lorene, and Serra, Mary: *The New My Word Book* Spelling Series. Chicago, Lyons and Carnahan.
22. *Spell Correctly.* Morristown, N.J., Silver Burdett.
23. Tudyman, Al, and Grolle, M. C.: *A Functional Basic Word List for Special Pupils.* Pittsburgh, Stanwix House.

10

MUSIC

PURPOSE OF THE PROGRAM

Tʜᴇ purpose of teaching music to the educable mentally retarded is to assist them to a greater enjoyment of music. This enjoyment of music may be produced through listening, participating, or creating. Music appeals to the emotions and to the mind. The listener will gradually feel the rhythm of the music. When he begins to move his hands or feet to the rhythm he is having a new experience, developing confidence, beginning coordination of the mind and the body, and releasing tension and energy.

The withdrawn, fearful child may find a pleasant security in the sound of music, become animated and a part of the social group. The noisy, hyperactive child may be soothed by quiet tones, relax, and be cooperative.

Music used in a planned program for the classroom and as the need arises, to stimulate or to relax, may become an important factor in the social development of the children. They may attain satisfaction through self-expression and emotional release through listening or participating in musical activities.

Basis for Planning a Music Program. The teacher, in planning a music course for mentally retarded children, must consider their mental, physical and emotional status, as well as their environmental background. She must have a knowledge of their char-

195

acteristics, abilities, and disabilities. She must know their peculiar problems learning, discipline, humor, social situations, and group activities in order to have success with them. She must have an understanding of their mental, physical, and emotional needs as opposed to the normal child's needs.

She must learn how to hold their interest, to present adequate materials, and to assist in comprehension. She must learn ways to care for the maladjusted or the physically handicapped in the class. She must learn to recognize when a child has reached the saturation point with a certain type of music and change to another activity.

There may be a child in the group who responds to loud music and a fast tempo with shrieks of laughter or tears. He may require special care, even to being removed from the group before such an activity is started, because he has a low tolerance for this type of sound. Enlist the help of the librarian for a fifteen minute visit to the library at this time. Some definite activity should be

42. Rhythm band.

prepared so the child will feel useful and will be kept busy and happy.

The teacher must also remember that the educable mentally retarded child has a short attention span; therefore, she should vary the instruction period with several types of activity, commensurate with the child's ability. Understanding of the children's ability and careful preparation by the teacher should allow the music period to be an enjoyable experience.

The musical experience should be carefully selected to be within the understanding and ability of the group. The teacher of the primary or the intermediate groups must select the songs or activities, since few of the children will know what is suitable and available. Then the children by their interest or lack of interest, let the teacher know if she has chosen wisely.

As the children mature and gain experience they will request music, songs, and rhythm band activities they have enjoyed. They will also bring into the classroom their favorite records to be shared with the group.

Familiarity with the rhythm band instruments and the activities connected with their use appears to engender self-confidence. One child may direct the rhythm band, another may turn on and off the record player, one may jingle the bells, and another may be able to tap the tambourine correctly.

Some children are able to sing well and to remember the words of many songs. The words of favorite songs seem to stay with these children through the years.

PRIMARY GROUP ACTIVITIES

Music and activities for the primary level slow-learner or educable mentally retarded should be simple and repetitive. A list follows of some activities primary educable mentally retarded children are able to perform.

1. Sing *America,* first verse.
2. Sing primary songs with recordings.
3. Listen to recordings.
4. Draw with crayon or chalk as a record is played.
5. Finger paint to music.
6. Take exercises to rhythms. These may be played on the piano, or may be recordings. Some albums of rhythms have

special records for walking, hopping, skipping, galloping, marching, or running.

7. Play musical games.
8. Sing by rote.
9. Watch a short film or film-strip, picturing the story of a musical score or story.
10. Perform action songs.
11. Make up little jingles and tunes.
12. Learn the names of several musical instruments as a drum, violin, horn. Let them see, handle, hear a demonstration, of the actual instrument. Then follow through by showing pictures of these instruments.
13. Make a scrapbook of pictures of the instruments. Pictures may be obtained from musical supply houses.
14. Listen to rhythms and act them out by clapping, tapping on the desks, shuffling the feet, marching, or swinging the arms.
15. Try to imitate the sounds of the musical instruments as heard in the recordings.
16. Make simple instruments for rhythms: sand blocks, strings of bells, strings of bottle caps, dried gourds, round cereal boxes may be decorated and used as drums or rattles. Many kitchen utensils can be utilized as rhythm band instruments.

Source Materials for the Primary

I. Music Series with Record Albums
1. New Dimensions in Music Series, Chicago: American Book, 1970.
2. Arthur, Sister Mary, and Elaine, Sister Mary: We Speak Through Music, Manual and three L.P. records. Valhalla, New York, Stanbow Productions, Inc.
3. Making Music Your Own Series: Chicago, Silver Burdett, 1964.
4. This is Music Series: Chicago, Allyn, Bacon, 1967.
5. Magic of Music Series: Chicago, Ginn, 1966, 1968.
6. RCA Victor, New York, Educational Record Sales Company:
   a. Rhythm Program for Primary Grades.
   b. Listening Program for Primary Grades.

c. Singing Program for Primary Grades.
d. Adventures in Resting, L.P.
e. Everybody Sing, L.P.
f. Magic of Music, L.P.
g. Music for Relaxation, L.P.
h. Rodgers and Hammerstein (selected songs for children), L.P.
i. Quiet Music, 2 Vol., L.P.
j. American Folk Songs for Children, L.P.
k. Johnny Can Sing Too, 2 Vol., L.P.
l. Activity Songs, L.P.
m. The Rhythms Hour, L.P.
n. Adventures in Music, Tipton, Tipton.
7. Discovering Music Together: Chicago, Follett, 1966.
8. Steck Music Series, Worktests: Austin, Texas, Steck Publishing Company.
9. *Songs for Children with Special Needs*, Albums 1, 2, 3. North Hollywood, Calif. Bowman Records, Inc.
10. Concept Records: *Basic Songs for Exceptional Children.* North Bellmore, L.I., N.Y. (Three LP records.)

Most music series now have records available following the songs listed in their series of song books. This allows the teacher freedom to direct and help the children learn to sing. The record player should have a variable speed adjustment. This enables the children to be instructed at a slower speed until they learn the words, then the tempo may be increased.

II. Filmstrips and Records
Music Stories: Hansel and Gretel, Peter and the Wolf. Detroit, Mich., Jam Handy Organization.

III. Geri, F. H.: *Illustrated Games and Rhythms for Children in the Primary Grades.* New York, Prentice-Hall.

INTERMEDIATE GROUP ACTIVITIES

Musical activities for the intermediate age educable mentally retarded should be an extension and enrichment of the primary activities. More difficult material should be gradually introduced as the pupils mature and develop in ability and interests. The simple songs with a repetitive feature continue to be important for ease in learning and retaining the words. The children will continue to enjoy many of the activities initiated in the primary class. These may be an extension of former activities.

1. Learn the last stanza of *America*.
2. Start to teach the *Star Spangled Banner*.
3. Start to teach the first stanza of *America the Beautiful*.
4. Teach seasonal songs and other patriotic songs.
5. Teach popular new songs.
6. Recordings of popular musical plays are enjoyed for listening.
7. *Classics for Children*, Capitol Records, is suitable listening material.
8. Music book series with record albums listed under the primary materials are also available for the intermediate age pupils.
9. Stories of music classics and music stories with filmstrips are available from the Jam Handy Organization (see primary list). Intermediates enjoy The Nutcracker, The Sorcerer's Apprentice, The Sleeping Beauty, William Tell, Swan Lake.
10. Play records and let the pupils make drawings to the music.
11. Make drawing or painting to illustrate the stories of the recordings.
12. Play records for listening to recognize the melody.
13. Sing to recordings, piano, auto harp, or without accompaniment.
14. Exercise to rhythms.
15. Listen to quiet music for relaxation.
16. Play rhythm instruments to recordings. These may include class-made instruments as well as commercial items.
17. Introduce the resonator bells for group work.
18. Review the musical instruments taught in the primary and introduce new ones.
19. Teach about the woodwinds, percussion and string instruments and how they are used in the orchestra and in the band.
20. Make a scrapbook showing the instruments studied.
21. Learn to play a musical instrument. Simple tunes may be played on the chord organ, auto harp, tonette or recorder, or piano. There are simplified music texts for all of these instruments. Many use color codes.

22. Make an Indian drum from a wooden nail keg. Cover the open end with a piece of inner tube from a truck tube. This requires stretching the tube tightly and fastening it securely around the top. The keg may be painted in bright colors with an Indian type design before stretching the tube over the top of the keg. Tap on the rubber top with the fingers or palms of the hands.

23. A soft sounding rhythm instrument may be made from two small tea strainers partially filled with uncooked rice or gravel. Put the gravel in one tea strainer. Place the other tea strainer over it, up-side down. Tie the two together. (Courtesy Helen McCallom.)

24. Teach folk dances from our country and from other countries.

25. Teach square dancing. Find an album with simple uncomplicated movements and calls. Each step of the dance must be mastered independently, then step by step they are taught in sequence. All of this is done without music. When the pupils have some confidence in the routine, the music with the calls is played. This is a critical time in the learning process. Try to guide the children through the routine with a minimum of errors. Keep the group moving. Watch the child who appears uncertain and turn him around and send him along in the right direction.

The group will soon become proficient as the square dance music has a strong, steady, repetitive rhythm that is enjoyable. Interest may be stimulated by a few additions to the pupils' everyday clothes, of head scarves for the girls and neckties for the boys. The girls may eventually make full skirts to wear for variety.

JUNIOR HIGH ACTIVITIES

At this level the young teenage pupils are not interested in former primary activities. Usually there is good interest in group activity that includes popular items similar to that enjoyed by any teenage group. They like popular songs, records, dances, and activities. They will sing seasonal and patriotic songs. They will listen to recordings of good music. They enjoy band music and lively orchestra music.

Square dancing is popular and more intricate dance sets may be introduced at this age. Social dancing etiquette should be taught along with the dancing steps. The young man should be instructed in the proper way to ask a girl to dance with him, how to escort her to the dance floor, and how to return her to her group when the dance is over. The girl should also be instructed in the proper way to accept or refuse as a partner any one who asks for a dance, and how to thank the partner when the dance is over.

At this age more of the pupils should learn to play musical instruments. The chord organ, piano, recorder, drum, xylophone or auto harp are good choices for beginners. A xylophone chorus arouses interest, especially if the instruments have been made by the group. The wooden xylophone has a pleasant tone and is satisfactory to teach simple rhythms.

DIRECTIONS FOR MAKING A WOODEN XYLOPHONE

The frame may be constructed of scrap material. The blocks should be of a hardwood with a fine even grain. The blocks may be slightly tuned by hollowing out the center of the underside or sandpapering the ends. Hollow out to raise the tone, shorten the block to lower the tone (Courtesy of Lowell Kuntz). The density of the wood affects the tone. Working directions with dimensions are pictured in the text.

Assemble the frame and glue a felt strip the width of the runners to each runner. Cut the tone blocks from the hardwood strip. The eleven blocks should be cut in these lengths: G-9″, A-9½″, B-10½″, C-11″, D-11½″, E-12″, F-13½″, G-14″, A-14½″, B-15½″, C-16½″. Drill a hole in each end of each tone block to allow it to fit easily over the opposing nails that have been spaced in the top of the frame. Fit the tone blocks over the nails. Make a mallet from a 12″ length of dowel rod, fitted with a large pencil eraser. (Courtesy of Beulah Wildermuth.)

HIGH SCHOOL ACTIVITIES

The musical activities for the senior or advanced age group of educable mentally retarded will generally follow the pattern set by the junior high school. Some integration will have been made in the junior high school, and more should be made at this time

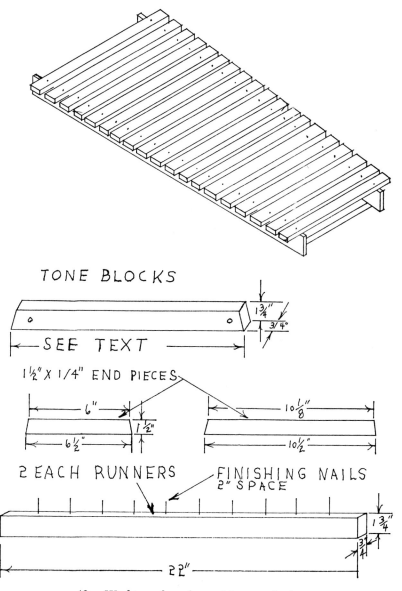

43. Working plans for making a xylophone.

as pupils' ability and maturity allow freer participation and integration with regular classes. It should be noted that pupils will have less time for such activities in senior high school as preparation is intensified for training on the job and for eventual separation from school.

The homeroom teacher should keep interest alive by class discussion about new songs, recordings, dances, school programs, community musical programs, and band concerts. Class parties provide an opportunity for the young adult to keep in practice singing and dancing.

Teaching Songs with the Words and Music. The teacher should observe the following order for the older pupil who is able to read.

1. Write the words of the song on the chalkboard or chart paper.
2. Use the words of the song as a reading lesson, explaining the meaning of the words and phrases.
3. Present the tune by humming or playing on a musical instrument.
4. Have the pupils hum the tune.
5. Sing the words to the pupils.
6. Have the pupils sing the words with you.
7. This procedure should be repeated until the song is memorized.

A FOLK DANCE

The Tinikling Dance. The Tinikling Dance was introduced to a group of intermediate age educable mentally retarded children. The unusual Tinikling Dance from the Philippine Islands is an example of a folk dance that was successfully taught to an intermediate age group of slow learners. The dance was introduced by a graduate student teacher from the Philippine Islands. This dance provided the focus of interest for a unit of work about the growing of rice. The teacher used the music and words in both Spanish and English. The Tinikling is a Samar-Leyte folksong with the English version by Nancy Byrd Turner. The name of the song and dance, Tinikling, differs in its spelling from the name of the bird, tikling. The teacher demonstrated and explained how the tikling runs and hops around as it pecks at the rice and tries to keep out of the trap which is represented by two poles.

44.   The Tinikling—a folk dance.

The directions and explanation of the meaning of the dance are simple as given in the music text, *The Philippine Progressive Music Series,* Primary Grades, Copyright, 1948, by Silver Burdett Company, in the Republic of the Philippines. "The name 'Tinikling' suggests the imitation of the way in which the bird 'tikling' walks. Use the right foot for four measures, then the left for four and keep alternating."

The dance is easy to learn. The three-quarter time provides an easy rhythm for the dancers as they hop on one foot as the poles are brought together, and tap that foot inside the "trap" as the poles are separated on the counts of *two* and *three.*

The teacher and the children may make up a story about the tikling bird and the trap and act it out to the music of the song. The children enjoy an activity such as this one in which they learn something that their brothers and sisters have not learned at school. Every community has some members from other nations who are usually delighted to teach folk songs and dances. Perhaps some of the children's parents or relatives might be willing to help in such a project. The teacher could first learn the song, game or dance from the person and do the actual presentation, while the other person assisted.

The teacher must assume the responsibility for locating songs, recordings, films, film strips, and instruments and for locating books of instruction to help her become an authority in presenting games, songs and dances from her own as well as from other countries.

SUMMARY

The educable mentally retarded enjoy music. With a patient teacher they can learn many songs, rhythms, musical games, and dances. Through these activities they improve their ability to socialize, release energy, and become happier, more stable people.

REFERENCES

1. Berel M.: *Bibliography on Music Therapy.* New York, United Cerebral Palsy Association of N.Y., 1969.
2. Bowman Records. North Hollywood, Calif.
3. Catholic University of America: *Workshop on Music Education,* 1953 and 1954. *Workshop on Special Education of the Exceptional Child,* 1954. Washington, D. C., Catholic University of America.
4. Coleman, Jack: Music for Exceptional Children. Evanston, Summy Birchard.
5. Concept Records: *Basic Songs for Exceptional Children.* North Bellmore, L.I., N.Y.
6. Educational Records, New York.
7. Ernst, Karl D., and Gary, Charles L.: *Music in General Education.* Washington, D.C., Music Educators National Conference, 1965.
8. Ginglend, David R.: *The Expressive Arts for the Mentally Retarded.* New York, NARC, 1967.
9. Ginglend, David R.: *Using Records with Retarded Children.* A list of records and albums and resources for leisure time activities. New York, NARC, 1966, p. 106.
10. Ginglend, David R., and Stiles, Winifred E.: *Music Activities for Retarded Children.* New York, Abingdon, 1965.
11. Haynie, William S., and Red, Buryl A.: *Headstart with Music.* Chicago, Systems for Education, 1966.

12. McCall, Adeline: *This is Music.* Rockleigh, N. J., Allyn and Bacon, 1965. (Kindergarten songs, listening activities.)
13. National Association for Music Therapy: *Music Therapy.* Chicago, National Association for Music Therapy, 1951.
14. New York State University: *Children the Music Makers.* Buffalo, Bureau of Elementary Curriculum Development, 1953.
15. Nye, Robert E.: *Music for Elementary School.* Washington, D. C., American Council on Education, 1959.
16. Society of Brothers: *Sing Through the Day.* Rifton, N. Y., Plough.
17. Wessells, Katherine Tyler: *The Golden Song Book.* New York, Golden Press, 1963.
18. Wylie, Evan McLeod: Pied Piper from Peoria. *Readers Digest,* 93(5):58, 1968.

11

HEALTH

HEALTH, RECREATION, PHYSICAL EDUCATION AND SAFETY

THE importance of a good program of health, recreation, physical education, and safety for the mentally retarded
cannot be overemphasized. The success of the entire program
depends entirely upon the physical condition of the child, and is
contingent upon his mental health. The physical condition has
an important influence upon the mental health. The child with a
tendency to emotional instability becomes easily discouraged,
depressed, or angered.

A healthy child has a better chance to make friends, to have a
vocation, to merge into the school life, and to adjust to the community. Better emotional health and social adjustment may be
aided through the development of special health and nutrition
courses and through proper physical education classes. This is
aided by the appropriate knowledge of good safety rules and
pleasant recreational activities. Many opportunities for personality growth should be provided through the areas of music, arts
and crafts, industrial arts, dramatization, play therapy, and homemaking.

There are many complete diagnostic clinics as well as treatment
centers throughout the country. These clinics and treatment
centers are often combined. Sometimes several agencies in a community will go together, as in Peoria, Illinois, and house their

services in one building. This provides easy access to the agencies
for the concerned persons.

SOME TESTED PROGRAMS

The mentally retarded, or slow learner, sometimes with attention, love and help, moves into a regular classroom. The so-called
trainable child may be able to function in the educable class. In
some residential institutions, love and companionship, a variety
of experiences, and much communication with selected adults,
proved to be key that unlocked the door to these closed lives.

The Denton State School, in Denton, Texas, under the direction of Superintendent E. W. Killian, has in operation an elaborate
"Grandmother and Grandfather Plan." Each day, six days a week,
for two hours, the same elderly person comes to the residence
school. This substitute grandparent has complete charge of the
same child each time. They take walks, they play, they talk. If
the child is not able to do this, the "grandparent" holds the child,
pets and talks to him, so the child feels loved and wanted. The
child improves, becomes interested in life. Some who have never
walked or talked are now doing both.

The Arkansas Children's Colony at Conway has a similar program, with trained therapists working daily with children who
were not talking, not even moving, with astonishing results. The
Dixon State School, Dixon, Illinois, in the early sixties was ex-
perimenting with adult patients as substitute mothers in the infants wards with good results.

This kind of program is spreading across the country in the
residential schools. The lesson is important for the teacher of the
retarded in the public school. Special pupils must have their
rightful share of time in the gymnasium and on the play grounds.
Where the special teacher must be the instructor as in the usual
primary grade situation, special play equipment must be provided.

All of the facilities of a school should be available for the slow
learner. Teachers in other special areas should be willing to spare
their specialized knowledge a few times each week for these
youngsters, who are frequently quite adept with tools and homemaking equipment. Most schools have enough sections in every
area, the slow track section could accommodate the retarded, if a

special section is not available for them. The teachers should be flexible enough to adapt materials for the slow learner.

Lessons in health care and safety should be presented regularly, as these children need many repetitions to reinforce retention of any material. The physical education program should be on a regular schedule to build good muscle coordination.

In the primary group, the children love the simple games that may be played out of doors in good weather. Usually by the second grade the group is able to be in a class of their own in gym, or to be integrated in different regular classes according to their age and physical ability. This schedule may be worked out by the principal with the special teacher and the physical education teachers. With all of this, remember to love these children, then you may expect them to respond.

The pupils from the primary and intermediate groups, in the special classes at Whitaker Elementary School, Finneytown School District, Cincinnati, Ohio, were placed in regular classes of physical education. These classes ranged from the second through the fifth grade.

The Intermediate pupils were from eleven through thirteen years of age, with the usual range of academic ability. All of this group attended some regular gym class.

The primary pupils were aged seven through ten years. The youngest ones had some form of play and exercise with the teacher. The older ones were placed with the regular second and third grade classes. Sometimes a child should be changed from an assigned class because of inability to perform physically, or because of an emotional disturbance. Special therapy may be indicated.

The child's health should be constantly checked. Often the mentally retarded child is unable to explain what is wrong. He seems to lack the sense of knowing when he is really ill. The teacher might watch for unusual trips to the rest room, flushed faces, sleeping in school, not eating lunch, many trips to the drinking fountain, paleness and the like. If the child makes a complaint about an actual pain, do listen, closely observe the child, and if possible, contact the school nurse or parent. Send a note home alerting the parent to the observed symptoms.

The noon lunch is often an important part of the child's daily nutrition. It is important to help the child see the value of eating a variety of foods, to observe good manners, to be clean, and to be considerate of others. These things make for a better attitude and aid digestion.

The importance of diet on intelligence has been demonstrated by studies such as that undertaken by the Child Development Day Activity Center, St. Louis University, Missouri. This study brought out the importance of a well-planned diet for the mentally retarded child. Other studies have presented implications for proper food during the first few weeks of the life of the infant as well as later. Lack of proper nutrition can cause irreparable damage to the infant's brain.

Proper recreation for children and youth must be a part of any program. The person who undertakes to direct such a program should be understanding, energetic, and enthusiastic. Sometimes local clubs help, other times a community center, or a parents group form the background, offering recreation facilities to the handicapped on assigned afternoons or evenings.

Scouting is a good outlet for both boys and girls. There are special manuals to assist sponsors of these organizations for the retarded. The various associations for the slow learners and the retarded usually provide regular recreational and social meetings for the young people. In Ohio, The Hamilton County Association for the Retarded, provides special nights for bowling, dancing, and other parties. These are well attended. They are enjoyable social affairs and fill a deep felt need of the young people.

ACTIVITIES FOR INDOOR RECREATION

Keep some materials and activities for those days when the weather will not permit the very young to play outside. Try some skill games: ring toss, toss the bean bag into a box, drop a clothes pin into a jar, drop a marble into a hole in a box top, walk the beam, crawl through the tunnel, build a block house, use the tinker toys, match blocks for color, work on scrapbooks, cut out paper for chains and make the chains, weave paper mats, play house, pop corn, bake cookies, weave yarn or loop mats, knit on spools, or use sewing cards.

Some of the pupils may enjoy coloring. Help them to crayon properly by starting at the outer edges and working in to the center. Show them how to color smoothly. If not taught properly, they will make random marks across the page, not even looking at the form of the object to be colored. They must be shown the shapes of things.

Making a chain in a sequence of colors requires patience and careful instruction by the teacher. The results are pretty and the pupils have learned to follow directions carefully. Start with alternating colors and advance to three colors slowly. Teach the correct way to paste, to use a small amount on both ends of the paper and press the ends together.

Use modeling clay. One kind may be made by a class of older pupils for the younger classes. This should be supervised and safety rules for hands around hot pans should be stressed. 1 cup salt, ¾ cup corn starch, ½ cup water. Mix and put in a double boiler over boiling water. Stir into a ball. Remove from the fire. Turn the ball out onto wax paper and cool slightly. Store in wax paper until used.

Stencil drawing is fun, the shape drawn may be colored. A flannel board is useful for matching colors, shapes, materials, or pictures. Objects and other items may be matched on a table. Small boxes may be used for sorting objects into groups or sets.

REFERENCES

1. Arbuckle, Wanda Rector, Ball, Eleanor Hill, and Cornwell, George L.: *Learning to Move and Moving to Learn—Book I; Insects.* Columbus, Ohio, Merrill, 1969.

2. Barclay, Marion S., and Champion, Frances: *Teen Guide to Homemaking,* 2nd ed. Manchester, Mo., Webster Division of McGraw-Hill, 1967.

3. Birenbaum, Arnold, and Schwartz, Arthur L.: *Recreation for the Mentally Retarded: A Community Program.* New York, AES, Association for the Help of Retarded Children, New York City Chapter, 1967.

4. Canner, Norma: *". . . . . and a time to dance."* Boston, Beacon, 1968.

5. Carlson, Bernice Wells, and Ginglend, David R.: *Recreation for Retarded Teenagers and Young Adults.* New York, Abingdon, 1968.

6. Carlson, Bernice Wells,. and Ginglend, David R.: *Play Activities for the Retarded Child.* New York, Abingdon, 1961.

7. Carson, Byta, and Ramee, McRue Carson: *How to Plan and Prepare Meals*. Manchester, Mo., Webster, Division of McGraw-Hill, 1968.
8. Choromanski, Frederick: Pilot swim program successful in Norwalk. Norwalk City Schools, Conn., Dept. of Special Education. *CARC News, 3*(5):3, 1968.
9. Community Playthings, Rifton, N.Y.
10. Creative Playthings, Inc., Princeton, N.J.
11. Crane, Helen: *Easter Seal Guide to Special Camping Programs*. Chicago, National Easter Seal Society, 1968.
12. Daniels, Arthur S.: *Adapted Physical Education*. New York, Harper, 1954.
13. Duncan, Ray O., and Watson, Helen B.: *Introduction to Physical Education*. New York, Ronald, 1960.
14. Dunham, Paul Jr.: Teaching Motor Skills to the Mentally Retarded. *Exceptional Child*, 35(9):739, May 1969.
15. Endress, Jeanette and Thaman, Audrey: New Perspectives in Applied Nutrition for Mentally Retarded Children. *Ment Retard*, Feb. 1969.
16. Fait, Hollis F.: *Physical Education for the Elementary School Child*. Philadelphia, Saunders, 1964.
17. Freeberg, William H., and Luan, Bert: *Recreation for the Handicapped: A Bibliography*. Carbondale, Southern Illinois Univ., 1967.
18. Health, Physical Education and Recreation. Joint Committee of the Council for Exceptional Children and the American Association for Health, Physical Education, and Recreation. Washington, D. C., 1968.
19. Hunt, Valerie V.: *Recreation for the Handicapped*. New York, Prentice-Hall, 1955.
20. Kephart, Newell C., and Radler, D. H.: *Success Through Play*. New York, Harper and Row, 1960.
21. Kirk, Samuel A., Karnes, Merle B., and Kirk, Winifred D,: *You and Your Retarded Child*, rev. ed. New York, Macmillan, 1968.
22. Ladoca Aids for Teaching the Mentally Retarded: Originated by Roy McGlone and manufactured at the Ateliers of Larandon Hall School for Exceptional Children, Denver, Colo.
23. LeCrone, Harold, and Mary Jane: *Fun While Learning*. Dansville, N.Y., Owen, 1963.
24. McDonald, Eugene T.: *Understand Those Feelings*. Pittsburgh, Stanwix House, 1962.

25. McLellan, Margaret: Home economics and the slow learner. *Special Education in Canada*, 42(4):23-28, 1968.
26. Montessori, Maria M.: *Fantasy and Reality in Children's Games*. Children's House, Nov./Dec. 1966.
27. National Recreation and Parks Association: *A Guide to Books on Recreation*, Twelfth Annual Edition, 1968-1969. Washington, D.C.
28. National Association for Retarded Children: *Guidelines for Helping Local Units Initiate and Strengthen Recreation Programs for the Retarded*. New York, NARC, 1969, p. 106.
29. *Nutrition and Intellectual Growth in Children*. ACEI, 1969.
30. Olson, Huber, and others: *Elementary Physical Education*. Bloomington, Minn., School Dist., 1962, p. 271. (Good activities, games, rhythms, and plays.)
31. Project on Recreation and Fitness for Mentally Retarded. A guide for programs in recreation and physical education for the mentally retarded. Washington, D. C., AAHPER, 1968.
32. Robinson, Christopher M.: Physical education of the mentally handicapped child. In Boom, Alfred B., Ed.: *Studies on the Mentally Handicapped Child*. London, Edward Arnold, 1968.
33. Salt, Benton E., Fox, Grace I., and Stevens, B. K.: *Teaching Physical Education in the Elementary School*. New York, Ronald, 1960.
34. Schneider, Herman and Nina: *New Health Science Series*, Grades 1-6. Chicago, Heath.
35. *Scouting for the Mentally Retarded*. New Brunswick, N.J., BSA, 1968.
36. Barnett, M. W.: *Scouting: Handicapped Girls and Girl Scouting*. Girl Scouts of the USA, 1968.
37. Sisters of St. Francis of Assisi, St. Colette Schools: *Physical Education Curriculum for the Mentally Handicapped*. Milwaukee, The Cardinal Stritch College, 1962.
38. *Swimming for the Mentally Retarded*. New York, NARC, 1958.
39. U. S. Department of Health, Education and Welfare: *Feeding the Mentally Retarded Child*. Washington, D. C., 1964.
40. U. S. Department of Health, Education and Welfare, Children's Bureau: *Guide to Nutrition Services for Mentally Retarded Children*. Washington, D. C., 1967.
41. Wallace, H. M., and others: Comprehensive health care of children. *Jr. P.H.*, 58(10):1839, 1968.

12

ARTS AND CRAFTS

PURPOSE OF THE PROGRAM

THE purpose of teaching arts and crafts to the educable mentally retarded is to give them an opportunity to learn about some of the materials used in art and construction activities. It should increase their appreciation for arts and crafts, lessen their fears, tensions, and feelings of inadequacy, aid in better physical coordination, improve manual dexterity, social adjustment, and provide leisure time activities.

PLANNING THE ART PROGRAM

Art activities should be planned so that the mentally retarded are able to achieve success and attain a degree of pleasure. Therefore, the program must be adapted to the children's ability to understand and to follow directions. The teacher must remember that a simple direction may contain words that have no meaning for the children. Their useful vocabulary is limited because of a dearth of experiences.

Mentally retarded children usually have a feeling of frustration whenever they are introduced to any of the tools used in creative endeavor. Their undertakings have been unsatisfactory compared to those of their chronologically aged peers. Any plan or directions should be carefully prepared by the teacher so that the directions and the skills needed to complete the task do not frustrate the child before he even attempts it.

Basis for Planning the Program. The teacher must consider the chronological age of the children, as well as their mental age and emotional tone in the preparation of an art lesson. A child cannot respond to this instruction when he is terrified, insecure because of parental rejection, or is angry at misunderstood or cruel treatment. Such children are unable to verbalize their feelings or to interpret to themselves the treatment they have received at home, at school, or at play; hence a free period of art activity should be substituted for the regular class lesson.

The teacher must be aware that in every educable mentally retarded class there are at least three groups with as many years of experience in that room. Since each pupil remains there approximately three years, about one-third of them are new to the program, one-third have had one year's experience, and the other third have two years' experience.

The teacher should carefully list the skills needed to complete the project before deciding whether all of the group can complete it or whether this is a project for a few of the older children. The mentally retarded do not notice how things are done around the home; they do not have a supply of miscellaneous information that helps them in carrying out directions; their environment usually does not provide them with experiences in cutting, sewing, ironing, stirring things with spoons, or rolling out pie dough. Any such skill must be taught by the teacher before the child is ready to proceed with directions calling for cutting, pressing, mixing, rolling out or sewing.

The teacher inexperienced in working with the mentally retarded is often misled by the appearance of these children, for physically they differ little from the normal children. Therein lies the danger for the children and for the teacher. Since they do not appear to be handicapped, she expects them to perform as does the usual child, but they are unable to meet even the ordinary competition of their peers.

The mentally retarded lose their self-esteem because of their many failures to meet with approval and success; as a result, they sink into apathy or indulge in tantrums, bullying, or other overt actions. However, success in even a small measure contributes to building their ego by compensating for failure in many endeavors.

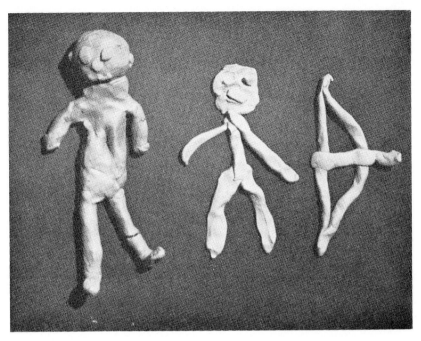

45.   The clay images show a lack of self-confidence.

The educable mentally retarded are often blessed with an imitative ability, and are able to enlarge upon things they see and experience with a delightful fantasy. They love gay colors, and when they feel free to do as they desire with a medium, they obtain much joy and pleasure from their efforts.

DEVELOPING SELF-CONFIDENCE

The teacher will observe that once the child feels unrestricted and free to paint, the urge to do so occurs frequently. Some children have repressed their feelings so long that it takes much time, patience, understanding, and encouragement to get them to realize that the teacher wants them to be unrestrained.

Children who have been in regular rooms find it difficult to abandon their previous peers' standards of perfection. It is only after they accept the new evaluation and relax that they can tell their story through their own fantasy of painting or modeling in clay.

46.   The clay images show developing self-confidence.

For many months Joe was rebellious toward every school activity, his modeling in clay was flat, immature, and repetitious. Gradually, his appearance became that of a happy youth, his progress in the basic school subjects improved, his modeling became three dimensional, varied and coordinated with units of study.

The teacher can help the emotionally disturbed child by giving him materials and a place to work in privacy. He then may gain confidence not only in himself, but in the teacher. This confidence cannot be forced, but must grow slowly as rapport is established.

The child's confidence in the teacher may cause him to take a painting to her and even try to tell her a little story about it. If possible, she may write down the story and later use it as a reading lesson with the child. If it is not a suitable story, she may want to pin it to the picture or model for future reference. These acts on the teacher's part usually give the child a sense of importance which makes the painting and story valuable to him. Such rapport between pupils and teacher may take weeks or months to be established.

Such was the case of Gladys who was a product of a broken home and of several unsatisfactory foster home placements. Gladys was a pale, withdrawn child who refused to speak except in monosyllables. She was five years educationally retarded and was not interested in any school activity. She would sit at a table with a ball of clay and withdraw from the activity of the classroom. She made a few objects but quickly destroyed them.

It was the middle of February before she brought one of her modelings to the teacher. She called it "Little Mouse." Later she made some objects she identified as "Little Boy and Kitty," and "Cat and Kitten." It was almost a month before she saved another object. She worked for about an hour rolling, patting, destroying, and again shaping the object. She brought this to the teacher and said, "This is Little Boy sitting in his bed."

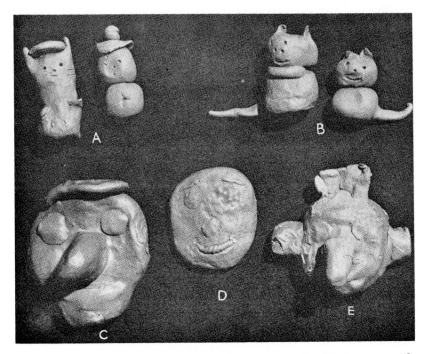

47. At the time the clay figures A and B were made, Gladys was withdrawn and spoke only in monosyllables. Figures C, D, and E, were made by Allan.

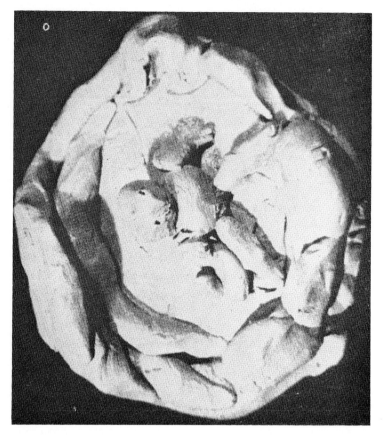

48.   Gladys spoke her first sentence after she made this clay image.

This was the first long statement she had made and the teacher was elated. After that Gladys began to take part in class discussions and other activities.

In working with the children on a free basis, the teacher instructs them to put their names and the date on the back of the paper. A mark of their name or initials on the clay will establish ownership. The mentally retarded frequently refuse to acknowledge as their own production a painting in as short a time as a few hours. The child cannot recall the emotion that produced the painting. Since he has painted it out of his system, he does not feel kinship with the painting.

Allan never claimed any of his clay models. However, his modeling seemed to help him relax sufficiently to participate in class discussion as well as make progress in the basic skills of reading, writing, and arithmetic.

The painting of a picture or the modeling of an object appears to be the releasing of subconscious drives. Sometimes the child appears lost to his surroundings as he works, whether he is at the easel using the large brushes with poster paint or at his desk with crayons or at a table with finger paint or clay. At such a time no one should approach him to speak about or to direct his activity. The release of tension is the important thing at this particular time. For this child as with everyone else, the joy is in the making of the object. Any interruption of his absorption in his activity blocks the release of tension.

INSTRUCTING THE PUPILS

The child will get more satisfaction and emotional relief from a misshapen little bowl that he did alone than from a beautiful product largely shaped by the teacher's guiding hand. Teachers often both consciously and unconsciously structure the children's work.

The teacher does the child a disfavor when she smooths out the clay dog, suggests the color it should be painted, and even paints it for him. She is not helping his mental health when she adds a knowing line to a drawing or reshapes a face or form. The child immediately knows that his product has been rejected. It is no longer his very own. He must be allowed to complete the project in his own way from the first brushful of paint or lump of clay to the finished product.

Because of their inability to sustain interest over a long period of time, any project that is planned for the educable mentally retarded should be one that can be completed within two or three lessons. The teacher must also remember that, since these children have a very short attention span, lessons should not extend over thirty minutes. Extra time should be allowed for cleaning up and putting away materials. Older pupils will be able to enjoy a longer art period. Frustrated by an activity that continues over a prolonged period of time, they often show their resentment by tantrums, sulking, spoiling materials, or being absent on art days.

Lessons of instruction on how to use the different art materials

49.   The girls are weaving place mats.

should be just a trial period with plenty of time for informal questions and answers. The teacher must remember, when giving the directions, that each detail must be explained, for these children frequently do not understand but hesitate to ask for explanations, even saying they understand when they do not.

The directions should be given orally, as few of the written words used would be in the children's sight vocabulary. Any direction on the chalkboard must be in clear round letters with well-separated words which must be explained. These words must be taught as patiently as in any reading lesson. For many of the younger children in the group even these simple directions will usually be incomprehensible.

The Classroom Teacher and the Special Art Teacher. If the classroom teacher is directing the art and crafts class, she can control the presentation of the work to the children. Since she is in constant contact with the pupils, she knows their abilities and potentialities. However, if there is an art teacher who comes

50. Crafts produced in the classroom by educable mentally retarded
children, whose ages were 10 to 13 years.

in once or twice a week, it is usually better to attempt no coordination between classwork and the art program. The homeroom teacher must find time in her schedule to do the art and craft work that she feels is required to complete a unit of study.

WEAVING

Weaving in a Classroom. The simple loop looms that may be purchased at a variety store are good for beginners. The loops are in bundles of solid or mixed colors. Instructions come with each little loom. Squares about 6″ x 6″ are woven on the frames. These may be made of cotton or rayon and used as hot pads or pot holders. They may be woven of wool and the squares stitched together to form an afghan, or a small rug.

A cardboard frame may be used to make a small round mat for hot dishes. To make one, draw a circle on a piece of card board. Punch a hole in the center. Cut around the circle to secure a disk. Make small V-shaped notches around the circumference about one inch apart.

With needle and thread, go in and out from the center hole to the notches until a basic "spider web" warp has been laid down. Then use heavy cotton roving or yarn to weave around under and over, each spoke of the web until the rim of the card is reached. Turn over the card and repeat the weaving process. Use a contrasting color thread to overcast the edges. The cardboard is left inside to hold the mat in shape and to give added protection to the table.

Weave a pocket book. Use a card about 6" x 10". Cut the notches on each end about one-half inch apart. Wind yarn or carpet warp up and down one side of the cardboard, holding the warp firmly in the notches.

Start with the heavier yarn or cotton roving and weave back and forth. Be careful to keep the edges straight with the edge of the cardboard. Use an old comb to press the yarn, or woof, down evenly, but do not pack it in tightly. Keep the weaving light and airy.

Stop weaving about 1½ inches from the top. Cut two strings at the top and tie them. This will keep the weaving from ravelling out. Continue cutting and tying across the card until that end of the weaving is free. Pull the weaving away from the bottom of the card. Handle it carefully. Cut the strings of the warp and tie the ends here as they were tied at the top.

This fringe may be turned under or left outside as a decoration. A piece of soft cloth, silk, satin, or nylon may be used to line the pocket book. Sew up the sides. Run a colored cord through it for a draw string. It may also be finished for an envelope style purse. Insert a piece of cardboard in one side under the lining to help keep the material in the proper shape.

Looms for Ties or Belts. Other looms may be fashioned from wood for weaving ties or belts. Where a narrow strip of weaving is to be made, a long narrow board, notched at each end is used in the same way the cardboard frame is used for the pocket book weaving.

Wooden frames for weaving mats are easily assembled from four strips of wood securely nailed together. One inch brads spaced at half or one inch intervals form the means for securing the warp. These frames may be in any convenient size for the age of the pupil. A small frame is easy to hold, and a mat is fin-

SMALL HAND LOOM

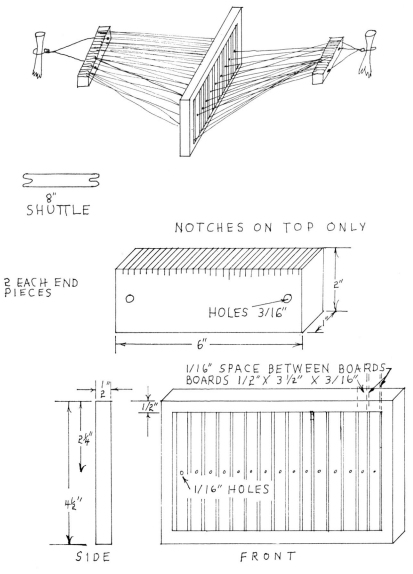

SHUTTLE 8"

NOTCHES ON TOP ONLY

2 EACH END PIECES

HOLES 3/16"

2"

1"

6"

1/16" SPACE BETWEEN BOARDS
BOARDS 1/2" X 3 1/2" X 3/16"

1/2"

1" 2"

2 1/4"

4 1/2"

1/16" HOLES

SIDE

FRONT

51. Working plans for making a belt loom.

ished before the young pupil tires of the project. The advanced pupil will want to make larger mats for use about the home.

Another type of small hand loom uses just the end pieces and a heddle. It is constructed from scrap wood. The heddle may be cut from plywood with a jigsaw and the use of a hand drill for the holes. Working plans are given with drawings of the parts for assistance in assembling the loom.

Thread the warp through the heddle. Alternate between the slot and the hole in the stave next to it. Fasten the warp securely to the notched end pieces. The warp may be stretched out on a table so the threads will be kept the same length. A thread may require lengthening or shortening to make the tension even when the weaving starts.

When ready to weave, tie a heavy cord in each end of the two end pieces and fasten the loom between two solid places with the heavy cord. Wrap some yarn or cotton roving around the shuttle and raise the heddle. This opens the warp, forming a space through which the shuttle is passed. This space is called a shed. The heddle is lowered and tapped lightly against the filler, and pushed lower to make a cross in the warp and prevent the filler or woof, from coming out. The shuttle is passed through this new shed, and again tapped against the filler. Raise the heddle and repeat with the shuttle. Each time after tapping the filler, slide the heddle back a few inches before raising or lowering it, this will provide sufficient room for the shuttle to pass through.

When the warp is used up, clip the ends from the end pieces of the loom and tie them to prevent ravelling. Fringe may be made separately and tied onto the ends of the sash or scarf.

Loom for Rugs. The standing type rug loom is easy to construct if one has some shop facility available. If not perhaps a father who has a workshop in the home may be willing to make such a loom for the class. Weaving on this type loom is interesting for the intermediate and older pupils. A working plan to make a standing rug loom is included in the illustrations. (Courtesy, Whitaker Elementary School, Finneytown, Ohio.)

Table Hand Looms. Small table hand looms with two harness arrangements are suitable for scarfs, dresser sets, place mats, chair sets. Intermediate age and older pupils enjoy using these looms.

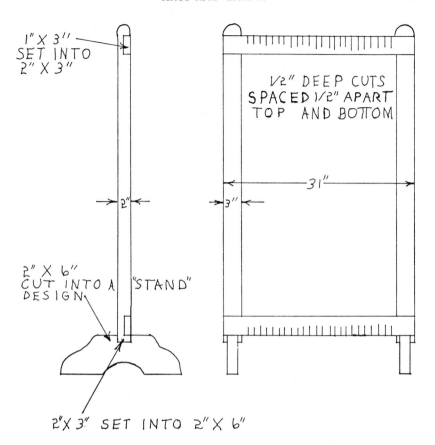

1" X 3" SET INTO 2" X 3"

1/2" DEEP CUTS SPACED 1/2" APART TOP AND BOTTOM

31"

2"

3"

2" X 6" CUT INTO A "STAND" DESIGN

"STAND"

2"X 3" SET INTO 2" X 6"

THE COMB

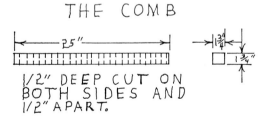

25"

1 3/4"

1 3/4"

1/2" DEEP CUT ON BOTH SIDES AND 1/2" APART.

THE COMB IS USED TO KEEP THE STRING STRAIGHT WHILE THE RUG IS WOVEN.

52. Working plans for making a standing type rug loom.

The twelve inch size is useful and the cost is moderate. Complete instructions accompany each loom.

Floor or Treadle Type Looms. The junior high and senior high school pupils are able to use these larger looms. They are expensive but are worth while for the therapy for these older pupils. They learn to make beautiful rugs, tote bags, drapery material, and many useful articles. If the program is integrated at this stage with regular art or craft courses there should be an opportunity for the use of the looms by these pupils on a regular schedule.

FINGER PAINTING

The inarticulate child, who is unable to express his emotion, finds a medium in finger painting that he can easily use. Because he can freely express his likes and dislikes with color and muscular action, he obtains great emotional relief and also a feeling of accomplishment through the manipulation of the paint.

When a child fully accepts finger painting, it is a satisfying and meaningful experience. There is the emotional impact of the chosen color mingled with the tactual and kinesthetic process.

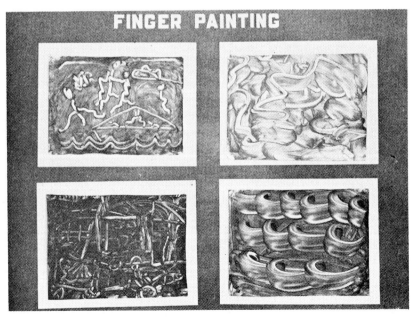

53.   Finger painting.

The child is unconsciously dramatizing his past in the swirls and lines of the slightly resistant medium of the paint.

The table that the teacher provides for the finger painting should be near a sink or a large pan of water. A pad of several newspapers may be placed at one end of the table to protect it from the paint. The paper for finger painting, which may be the regular kind or white wrapping paper, is dipped into water and placed, slick side up, on the pile of newspapers. The paint may be purchased in jars or made like starch and colored with powder paint. A large spoonful of the paint is placed on the wet paper, after which the child spreads the paint around with his hands. He forms such patterns and pictures as his fancy dictates.

Varied Results Produced by the Free Art Experiences. The educable mentally retarded will become absorbed in making pictures that repeat the same design over and over for many months with few variations. This design is a reflection of the child's personality and peculiar problem.

A change in environment may effect a change in a child's painting. He may be so sensitive to his surroundings that he quickly expresses his feelings in some form. If an art medium is convenient, he will use that form to express his insecurity, tension, hostility, happiness, or love.

Types of Arts and Crafts for the Educable Mentally Retarded. The educable mentally retarded like to work with things that seem useful. They also like to make pretty things. They are intrigued with such simple crafts as stick painting, making puppets from socks or paper sacks, knitting on frames, tooling leather or copper, or enameling on copper. They enjoy daubing water colors or poster paint on paper. After they have made a small ball of clay into a bird or rabbit, they can glaze it and place it in the kiln They enjoy watching it being transformed into a shining object in the color of their choice.

Some educable mentally retarded children have an ability for copying drawings or pictures in detail. However, the child who deviates from the pattern and shows originality may be a child who is not functioning as high as his true ability. Tim was a child who loved to copy faces he had seen in comic books or in the movies. He used clay as his medium for expression. He did not attempt to do original characters. This form of modeling does not

54.   Crayon drawings.

appear to result in much emotional release, but the pounding and shaping of the clay does seem to release muscular tension.

The mentally retarded enjoy using crayons. Many will illustrate their stories by imitating the drawings or pictures from books. Dependent upon a copy, they are seldom able to adapt a picture to a new purpose. They find it difficult to do freehand paper cutting, because they lack the imagination to visualize an object in its true proportions when greatly reduced in size. They need to view a completed pattern from which to work.

ARTS AND CRAFTS FOR THE PRIMARY CLASS

Each child should have a coverall to wear when using art or crafts materials. A few suitable activities for the primary educable mentally retarded are suggested.

1. Scribble on the chalkboard.
2. Scribble on 24″ x 36″ newsprint with chalk at the easel.
3. Draw lines on the chalkboard: guide the child's hand.
    a. Curved lines-rounded slowly; sharply; circles; ovals.
    b. Straight lines-vertical, up and down; horizontal, across; oblique, slant; squares.

Teach the child to look at the line. Be sure he knows what you are talking about when you say "a line." As he gains coordination he will use the line to guide him in many activities. He will use a line as a base for cutting out a picture, for coloring within or outside of an area.

4. Easel painting: use large newsprint with large brushes for the poster paint. Start with one or two colors and change them frequently. As the pupils mature and learn how to use the materials let them use a greater variety of colors.

5. Teach the names of the colors.

6. Crayon drawing and coloring: use 12" x 18" paper at the desks. The older pupils may try using some design on the one inch squared manila paper. Teach the pupils to make the crayon strokes all go in one direction, and to use an even pressure.

7. Finger painting is discussed in detail in another section of this chapter.

8. Spatter painting: use screen wire over a box with a space open on one side to slide the paper and design under. Old tooth brushes or a spray gun are used to spread the paint across the screen. The tooth brush dipped in the paint and scrubbed across the screen by the child produces a nice print and is highly satisfying to the child.

9. String Prints: dip a string in poster paint of a creamy consistency and lay it on a paper's surface to form a line design. Fold the paper over the string and press with the hands; slowly pull out the string. This makes a symmetrical design when the paper is unfolded.

10. Clay modeling: use small balls of clay and let the child pull out the features; roll, flatten or shape with the hands; make small animals and bowls. More mature pupils may use a rolling pin to make a slab and from that form tiles, brooches, ash trays. These may be decorated with designs made by pressing a nail head, a paper clip, a bobby pin against the soft clay. Small articles may often be fired and later glazed. These make attractive gifts for mother.

11. Weave pot holder or mats on small frames.

12. Sewing cards: Use simple designs, bright colored thread, large, blunt needles.
13. Press leaves for booklets, or for posters for a border.
14. Stencil designs, animal forms, letters and numerals.
15. Draw or sculpture in the sand-box.
16. Make things for the play house or doll house.
17. Pound nails into a big block of wood.
18. Paper cutting and pasting: tear strips of one color and paste on another color; paste ready cut out squares, circles, pictures; more mature pupils may be able to cut out pictures and paste; practice cutting anything, then cut for a purpose—to make a poster, a mural.
19. Make masks, animals, from paper sacks.
20. Print with sticks of many sizes and shapes, with common and unusual objects, with designs cut into the end of a carrot or a potato. Use poster paint and apply it with a small brush to the stick to be used for the printing.
21. Plaster molds: make hand prints, leaf prints.
22. Draw with colored chalk on dry or wet paper, or use wet chalk on dry paper.
23. Bring small sculptured articles into the classroom for the group to observe.
24. Keep some interesting, colorful pictures on the bulletin board and talk about them to the children.

55. Leather craft. Industrial Arts, Special Education, Lyons Township High School.

ARTS AND CRAFTS FOR THE INTERMEDIATE CLASS

Review the techniques from the primary class regarding the use of materials, drawing lines and forms, coloring evenly, painting freely with large brushes, and modeling simple clay objects. A few additional activities and the enlargement of previous ones are suggested.

1. Draw: use pencils, crayons, chalk.
2. Murals: use chalk, poster paint, cut or tear paper.
3. Model: use coil, slab, or ball of clay; use flour and salt mixture for maps and beads; use papier-mâché for masks or puppet heads; use plaster of Paris for leaf or hand casts, or picture frames.
4. Stencil: use wax crayons on cloth, press with a warm iron to set the color. Cover the cloth with paper before pressing.
5. Make hand puppets from socks, papier-mâché; dress them.
6. Finger paint: try two colors.
7. Scribble a design on lightweight cardboard and color it smoothly and brightly with crayons. Add a little water to some detergent and whip to a creamy froth. Let each child spread a thin layer of this over the scribble design and use as finger paint. The bright colors will show through.
8. Water color: with a brush, wet a 10″ x 12″ sheet of white drawing paper. Drop a small blob of wet color on it and let it ooze out over the paper to form a design. The paper may be tipped slightly to add to the interest. Let this dry. Then trim and mount with a narrow border of construction paper of a contrasting color showing.

   Another way to use these water color free designs is to print designs on the dry paper using any printing sticks or odd-shaped articles available, dipped or brushed lightly with poster paint.
9. Tie and dye material for scarves and skirts.
10. Weave mats and baskets of reed or raffia.
11. Make woodburning designs.
12. Make designs on squared paper with crayons.
13. Decorate bottles or jars with wax or beads.
14. Make mobiles.
15. Make stuffed animals.

16. Make animals of plywood.
17. Make cross-stitch designs.
18. Make braided rugs.
19. Make hooked rugs.
20. Weave on small hand looms to make pot holders, table mats, dresser sets, belts, ties.
21. Weave on upright loom to make rugs.
22. Use wire to make figures.
23. Use needle and thread to sew on buttons, hem towels, sew rags for rugs.
24. Use a hammer to drive a nail.
25. Use a small saw and jigsaw.
26. Go to art exhibits.
27. Enjoy art objects brought into the room.
28. Study some works of art.
29. Make papier-mâché masks and animals.
30. Practice paper folding.

ARTS AND CRAFTS FOR JUNIOR HIGH AND SENIOR HIGH

These educable mentally retarded pupils should be in classes of industrial arts and homemaking. The boys should be learning how to use simple tools at first and later power tools, safely and efficiently. They can learn to handle these tools carefully and to produce good articles. The girls should be in homemaking classes where they are learning the basic principles of nutrition, practicing food preparation, simple sewing and mending, the use of

56. Making jewelry: a) cutting a stone for jewelry, b) polishing a stone. Industrial Arts, Special Education, Lyons Township High School.

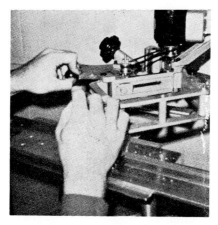

57. Making a name plate. Industrial Arts, Special Education, Lyons Township High School.

cleaning and laundry equipment, and the care of a house. If such courses are not available, much of this material will be taught by the classroom teacher. She should use every means to secure proper facilities for adequately preparing these young people for school termination. Much can be accomplished through an interested association of the parents of the pupils.

The art and crafts course for the junior and senior high pupils should include activities for pleasure at the present time and skills for future leisure time. Drawing, painting, designing, modeling, should be continued. Wood carving, modeling in metals, block printing, glazing and firing of ceramics, lettering, puppetry, weaving, book binding, making jewelry, leather craft, and learning to work with many kinds of plastic materials all may be included in planning activities for the older slow learner. These activities may hold the young adult in school and prevent a dropout before ready to go to work.

SUMMARY

The educable mentally retarded will benefit from an art program that is administered with patience and understanding. The mentally retarded cannot be forced to accomplish things for which they have little ability and in which they have no interest. The program that is best for the mentally retarded is one that does not restrict nor coerce, yet engenders enthusiasm. By careful direction, it increases skill in the manipulation of the art and crafts materials.

REFERENCES

1. Atwater, M. M.: *Byways in Handweaving*. New York, Macmillan Company, 1954.
2. Benson, Kenneth R., and McNice, William: *Arts and Crafts for the Mentally Retarded*. Union, N. J., Newark State College.
3. Boehemer, Susan E., and Groneman, Chris H.: *Making Things Is Fun*, Handcraft Series, Book I and Book II. Austin, Texas, Steck.
4. Conant, Howard: *Art Education*. New York, Center for Applied Research in Education, 1964, 1965.
5. D'Amico, V. E.: *Art for the Family*. New York, Simon and Schuster, 1954.
6. Faber, M. E.: Handcraft Series—*Knots and Braids; Metal Modeling; Modern Felt Handicraft*. Waupun, Wis., The Handcrafter.
7. Gaitskill, C. D.: *Art Education for Slow Learners*. Peoria, Ill., Bennett, 1953.
8. *Highlights Jumbo Handbook*. Columbus, Ohio, Highlights for Children, 1967.
9. LaMancuse, Katherine C.: *Source Book for Art Teachers*. Scranton, Pa., International Textbook Co., 1965. (A Dictionary of art terms, well illustrated.)
10. Lindsay, Zaidee: *Art is for All*. New York, Taplinger, 1968.
11. Miller, Josephine V.: *Paper Sculpture and Construction*. Peoria, Ill., Bennett, 1957. (Excellent suggestions for classroom use.)
12. Moore, F. C., Hamburger, C. H., and Kingzett, A. L.: *Handcrafts for Elementary Schools*. Chicago, Heath.
13. Murray, William D., and Rigney, F. J.: *Paper Folding for Beginners*. New York, Dover, 1960.
14. Myers, Jack, and Myers, Louise: *Easy Paper Folding*. Racine, Wis., Whitman, 1963.
15. *Resource Manual for Educable Mentally Retarded Children (Part II)*. In a series of Resource Manuals for Teachers of Exceptional Children. Vancouver, B.C., 1967.
16. Schein, Jerome D., and others: Color blindness in mentally retarded children. *Exceptional Child*, 35(8):609, 1969.
17. Schmidt, Alfred: *Craft Projects for Slow Learners*. New York, John Day.

18. Sisters of St. Frances of Assisi, St. Coletta Schools: *Crafts Curriculum for the Mentally Handicapped.* Milwaukee, Department of Special Education, The Cardinal Stritch College, 1960.
19. Wankleman, Willard, and others: *A Handbook of Arts and Crafts.* Dubuque, Iowa, W. C. Brown, 1961.

13

ARITHMETIC

ARITHMETIC FOR THE EDUCABLE MENTALLY RETARDED

THE educable mentally retarded child should be taught arithmetic when he has a need for it and when he has developed a readiness for it. This usually occurs when he has a mental age of six or seven years. The normal child is ready for numbers when he is six to seven years of age chronologically. The mentally retarded child will be much older chronologically than the normal child when he arrives at a readiness age. Besides mental age, mental and physical health are factors to be considered in determining the child's readiness for arithmetic.

Disabilities that Affect the Understanding of Arithmetic. The mentally retarded are severely handicapped in the study of arithmetic because of certain disabilities which have been discussed in detail in previous chapters. The following characteristics are especially applicable to the study of arithmetic: low transfer of learning; low abstract thinking ability; poor comprehension and observation of details and situations; slow absorption of facts; little initiative, and lack of ability to concentrate.

OBJECTIVES

The teacher must face the above disabilities and plan methods to achieve objectives desirable for these children both for the present and for the future. The objectives should include teaching the essentials in arithmetic that will enable the person to preserve his personal diginity in ordinary business transactions.

The fundamental processes of arithmetic should be made automatic so that they are incidental in solving problems. Through the development of good work habits and a feeling of security in his ability to solve arithmetic problems, the pupils will develop independence and self-reliance in other areas.

Basis of the Program. The program must not be a "watered-down" version of a regular class, but one pared of non-essentials, devoted to basic skills and learnings. The teacher must build this program on lifelike situations and problems structured with oral problems for drill and fixing facts. These should be interspersed with simple written examples for practice that will facilitate accuracy and develop speed in using fundamental processes. Hence, it becomes a teaching situation involving an individual or a small group.

READINESS

As with normal pupils, the mentally retarded must achieve a readiness and a mental age for a process before it is presented to them. Children in the regular primary room are in the process of acquiring readiness for numbers. This is developed through play activities, games, touching and handling materials, and directing class activities. The mentally retarded are given similar preparation, but it must be simplified, explained in detail, and continued for a longer period of time. Because of their mental age, many are still in the readiness stage when they are advanced to the intermediate group.

Intermediate Group Age Span. Children in the intermediate group are usually from ten to thirteen years of age chronologically. Their mental ages are from four or five to eight years. The age for number readiness for the normal child, as previously listed, is 6-0 to 7-0 years chronologically. The age of six years and six months or even an older mental age is preferred by many teachers before starting number activities. The mentally retarded child should be at least that age mentally before he can be expected to have the understanding to make any growth in his ability to use numbers.

The basic skills are established and maintained during the three or four years the children remain in the intermediate group.

The pupils will need these skills when they are advanced to the older group where they will have an opportunity for experiences in problems dealing with wages, jobs, installment buying, upkeep of a car and a home, trips, insurance, taxes, using banking facilities, writing orders for merchandise, managing an income, and taking care of household expenses.

Attention Span. Although a group of mentally retarded may work together for a short time, the best teaching is done individually. Most of the mentally retarded are easily distracted. They are unusually distractible when tired, angry, frustrated, or grouped with several other children. After the regular group work has been presented, the teacher should devote some time to each child. This individual help will develop greater understanding of a process than half an hour of group instruction.

Since the mentally retarded child's attention span is short and his interest wanes with each passing moment, the problem should be immediately explained and demonstrated. A new objective should be set up for the child, and he should be sent back to his seat to work.

Length of Drill. Five minutes is as long as the child's interest can be held in a drill on number facts. He should be given something else to do while the teacher works with another child. This whole program of training the educable mentally retarded for a useful life is a slow process which cannot be hurried.

Counting Devices, or "Crutches." "Crutches" in arithmetic refer to little methods and aids for working examples without memorizing facts. Some children count on their fingers; some make a series of dots; some make marks; others use beans or an abacus to arrive at an answer.

The child should be weaned from his need to count objects or fingers to find sums as soon as possible. He should be made to feel confident of his ability to recall the sums and differences between groups. He should be impressed with his ability to perform without these helpers, and to rely on his ability to recall the sums and differences between groups of objects. Before presenting new material the teacher should review until the child has a feeling of security, or until she is satisfied he will be able at this stage to retain the basic facts.

If he continues to use "crutches," he will soon arrive at a

plateau in his learning ability. It will require many long patient hours of explanation of new processes, with good motivation, to induce the pupil to proceed using immature, slow methods of computation. Knowing how to add, subtract, and divide, even though relying heavily upon mechanical aids, is satisfying and useful to the child.

Making Numbers Meaningful. The teacher may utilize school situations to make numbers meaningful. This will help prepare the pupils for actual instruction in specific skills. She must take the time to explain every detail of a process, to drill on the facts, and to work for comprehension of number values.

The teacher must prepare many pages of examples for oral and written work. She must present the same facts and skills in many ways so that they become workable concepts for the mentally retarded. Concrete objects—such as pennies, small blocks, books, or clothes pins—should be used first, followed by semi-concrete materials, such as pictures on cards, dots on cards, and finally the number symbol alone.

Limitations of the Regular Work Books. In preparing a program for the mentally retarded, one encounters difficulties in using a regular series of work books. These books were prepared for children with normal intelligence, who are able to use abstract ideas, to analyze a situation, and to use the reading vocabulary of a particular grade level. The teacher of the educable mentally retarded will be able to use some of the pages from many sets of work books. Teacher-made work sheets should be substituted for the too abstract and too difficult ones.

NEED FOR REPETITION

The findings of the "Committee of Seven," as reported in the *Thirty-eighth Year Book of the National Society for the Study of Education,* shows that for the average person sixty-seven repetitions were required to fix an easy addition combination; over 100, for a moderately difficult combination; and 150, for a difficult combination. The teacher of the mentally retarded should keep these facts in mind when preparing lesson plans. She should remember that perfecting skill in numbers takes patience and persistence.

Inventory of Ability. The teacher should take a semi-yearly inventory of the number ability of the children and start teaching where their understanding ends. If there seems to be a weakness, she should re-teach and review until there is a solid base from which to proceed. A check list is given in this chapter.

Types of Materials. As in all work with the mentally retarded, the simple approach is the most effective in the development of number concepts. The use of familiar materials for counting, such as blocks, buttons, spools, and the abacus, will not distract the children from the number lesson. The teacher should also provide simple play materials for the children who do not have the ability to proceed with the regular training program.

PROGRESS CHART AND CHECK LIST

Mental Age of 6-6 to 7-0. At a mental age of 6-6 to 7-0, the child should be ready to understand and to assimilate the following concepts:

Rote counting—1 through 5.

Values of the numerals 1 through 5.

Grouping—1, 2, 3.

Writing numerals—1, 2, 3, 4, 5.

Ordinals—first, second.

Meaning of terms—more than, last, and, put together, altogether, day, night.

Addition—with no sum greater than 5.

Subtraction—none.

Sight recognition of the words *one*, and *two*.

Time—meaning of o'clock, clock, hour.

Money—one cent, 1c, 2c, 3c, 4c, 5c, nickel.

Use of 1 and 2 in simple oral additive examples.

Recognition of a circle.

Calendar—practice in locating the day of the week and the date of the month.

Recognition of the signs + and =, for *and*, and *equals*.

Measurement—cup, teaspoon, tablespoon, dozen.

All of the above should be completely mastered before proceeding to the next steps in arithmetic.

Mental Age of 7-0 to 7-6. At a mental age of 7-0 to 7-6, the child should be ready to understand and to assimilate the following concepts:

Rote counting—6 through 10.

Grouping—1, 2, 3, 4, 5.

Writing numerals—6, 7, 8, 9, 10.

Ordinals—third, fourth.

Meaning of terms—take away, less, subtract, plus.

Addition—with no sum greater than 10.

Subtraction—presentation of the facts from 1 through 5 as a unit; then the presentation of the facts from 6 through 10, parallel with each new addition fact.

Sight recognition of the words *three, four,* and *five.*

Time—half-hour, afternoon, morning, evening, noon; counting the hours to 10.

Money—dime, 10c, making change from 1c through 10c.

Recognition of the square, and of the sign — for take away or subtract.

Calendar—days of the week, the date, the weather.

Zero—as a place holder.

Measurement—pint, inch, half-dozen, ½ of each, ½ of a group up to 10.

Child's telephone number and street address.

Mental Age 7-6 to 8-0. At a mental age of 7-6 to 8-0, the child should be ready to understand and to assimilate the following concepts:

Rote counting—1 through 50.

Values of the numerals 1 through 50.

Grouping—easy addition and subtraction facts.

Counting by decades—10 through 50.

Writing numerals—1 through 50.

Ordinals—fifth, sixth.

Meaning of terms—tens, teens, ones, units, 30 minutes.

Addition—simple oral and written examples with sums of 19 or less.

Subtraction—simple oral and written examples with remainders of 19 or less.

Sight recognition of the words *five, six.*

Time—minute, counting of minutes from 1 through 50.

Money—quarter, 25c, making change to 25c.

Recognition of a triangle.

Calendar—days of week, date, weather report.

Zero—as a place holder.

Measurement—quart, foot, 12 inches, ¼ of each, ¼ of a group.

Mental Age 8-0 to 8-6. At a mental age of 8-0 to 8-6 the child should understand and be ready to assimilate the following concepts:

Rote counting—50 through 100.

Values of the numerals 50 through 100.

Grouping—more difficult addition and subtraction facts.

Counting by decades—50 through 100.

Counting by 5's—5 through 50.

Counting by 2's—2 through 10.

Writing numerals—1 through 100.

Ordinals—seventh, eighth.

Meaning of terms—review.

Addition—more difficult addition facts, simple oral and written examples with no carrying, one-place column of three numbers with no sum over 10.

Subtraction—more difficult subtraction facts, simple oral and written examples with no borrowing.

Sight recognition of the words *seven* and *eight*.

Time—quarter hour, 15 minutes, days of the week, date, midnight, A.M.

Money—half-dollar, 50c, making change for 50c.

Recognition of a rectangle or oblong.

Calendar—day of the week, date of the month, the month, the year, the weather record.

Measurement—yard, 3 feet, 36 inches, ⅓ of each, ⅓ of a group.

Place values in numbers—ones, tens, hundreds.

Mental Age of 8-6 to 9-0. At a mental age of 8-6 to 9-0, the child should be ready to understand and to assimilate the following concepts:

Counting—100's to 500.

Counting—5's to 100; 2's to 50; 3's to 21.

Reading and writing numerals—1 to 500.

Ordinals—ninth, tenth.

Meaning of terms—review; times, multiply, multiplication.

Addition—two-place numbers in examples with carrying, single column examples with no sum over 10, simple oral situation problems.

Subtraction—two-place numbers in examples with borrowing, simple oral situation problems with no remainder over 10.

Sight recognition of words—*nine* and *ten.*

Time—month, names of months, 12 months in a year, days of week, date, hour, minute, second.

Money—one dollar, $ for dollar, $1.00, decimal (.) sign, making change for one dollar, reading money in dollars and cents.

Calendar—day of week, date of month, the year, weather record.

Measurement—city block, mile.

Place values in numbers—ones or units, tens, hundreds, thousands.

Multiplication—the two's and the sign $\times$ for times or for multiply.

Mental Age of 9-0 to 10-6. At a mental age of 9-0 to 10-6, the child should be ready to understand and to assimilate the following concepts:

Reading, writing numerals—to 1,000.

Addition—100 facts; problems with carrying.

Subtraction—100 facts; problems with borrowing.

Multiplication—1's, 2's, 3's, 4's, 5's; simple problems with no carrying.

Problems—simple familiar situations.

Examples—two-place and three-place numbers.

Division—simple examples with one-place and two-place numbers.

Recognition of signs—division signs— $\lceil$, $\div$.

Ordinals—auditory familiarity with tenth through twentieth.

Cardinal names—sight recognition—one through twenty.

Time—365 days in a year, 7 days in a week, 52 weeks in a year, names of holidays, names of months in a year.

Money—five dollars, $5.00, ten dollars, $10.00, making change to ten dollars, know amounts to hundreds of dollars.

Measurement—2 pints equal 1 quart, 12 inches equal 1 foot, 3 feet equal 1 yard, 16 ounces equal 1 pound.

Abbreviations—qt., lb., yd., in., pt.

Thermometer—telling temperature.

Scales—reading pounds and ounces.

Recognition of a cube, a cylinder, and a sphere.

Reading and writing Roman numerals from I to X.

Mental Age of 10-6 to 12-0. At a mental age of 10-6 to 12-0, the pupil should be in an advanced group of junior high or high school pupils. He should be ready to understand and assimilate the following concepts:

Reading, writing numbers in the thousands, be familiar with the more commonly used names of the decimal system: unit, tens, hundreds, thousands, millions, billions.

Addition—series of 2-, 3-, 4-, and 5-place numbers in reasonable length columns, with carrying.

Subtraction—2-, 3-, 4-, and 5-place examples with borrowing.

Multiplication—6's, 7's, 8's, 9's: simple exercises with carrying; use the three place multiplier.

Division—simple exercises with one-and two-place divisors.

Make up practical problems using the fundamental skills. These problems should relate to advertisements in the newspaper of articles of food, furniture, cars, homes, and clothing. Money transactions in large or small amounts could be incorporated into the problems as the pupils became proficient in using the basic skills.

Measurement may be studied by working with road maps, planning trips, figuring mileage, and the amount of gasoline needed for a trip. Monetary problems will grow out of these situations. The cost of the trip must be figured before it is undertaken. The cost of lodging, food, recreation, possible repairs to the car must be included in addition to the gasoline and oil.

Budgeting should have a place in the high school mathematics study. Keep the situations and the figures simple as the peak of ability will be about the fifth or sixth grade level, with the majority on a third grade level.

TEACHING NUMBER CONCEPTS

Methods for Rote Counting. When the child has attained the mental age of 6-6 to 7-0, he should have achieved a readiness for understanding numbers. At this time the teacher may begin presenting rote counting. Number rhymes are good for this purpose.

New pupils or those with readiness will enjoy participating in the singing and easy choral readings. The more mature children, who also enjoy rhymes, will help the others to learn them.

The children may sing "Ten Little Indians," then dramatize it. The child who is starting to learn the meaning of a number may be at the head of the line. He may be named One. As the children sing the song and name the numbers, Child One will step forward and then back into place in the line. As the children sing about the number two, Child One takes the hand of the child next to him and they step forward. Both children step back into line as the song proceeds.

The teacher must be careful to emphasize the idea of *one*, the group of *two*, or the group of *three*, to show the values of *one*, *two*, and *three*. She must not allow the children to confuse the number values with ordinal values of *first*, *second*, or *third* places. Following are some examples of old nursery rhymes and finger plays with simple directions that may be used to help teach the values of numbers. The teacher leads the rhymes and indicates the values and the actions.

One for the Money

One for the money, (Hold up one finger.)
Two for the show, (Hold up two fingers.)
Three to make ready, (Hold up three fingers.)
Four to go. (Hold up four fingers.)
—Anonymous

Hickory, Dickory, Dock!

Hickory, Dickory, Dock!
(Raise the left arm over the head to
represent a tall clock.)
The mouse ran up the clock;
(Raise right hand and imitate a mouse
running up the clock.)
The clock struck one, and down he ran.
(Clap hands as *one* is said.)
Hickory, Dickory, Dock!
—Mother Goose

Two Little Blackbirds

Two little blackbirds sitting on a hill.
  (Close fists, thumbs up.)
One named Jack and one named Jill,
  (Waggle thumbs.)
Fly away, Jack! (Move right hand behind back.)
Fly away, Jill! (Move left hand behind back.)
Come back, Jack! (Bring right hand in front.)
Come back Jill! (Bring left hand in front.)
Two little blackbirds sitting on a hill,
  (Closed fists with thumbs up, bobbing in front of child.)
One named Jack and one named Jill. (Waggle thumbs.)

—*Mother Goose*

Two Little Blackbirds may also be played as a game with a boy and a girl taking the parts of the birds, Jack and Jill. They may act out the movements of Jack and Jill as the rhyme is repeated. The *two* value is more evident when the rhyme is dramatized in this manner than when using it as a finger play.

Five Little Squirrels

Five little squirrels sitting in a tree,
  (Hold left hand up, fingers limp from the wrist.)
This little squirrel says, "What do I see?"
  (Begin with thumb and hold up a finger as
    each squirrel is named.)
This little squirrel says, "I see a gun."
This little squirrel says, "Let us run."
This little squirrel says, "I'm not afraid."
This little squirrel says, "Let's hide in the shade."
Along came a man with a great big gun.
  (Right hand moves up as finger points in imita-
    tion of a gun.)
Bang! See those little squirrels run.
  (Clap hands and hide left hand.)

—*Anonymous*

The above rhyme may also be used as instructional material for teaching the ordinals by substituting *first* through *fifth* for the word *this* at the beginning of each line.

Mother Hen and Chickens

(Point to each finger to indicate the *first, second, third,* etc.,
as the rhyme is repeated.)

Said the first little chicken with a queer little squirm,
"I wish I could find a nice fat worm."
Said the second little chicken with an odd little shrug,
"I wish I could find a nice fat bug."
Said the third little chicken with a sigh of relief,
"I wish I could find a nice green leaf."
Said the fourth little chicken with a queer little squeal,
"I wish I could find some nice yellow meal."
"Now see here," said the mother hen from the green
　　garden patch,
"If you want any breakfast, come here and scratch."
　　　　　　　　　　　　　　　　—Unknown

Grouping of Numbers. Grouping consists of arranging all of the
possible combinations of numbers whose sums equal a given
amount, as in the combinations 1 and 4; 2 and 3; 4 and 1; 3 and 2;
the sums all equal 5. The concept of each number in the series of
one through five with all of the grouping combinations should be
presented parallel with the teaching of rote counting.

Many of the rhymes used as choral readings will assist the children in understanding the real meaning of numbers. However,
there must be many other activities to fix the concept of the value
of the numbers: how its place in the number system is related to
the numbers before and after it; whether it is larger or smaller;
between which numbers it occurs; how it is composed of various
groupings; and in turn how it is part of another number.

Using Concrete Materials. Concrete materials are those which
may be actually used by the child to make definite problems.
These may be clocks, buttons, sticks, blocks, or any objects that
are easy to handle. The use of this type of material helps to structure the meaning for the child. The muscular activity used in
touching, lifting, pushing and moving objects contributes im-
measurably to the retention of the idea of the value of a number.

Teaching the Concept of One. A method of presenting the idea
of *one* is to give directions to the children, using the term at every
opportunity. A sample follows:

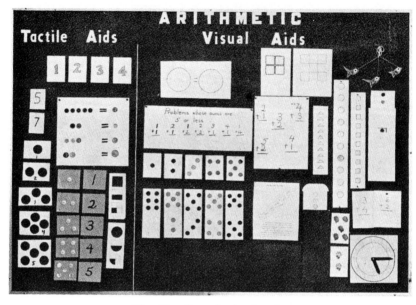

58.   Tactile and visual aids.

Move one chair away from the table.
Bring one sheet of paper to the desk.
Give one pencil to Sue.
Give each pupil one napkin.

Blocks are useful in presenting an activity of this type. They should be large enough to handle easily, but not too bulky for grouping. Blocks of the same color are suitable for this kind of instruction. The teacher directs the children's play as follows:

Pick up one block. Lay it on the table.
Give Tom one block.
Sue, take one block out of the box.
Bill, I will give you one block.
James, give one block to Sue.

Each child should be encouraged to reply, "One block," or "Here is one block." In the beginning of the drill the teacher should not suggest complete sentences in responses to her directions; but wait until the number concept is established. Thinking of the correct sentence form might so frustrate the child that he would be unable to answer the basic question.

The teacher should contrive variations of the play with the blocks. She should use dolls, pennies, books, marbles, chalk, crayons, or any familiar objects available in the room. When the child has a concept of the number value and is familiar with the oral name of the number, the visual symbol may be presented for sight recognition.

Presenting the Symbol for One. The teacher may find some of the following suggestions helpful in presenting the cardinal number 1:

Draw the symbol 1 on the chalkboard.

Make the line thick and several inches long.

Give the child a piece of chalk. Help him to make the symbol 1.

He should practice making the number and repeat the name for it as he draws.

The teacher should help him make the 1 on paper with a pencil.

He should use a pencil with a soft lead.

Give the child a stencil form or a plastic number 1 to trace around, and then let him color the pattern he has drawn.

Draw the number 1 on clay in the clay pan and let the child use a stylus to trace over it.

He should repeat the name, *one*, as he traces.

Draw the number 1 on cardboard or heavy drawing paper with different colors of crayon.

Clip tracing paper to the page and let the child trace the numbers with the same colors of crayons as the original while he repeats name of the symbol, *one*.

Training the Auditory Sense. Understanding of the number values may be intensified by the teacher's use of auditory training: clap the hands; sound a bell; tap on the desk; sound a note on the piano, at the same time naming the action or object in connection with the number being presented to the child.

Using Semiconcrete Materials. Materials classified as semiconcrete are such things as pictures, dots or simple marks on cards. The flash cards should be white or buff with blue or black dots about an inch across for quick recognition. After three dots have been used on the cards, dots that are too small or too large are confusing. The child is better able to form a mental image if the dots are arranged in a domino pattern which will assist him in grouping and in computing accurately and more rapidly.

Clear, distinct pictures should be used for flash cards. There should be nothing to distract from the idea of the value of the 1, 2, or 3. A picture should leave no doubt in the child's mind that this means one cat, one dog, two fish, or three apples.

If a fish picture is used, there should be no part of a fish line showing. The fish should neither be shown on a dish, nor be held by someone. Pictures of two dogs must be identical. A picture of a dog and a cat would be confusing. The child would say," A dog and a cat." He would not usually respond, "Two animals." The mentally retarded child would see one dog and one cat. This necessitates cutting out all extraneous matter, without mutilating the picture. In groups of such pictures as five apples, each apple should be identical, with the pictures of the apples arranged in domino pattern.

The following directions may be of assistance to the teacher in presenting semiconcrete materials to the pupils: Show the child a card with one dot on it. Say, "One." The child should pick up the card and repeat, "One."

Take a card from the child and say, "One dot." The child should repeat, "One dot." Put the card with other cards having more than one dot on them. Instruct the child to find the one dot card. When he finds it, he repeats, "One dot." If he does not remember the one dot from more than one dot, go over the cards again as before.

Use the same routine for pictures on flash cards. The child must give back verbally the exact information the teacher has given him in order to fix the concept in his mind. This can be accomplished only through dozens of repetitions.

Stimulating the Visual Memory for Numerals. Children enjoy coloring large numerals. These should be dittoed, as the children will use many of them. The numbers should be large enough to be outlined first with a crayon and then colored solidly. The child should say the name of the numeral as he colors it.

A stencil should be cut from heavy cardboard for the use of any

Numbers to be traced

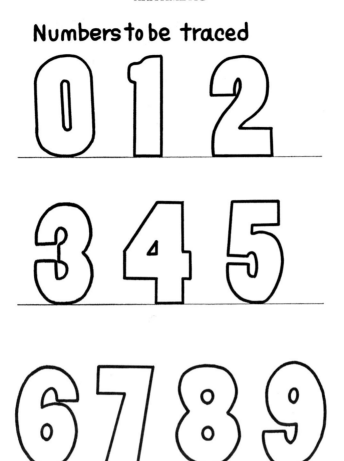

59. Stimulating the visual memory for numerals.

child who has trouble staying inside the lines. He should use a black pencil or crayon; then when he lifts the stencil the number is outlined and heavily colored so that he can see its correct shape.

Numbers cut from emery paper and pasted to cards are used for training the tactile sense. The child lightly traces over the number with his forefinger as if writing the number. He repeats the name of the number as he traces over it.

While the child is learning the concept of *one*, he may be given a page of all of the numerals to trace around and to color. At this time no attempt is made to teach him the names of the other numerals. He is merely becoming familiar with their shapes. However, as he participates in activities, he will become aware of the names of the other numerals.

Use a peg board and have the pupil select the color of sticks or pegs he prefers. Arrange the pegs in sets of 1, 2, and 3, and point to them at random to discover if he is able to distinguish the value of each group without counting. Continue with this material until the child is able to recognize up to five without pointing and counting.

Blocks of various colors or squares of colored paper may be used in the same manner to vary the material. The pupil may need to practice with just one thing many times to become aware of it as a fact. Vary the situation from day to day with different materials for the counting, going on to 2, 3, 4, and 5.

Count as you have the pupil count, and as you show him the sets of objects. As he advances begin "drawing" outlines of the name of the numeral as you say it. You may need to hold the child's hand as you help him draw or trace, or feel of the shape of the numeral. A beaded outline is helpful for this purpose, or a stencil is useful. The clay pan may again be used here.

Large square beads may be used to count and string, as coordination progresses and ability to count advances, smaller beads and various shapes may be added to the strings. Color may be taught at the same time, and as the pupil gains confidence, the beads may be used to show sequence and to repeat patterns of form and color.

Presenting Subtraction After Addition. In presenting the meaning of subtraction, the teacher should wait until after the concept of the sums of the numbers whose addends equal five or less is firmly established.

Teaching the Concept of Two. As confidence increases and the child uses *one* with meaning, *two* may be introduced in the same manner as *one* was presented. The teacher should use the same materials and proceed through the same steps. She will insist that the child repeat the name of the numerals with the name of the object or action, such as two blocks, two dots, two marbles, two bounces of the ball. This precaution will prevent a fixation that connects any number with an object. Numerical songs, number games, and choral games will also emphasize the number being taught.

Presenting One and One are Two. When the child can recognize two objects and can pick two things out of a group, he is ready to be made aware that *one and one are two.* This is accomplished with objects, little oral examples and problems, and finally with numbers on the chalkboard. At this time the children may be shown the sign for plus, and told to call it *and.*

Column addition is easier for the children to understand than the equation form. After they become familiar with column addition, the equation form is presented. Also, one-place column addition with three numbers should be taught parallel with grouping as well as the combinations of numbers whose sums are equal to or less than three.

The child should be shown how to make the equal sign. He must practice writing an example and reading it aloud many times, to become familiar with the form and content. He will learn how to write it and how to read it only after a long period of instruction. This stage in arithmetic is a great achievement for the mentally retarded. After practice on the combination *one and one are two,* the teacher may present the same example in column form again and continue the drill.

The examples may be scattered in irregular form over the page with a large space left around each one to break up the tendency of the child to skip or to do only one example. Only three to five examples should be used to a page at first. Crayons or a felt-tipped pen may be used to make the large numbers all of one color. The child should write the answers with a different color crayon. This allows him to see his progress.

Teaching the First Ordinal. The child is now ready to have the meaning of the ordinal *first* demonstrated. Stand several children in a single file facing the front of the room. Ask, "Who is first?" Some of the children may know the answer. If not, indicate the one who is *first* in the line.

Move another child up to first place and ask the same question. Have each child turn around in place and face the back of the room. Ask, "Who is first in line?" Touch the child who is the first one in line to be sure the group understands the meaning of the word.

Use objects in the same manner to continue the teaching of the meaning of the term *first*. Place in rows; books, toys, pennies, blocks, pictures, buttons, or crayons. Ask the child to touch the first block in a row and to say, "This is the first block."

After each child is confident of the pronunciation of the word *first* and of its correct use, he should make a complete sentence and say, "This is the first block in the row."

Teaching the Meaning of Last. The concept of *last* should be presented after the teaching of *first*. Use the same procedure as for teaching the concept of *first*.

Teaching the Ordinals, Second through Tenth. There must be a delay of several months between teaching the meaning of the different ordinals in order that the concept may be thoroughly assimilated and made useable.

Teaching Three. When the child knows the value of *one* and *two*, present *three* in the same detailed manner. Associate the number with concrete objects, but vary the material from day to day so that the child will not be convinced that it is only when he picks up purple spools that he has *three*.

The concept of three is so much more difficult than that of one or two for the child to understand that it will take much longer for him to assimilate the meaning, and it will necessitate many more presentations. A variety of objects may be collected by the children and used by the teacher to stimulate interest and understanding in counting. These objects, which should be kept within a size range that lend themselves readily to grouping and handling, may include spools, beads, beans, corn, blocks, buttons, acorns, pumpkin and sunflower seeds, or small boxes.

Testing for Readiness for a New Concept. The child now knows the oral and written forms for 1, 2, and 3. He recognizes or selects 1, 2, or 3 objects as directed. Now the teacher should particularly observe the child's ability to understand these groups by reversing the order of the groups before advancing to the next number.

There are maturity levels of comprehension for the numerical values of a group of objects. Unless the child has the readiness for this process, it is useless to try to force comprehension.

Introducing Oral and Written Examples. When the child is able to comprehend the values of *one* and *two* and can make the written symbols, give him written examples for seat work along with

Addition

NOTE THE LARGER NUMBER IS AT
THE TOP OF THE COLUMN. ADD DOWN.

$$
\begin{array}{r} 2 \\ +1 \\ \hline \end{array}
\qquad
\begin{array}{r} 1 \\ +1 \\ \hline \end{array}
\qquad
\begin{array}{r} 2 \\ +1 \\ \hline \end{array}
$$

$$
\begin{array}{r} 1 \\ +1 \\ \hline \end{array}
\qquad
\begin{array}{r} 2 \\ +1 \\ \hline \end{array}
\qquad
\begin{array}{r} 1 \\ +1 \\ \hline \end{array}
$$

$$
\begin{array}{r} 2 \\ +1 \\ \hline \end{array}
\qquad
\begin{array}{r} 1 \\ +1 \\ \hline \end{array}
\qquad
\begin{array}{r} 2 \\ +1 \\ \hline \end{array}
$$

60.   Addition examples for beginners.

little oral problems in class. Then, as comprehension develops for the number *three,* increase the range of examples. The child will need drill to establish procedures for working the examples and fixing the facts so that they will be automatic. Start this drill at the chalkboard, where every move of the child can be easily studied. Give him confidence by showing him how to do the work.

After the pupil has attained some confidence at the chalkboard, give him a page of examples. Sit by him often to help him establish good work habits. Teach the child to work from the left to the right on the page. He must learn to solve the first example in

61.   Introducing the equation form of addition.

the first row on the page. He must learn to solve the second problem, and then the third one in order, and to continue on row
after row until he solves the last example on the page.

Teaching the Word Add. The teacher should write the word
Add on the chalkboard. Let the child practice it on the board.
Then write *Add* on paper for the child to copy. Later use the
word in drills with the addition facts and with the signs used in
addition.

Preparing Examples for Beginners. The teacher should prepare the examples with a primary-sized pencil, felt-tipped pen, or crayon, so that the numerals are large and the signs are easily distinguished. Careful numeral formation is important. Nine to fifteen examples to a sheet, staggered and widely spread, is about right at this stage of ability for the pupil.

Many pupils are bewildered or frustrated by receiving a page closely covered with examples. Since the task looks formidable, they give up before starting. Sometimes a child will work only one example on the page. The teacher may outwit him by putting one example on a page. When he works the one example, she must praise him and write another one for him to work.

This is very trying for the teacher if she has a full case load of children in the room. Sometimes the child will accept a page of examples that has been folded into strips. Each strip is completed before the next one is unfolded.

Another method of handling this type of situation is to fold a paper into squares and to write an example on each square. The paper may be cut along the folds, and one example at a time may be given to the child. The examples should be collected as they are completed. When working with a group, the teacher may allow each child to keep his material in a box on his desk. This procedure will eliminate unnecessary movement around the room.

In preparing the examples, the teacher at first should use the larger number at the top and teach the child to add down the column. After the sum of the combination is fixed in the child's consciousness, the other corresponding fact may be included in the sets of examples.

Teaching the Place of a Number in a Series. The child must be taught to recognize that each number in the series has a special place and meaning. This may be accomplished by using objects placed in rows to show that a number is one more than the number it precedes and that it is one less than the number after it.

The give-and-take of dialogue between the teacher and the child is important for retention and eventual comprehension. The teacher may use a procedure similar to the following, using buttons, beans, blocks or cards to illustrate the problem: In the sample dialogue, T represents the teacher and C represents the child.

T: Two are more than one. Place one button beside another button.
   Take away the button.
C: Two are more than one.
   Repeat this procedure over and over, using many kinds of objects. Use sticks to demonstrate.
T: I will give you one stick. How many sticks do you have?

$$
\begin{array}{ccc}
1 & 2 & 1 \\
+1 & +1 & +2 \\
\hline
\end{array}
\qquad
\begin{array}{ccc}
2 & 3 & 2 \\
+2 & +1 & +1 \\
\hline
\end{array}
$$

$$
\begin{array}{ccc}
2 & 3 & 2 \\
+2 & +1 & +1 \\
\hline
\end{array}
\qquad
\begin{array}{ccc}
3 & 1 & 1 \\
+1 & +1 & +2 \\
\hline
\end{array}
$$

$$
\begin{array}{ccc}
3 & 1 & 3 \\
+1 & +1 & +1 \\
\hline
\end{array}
\qquad
\begin{array}{ccc}
2 & 3 & 2 \\
+2 & +1 & +2 \\
\hline
\end{array}
$$

$$
\begin{array}{cc}
3 & 1 \\
+1 & +3 \\
\hline
\end{array}
$$

$$
\begin{array}{ccc}
3 & 2 & 1 \\
+1 & +1 & +1 \\
\hline
\end{array}
\qquad
\begin{array}{c}
1 \\
+1 \\
\hline
\end{array}
\qquad
\begin{array}{ccc}
2 & 3 & 1 \\
+2 & +1 & +3 \\
\hline
\end{array}
$$

$$
\begin{array}{cc}
3 & 2 \\
+1 & +2 \\
\hline
\end{array}
\quad
\begin{array}{c}
1 \\
+1 \\
\hline
\end{array}
$$

1+3=
3+1=
2+1=
1+2=
1+ 1+1+1=

$$
\begin{array}{c}
1 \\
+1 \\
\hline
\end{array}
\qquad
\begin{array}{ccc}
1 & 1 & 3 \\
+3 & +3 & +1 \\
\hline
\end{array}
$$

$$
\begin{array}{ccc}
2 & 3 & 1 \\
+1 & +1 & +2 \\
\hline
\end{array}
$$

62. Introducing partial counting.

C: One stick.

T: Here is one more stick. Put this stick with your other stick. Now I will pick up a stick. Do you have more sticks than I have?

C: I have more sticks.

T: How many sticks do you have?

C: Two sticks.

T: Now, you tell me that two sticks are more than one stick.

C: Two sticks are more than one stick.

Repeat this type of drill over and over, changing the objects so that the child will not associate the *more than* with any one object. At the same time, the teacher should try to get the child to give a complete sentence as a response to her question.

When the child is ready for another number in the series, the same procedure is carried out. The concept of *less* should not be taught parallel with *more than* at this time, as it would confuse

63. Visual, tactile and kinesthetic teaching aids.

the child. Only after the concepts of the numbers 1, 2, 3, 4, and 5 have been established should the idea of *less than* be presented.

Teaching the Concept of Second. The procedure for teaching the concept of *second* is similar to that of presenting *first*. Review the ordinal *first*. Place the children in rows; sing the number songs; use blocks, marbles, and buttons; ask the children questions and let them echo the answers until there seems to be an understanding of the term *second*.

T: Give the second block to me.

C: Here is the second block.

These basic concepts cannot be hurried. The presentation of this simple material will consume weeks of time. The teacher must remember that the material, the objects, and the flash cards with pictures must be varied continuously to hold interest and to prevent the child from associating meaning with material.

Teaching Grouping and Partial Counting. When the child is ready mentally to understand grouping and partial counting, he will be able to recognize two objects and associates them with the name *two*. However, the child may be able to use the word *two* without knowing the meaning of the number two. He may revert to counting each object as he has not had enough drill on the recognition of groups before he begins to combine the groups.

Partial counting begins with naming the first number in a series without tapping or using counters, and continues from there to arrive at the sum, such as 4 and 2 are 6. Later he may be able to give the sum of 6 without counting out the last numbers. The child should be weaned of the habit of saying, "1, 2, 3, 4, and 5, 6," for 4 and 2 are 6.

Partial counting practices should begin with the previously mastered concepts of 1, 2, and 3 and be continued until they are automatic with the child. Then the numbers 4 and later 5 are presented. At this stage, partial counting is limited to the combinations taught and does not include other groupings. If the child is hurried too fast for his mental ability or if he has a lack of confidence he may manifest a reversion by using counters.

Aiding the Retention of Facts. Assimilation of the facts is accomplished so slowly by some children that it may be necessary to permit them to use counters in the manner of beginners, so that they may solve problems and have a feeling of success. Con-

$$
\begin{array}{ccc}
2 & 3 & 1 \\
+2 & +1 & +3
\end{array}
\qquad
\begin{array}{cccc}
4 & 1 & 4 & 1 \\
+1 & +4 & +1 & +4
\end{array}
$$

1+1= 1+2= 3+1=
2+2= 2+1= 1+3=

$$
\begin{array}{cccc}
3 & 1 & 2 & 2 \\
1 & +3 & +2 & +1
\end{array}
\qquad
\begin{array}{ccc}
3 & 2 & 1 \\
+1 & +1 & +1
\end{array}
$$

$$
\begin{array}{cccc}
1 & 1 & 3 & 1 \\
2 & 1 & 1 & 3
\end{array}
\qquad
\begin{array}{cccc}
2 & 1 & 1 & 3 \\
+2 & +2 & +3 & +1
\end{array}
$$

$$
\begin{array}{ccc}
4 & 3 & 2 \\
+1 & +1 & +1
\end{array}
\qquad
\begin{array}{ccc}
4 & 2 & 4 \\
+1 & +2 & +1
\end{array}
$$

$$
\begin{array}{ccc}
1 & 4 & 1 \\
+3 & +1 & +2
\end{array}
\qquad
\begin{array}{ccc}
3 & 4 & 2 \\
+1 & +1 & +1
\end{array}
$$

$$
\begin{array}{ccc}
1 & 2 & 4 \\
+1 & +2 & +1
\end{array}
\qquad
\begin{array}{ccc}
4 & 2 & 4 \\
+1 & +2 & +1
\end{array}
$$

$$
\begin{array}{ccc}
3 & 2 & 4 \\
+1 & +1 & +1
\end{array}
\qquad
\begin{array}{ccc}
1 & 2 & 1 \\
+4 & +2 & +3
\end{array}
$$

1+4= 3+1=
4+1= 1+3=

64. Introducing grouping.

tinued drill in competency would do more harm to the personality than the gain in skill would warrant. Examples should be prepared within the limits of the numbers formerly taught and upon which the children have been drilled.

Using the Flannel Board. Another way to vary the presentation of the lessons is to use the flannel board. This is effective in teaching number groups or the meaning of numbers. A flannel board is inexpensive to make and limitless in its use.

The base of the flannel board may be a piece of heavy cardboard with a cover of heavy outing flannel or felt stretched over it. The flannel is sewed across the back of the cardboard to keep it smooth and taut. White or black outing flannel is the best background for presenting numbers.

Circles may be cut from heavy flannel or from old felt hats of a contrasting color. These circles cling to the flannel board, yet they are easily moved about for grouping in teaching addition and subtraction.

The domino pattern should be used consistently in arranging the circles on the flannel board. Only the numerals the child has been prepared to understand through the previous use of concrete materials should be presented.

After this preparation, flash cards with the numerals may be used for a visual recognition drill. The teacher may use domino patterns of dots or squares for the semiconcrete problems. No decorated objects should be pasted on the flash cards, as they detract from the number group.

Matching Exercise. The teacher may prepare matching exercises for the children by drawing large numbers on mimeographed sheets of paper. The children match the numbers by drawing lines between the similar symbols with crayons. The numbers may be written on heavy cardboard, over which tracing paper is clipped. The children draw lines on the tracing paper to match the similar numbers.

Another method for matching is that of using shoelaces attached to the side of a plywood form on which the numbers and objects are painted. Holes are drilled into the plywood along the other side of the board into which the laces are strung as the numbers and objects are matched.

As each numeral is learned, it should be added to the list of numbers to be matched with objects. Matching may be used as a review. Place number flash cards on a table with groups of objects. Ask the children to match the cards to the groups. Also use picture flash cards or domino cards to match the objects or the numbers.

The mentally retarded child dislikes to do the same exercises over and over. Since he soon recognizes the same sheet of examples, rearrange the same material by using different pictures and designs. *Keep the materials simple.*

Teaching Number by Playing Games. Games are excellent to intensify learning and to assist in a socializing program. The use of games provides a practical experience in using number values. Change the points to be scored to suit the ability of the children, as in these games: beanbag, ringtoss, shuffleboard, hopscotch, or tenpins.

Make bean bags from any heavy material which can be sewed into bags about six inches square. Fill each one with six ounces of dried beans, which is the right weight for indoor use. Label shoe boxes and place them in a row as targets for the bean bags. Thumbtack the boxes to a piece of plywood so they will not slide about when the bags are tossed into them.

For beginners in counting, use *one box* for the bags to be tossed into. Label it 1. The players keep score by putting colored counting sticks beside their names. Each child should have sticks all of one color. Until the children are able to keep score, the teacher must count the sticks.

Make ten pins from round cereal boxes and paint them bright colors. Use a soft rubber ball to roll against the pins. Use as many pins in the games as the children are able to count. Start with one pin, if necessary, and add more as the children's counting ability increases. Keep scores with colored sticks as in the game of bean bag.

A toilet plunger makes a good peg for a ring toss game. The rings may be fruit jar rings, or they may be from short lengths of clothes line.

Teaching Tallying by Fives. The large sticks used for primary counting are excellent for teaching tallying by fives to the more advanced pupils who have learned to count by fives. Use the sticks instead of making pencil marks.

Using the Abacus. The abacus may also be used for scoring after the children are mature enough to understand how to manipulate it.

Teaching the Words One and Two. Sight recognition of the words *one* and *two* may be taught as the child becomes proficient

$$\begin{array}{ccc} 2 & 3 & 4 \\ -1 & -1 & -1 \\ \hline \end{array} \qquad \begin{array}{ccc} 2 & 3 & 4 \\ -1 & -1 & -1 \\ \hline \end{array}$$

$$\begin{array}{cc} 5 & 3 \\ -1 & -2 \\ \hline \end{array} \qquad \begin{array}{ccc} 5 & 2 & 3 \\ -1 & -1 & -1 \\ \hline \end{array}$$

$$\begin{array}{ccc} & & \\ 5 & 2 & 4 \\ +4 & -1 & -3 \\ \hline \end{array} \qquad \begin{array}{ccc} 4 & 2 & 5 \\ -1 & -1 & -1 \\ \hline \end{array}$$

$$\begin{array}{cccc} 2 & 3 & 4 & 5 \\ 1 & 2 & 1 & 1 \\ \hline \end{array}$$

$$\begin{array}{cccc} 3 & 5 & 4 & 2 \\ -1 & -4 & -3 & -1 \\ \hline \end{array} \qquad \begin{array}{cccc} 1 & 2 & 2 & 1 \\ +1 & -1 & +1 & +2 \\ \hline \end{array}$$

$$\begin{array}{cccc} & & & \\ & & & \\ & & & \\ \end{array} \qquad \begin{array}{cccc} 3 & 3 & 3 & 1 \\ -1 & -2 & +1 & +3 \\ \hline \end{array}$$

$$\begin{array}{cccc} 5 & 4 & 3 & 2 \\ -1 & -1 & -1 & -1 \\ \hline \end{array} \qquad \begin{array}{cccc} 4 & 4 & 4 & 1 \\ -1 & -3 & +1 & +4 \\ \hline \end{array}$$

$$\begin{array}{cccc} 5 & 4 & 3 & 2 \\ -4 & -3 & -2 & -1 \\ \hline \end{array} \qquad \begin{array}{cc} 5 & 5 \\ -1 & -4 \\ \hline \end{array}$$

65. Subtraction examples with some addition examples.

in the use of the addition combinations whose sums are five or less. Use the words as reading vocabulary. Write them on flash cards for matching with numbers, dots, or groups of objects.

Teaching Subtraction. Introduction to subtraction takes place *after* the complete presentation and understanding of the numbers 1 through 5. Introduce the minus sign as *take away*. This is an

Subtraction - Mixed

```
  4     2     1     3     0     4
 -0    -1    -1    -0    -0    -4
 ───   ───   ───   ───   ───   ───
```

2 - 1 =   2 - 0 =   2 - 2 =

1 - 1 =   1 - 1 =   0 - 0 =

3 - 0 =   4 - 4 =   5 - 0 =

3 - 3 =   4 - 1 =   5 - 5 =

3 - 1 =   4 - 0 =   5 - 1 =

66. Sample examples for practice in column and equation form in subtraction.

easily understood term and one with which the child is usually familiar. Present the numbers concretely, beginning with 2 and proceeding through the number series, 2 take away 1, to 5 take away 1. Zero is not presented at this time.

Present every step just as in addition, going from objects to the semiconcrete pictures and dots, and then to the number symbols. Give oral examples and problems first and then the worksheets of numbers to be subtracted.

Assimilating Each Combination. Work on one combination at a time until it is assimilated into the child's memory with a concept of its meaning. Review the addition facts continuously as the corresponding subtraction facts are being taught. As each subtraction fact is established for the child, give practice pages with

```
 2    3    4          2    3    4
-1   -1   -1         -1   -1   -1

      5    3          5    2    3
     -1   -2         -1   -1   -1

 5    2    4          4    2    5
-4   -1   -3         -1   -1   -1
```

```
 2    3    4    5          1    2    2    1
-1   -2   -1   -1         +1   -1   +1   +2

 3    5    4    2          3    3    3    1
-1   -4   -3   -1         -1   -2   +1   +3

 5    4    3    2          4    4    4    1
-1   -1   -1   -1         -1   -3   +1   +4

 5    4    3    2          5    5
-4   -3   -2   -1         -1   -4
```

67. Sample examples—subtraction with no remainder greater than 4,
and no zeros; addition and subtraction with no answer greater than 5,
and no zeros.

ZERO IN REMAINDERS

1	2	3	4	5	0
-1	-2	-3	-4	-5	-0

ZERO IN THE SUBTRAHEND

1	2	3	4	5
-0	-0	-0	-0	-0

6	7	8	9
-0	-0	-0	-0

USING ZERO IN SUBTRACTION

2	3	4	1	2
-0	-0	-4	-0	-2

5	1	3	4
-5	-1	-3	-0

68. Using zero in subtraction.

the corresponding addition facts. This is a tedious process for the teacher, but it is of great value to the child.

Presenting Zero in Remainders. Introduce zero as a remainder after the children understand subtraction facts whose remainders do not exceed four. These will need separate drill and must be

$$\begin{array}{cccccc} 2 & 2 & 1 & 3 & 4 & 5 \\ -1 & -2 & -1 & -2 & -1 & -1 \\ \hline \end{array}$$

$$\begin{array}{cccccc} 5 & 3 & 5 & 2 & 4 & 5 \\ -5 & -1 & -4 & -0 & -2 & -3 \\ \hline \end{array}$$

$$\begin{array}{cccccc} 4 & 1 & 5 & 2 & 4 & 3 \\ -0 & -0 & -2 & -2 & -3 & -3 \\ \hline \end{array}$$

$$\begin{array}{cccccc} 5 & 3 & 0 & 4 & 5 & 5 \\ -2 & -0 & -0 & -4 & -5 & -0 \\ \hline \end{array}$$

69. Practice sheet in subtraction.

taught as carefully as the preceding combinations. Proceed with the same methods and with step-by-step demonstrations with objects, then pictures, dots, and, at last, the number symbols.

Teaching the Value of Zero in the Subtrahend. The use of zero in the subtrahend should be taught with the same detail and care as in the preceding items, with objects, semiconcrete materials and the number symbols. Explain and dramatize every step to show the value of zero. The teacher should prepare many series of examples illustrating all possible combinations in the use of zero for the pupils' practice worksheets.

Teaching Grouping in Numbers 2 through 5. The educable mentally retarded find it difficult to associate the relationships

4   3   2 | | |
+1   +1   +1   +4   +3   +2

3+1=   2+1=   4+1= | | |
4+1=   4+1=   3+1=   +1   +4   +3
2+1=   3+1=   2+1=
4+1=   4+1=   4+1=   4   4 |
                            +1   +1   +4

3   4 | | | |
+1   +1   +1   +1   +3   +2

4 | 4   4   3   2
+1 +4   +1   +1   +1   +2

                             4+1= |
3 | 2   1+4=   +4
+1 +3   +1   2+2=
                             1+2=   3 |
| | 2   2+1=   +1   -1
+2 +1   +2   3+1=
                             1+3= |
4   3   2   1+1=   +3
+1 +1   +1 |
                                         +2

70. Practice sheet for addition—no sum greater than 5.

of numbers and to break numbers down into groups within a number. When the numbers have been thoroughly understood in their basic relationships of zero through five, it is important to start there with grouping and partial counting. Objects may be used to show the children all of the possible groups in each number. Then allow the pupils to write the group names as they recognize them. They should handle the groups of objects and talk about them.

Prepare practice sheets to review the previous instruction in partial counting. Try to proceed slowly so the child will have

$$
\begin{array}{cccccc}
3 & 5 & 1 & 6 & 6 & 4 \\
+3 & +1 & +5 & +1 & -5 & +4 \\
\hline
\end{array}
$$

$$
\begin{array}{ccccccc}
6 & 1 & 7 & 7 & 7 & 5 & 7 \\
+1 & +6 & -1 & -1 & -6 & +5 & +1 \\
\hline
\end{array}
$$

$$
\begin{array}{cccccc}
1 & 8 & 8 & 8 & 1 & 9 \\
+7 & -1 & -7 & +1 & +8 & -1 \\
\hline
\end{array}
$$

$$
\begin{array}{ccccc}
9 & 9 & 1 & 10 & 10 \\
-8 & +1 & +9 & -1 & -9 \\
\hline
\end{array}
$$

71. Practice sheet for addition and subtraction of numbers from 6 through 10.

confidence in his ability to name the sums. After the grouping idea has been established for the addition combinations, take up the subtraction facts. Demonstrate with objects for every group and continue drill on the combinations until the child can work them. This will include many, many lessons and many practice sheets.

Arousing the Child's Interest in Numbers. Interest and the will to accomplish a given goal is important in all areas of learning. The child needs adequate preparation, as well as maturation, to achieve this goal. Careful spacing of new steps will aid in the progress of the child.

Everyday situations should be used to impress the child with the necessity of knowing the fact being presented. The teacher must continuously question the children about experiences involving numbers to make them realize that numbers are an important part of daily living.

Introducing More Difficult Games. As the child advances in number recognition and ability to group and to count, he will enjoy playing a greater variety of games. An adaptation of parchesi may be made by the children. A story they have enjoyed may be the basis of the game. A route is marked on a large card along which the children draw or color episodes from the story. They may mark the route into sections and make a spinner on a card that is numbered for scoring. The numbers on the card must be within the child's computational ability. One spinner might have the numbers 1, 2, and 3; another, 1 through 5; and another 1 through 10.

Such games teach the children cooperation, honesty, and consideration for others; give experience in the use of numbers; and provide pleasant recreation.

Teaching the Numbers from 6 through 10. The teacher must take plenty of time to present the next group of numbers. The larger values will require more time for the memory and comprehension processes to function. The importance of the teacher's taking the work slowly cannot be overemphasized. Even though she has given meticulous presentations for the numbers 1 through

5, she must continue to do so for every item that is presented, *over-teaching,* if possible.

Large, tangible objects which the child can handle over and over should be used for counting. At first regular shaped objects, all of the same color, should be used so there will be no distraction. The teacher should check over the materials she has for counting and try to add some new ones for variety, using new colors to change the appearance of the old spools, sticks, and blocks.

She should begin using the abacus, now that the number concepts to five have been established. Small plastic toys are excellent to use for counters and to give variety to games and oral problems.

Other devices may be constructed to slow down the pupil in counting by rote, in order to attain comprehension of the value of the number in the series. One such device is a board about ¾ x 6 x 12 inches with 10 screw eyes lightly turned into the wood. As the child counts, he turns each screw eye in rotation.

Another device is a mobile abacus for counting. This may be made on a rod or suspended on a frame. Ten large wooden beads are individually strung on cords and hung from the rod or frame. The child grasps a bead and says the name of the number. Then he lets go of the bead and grasps the next one, repeating its number name in the series.

A child who has never been able to learn rote counting is thus slowed down by merely picking up each object as he names the corresponding number. As he matures and gains confidence, he is able to count without touching objects.

Presentation of Parallel Facts. At this stage of the presentation of numbers, the addition and subtraction facts for each number starting with six may be taught in the same lessons.

Teaching the Child's Telephone Number. When the child's mental age is 7-0 to 7-6, he should be able to give his address and telephone number. After he has learned them by rote, he can learn to write them. Then he should practice dialing the number in order to learn how to call his home. Later the number of the fire station should be taught for use in an emergency.

$$
\begin{array}{ccccc}
2 & 2 & 1 & 4 & 3 \\
+2 & +1 & +1 & +1 & +1 \\
\hline
\end{array}
$$

$$
\begin{array}{cccccc}
2 & 2 & 1 & 3 & 4 & 5 \\
-2 & -1 & -1 & -1 & -1 & -1 \\
\hline
\end{array}
$$

$$
\begin{array}{cccccc}
2 & 3 & 2 & 4 & 1 & 5 \\
-1 & -1 & -2 & -1 & -1 & -1 \\
\hline
\end{array}
$$

$$
\begin{array}{cccccccc}
1 & 2 & 2 & 3 & 1 & 4 & 3 & 1 \\
+1 & +1 & +2 & +2 & +2 & +1 & +1 & +3 \\
\hline
\end{array}
$$

$$
\begin{array}{ccccccc}
1 & 2 & 1 & 1 & 3 & 1 & 4 \\
+0 & +3 & +1 & +2 & +2 & +4 & +0 \\
\hline
\end{array}
$$

72.   Practice sheet—addition and subtraction with answers of 5 or less.

Teaching the 45 Basic Addition Combinations. Since ability to count is definitely related to the ability to add, adding and counting are two things that may be taught at the same time. There are forty-five basic combinations. It is better to teach the easier twenty-five combinations whose sums are ten or less first. Then teach the other twenty more difficult combinations and the zero combinations.

The teacher may adapt games to facilitate the retention of the combinations. These should be easy enough for enjoyment by the contestants, yet should be challenging. One such game may be called "Climbing the Stairs."

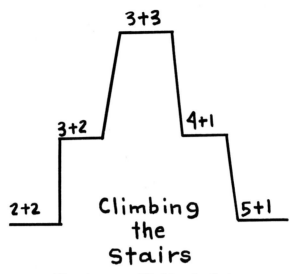

73.   A game—Climbing the Stairs.

Climbing the Stairs. The object of the game is to see who can go the highest on the stairs, or who can go up and down without missing a number. If the pupil misses, he is out of that game. If the child does all of the combinations correctly, he gains a point for his team.

Using Computational Skills. The child needs to have experiences with real situations to be able to solve problems. The children's own activities may be utilized for problem material. The children must be helped to visualize the situation or to act it out so that they will understand the situation and be able to arrive at a solution.

Action Problems. The teacher should compose for the children problems in which their names and activities are mentioned. These problems should be presented orally by the teacher. They should be simple in construction and easy to solve. The teacher is speaking.

1. Bob. please get 5 books from the table.
   Thank you, Bob. Now give 3 of the books to Sue.
   How many books do you have left?

2. Tom, please get 7 crayons from the box on my desk.
   Give 4 of the crayons to Sherry.
   How many crayons do you have left?
3. Mary, please give 4 blocks to Sue and 3 blocks to Bob.
   Who has more blocks, Sue or Bob?
   How many more blocks?

Teaching about Zero as a Place Holder. The abacus should be frequently used in teaching the position of zero as a place holder and in teaching the meaning of units, tens, and hundreds. It shows the regularity of the numerical system. The beads, manipulated on the wires, make it easy for the pupils to count off any given number and see what the number means.

Teaching Counting by Twos. When a child is able to count by rote and knows the meaning of *two,* he is ready to learn about pairs of things. As his ability progresses to 4, 6, 8, or 10, he should learn to count the even numbers and the odd numbers. The children like to play games or chant rhymes that help make the idea of pairs meaningful. Objects used in counting, such as disks, beads, buttons, blocks, toys or felt circles, should be utilized in practicing counting the *even* and the *odd* numbers.

Teaching Counting by Fives. To introduce counting by fives, the teacher may tell the children the old story of the shepherd who kept track of his flock with a pile of pebbles. As each sheep passed out of the fold, the shepherd put a pebble in his pocket. The shepherd carried the pebbles about with him all day as he guarded the sheep.

At night as the sheep went back into the pen, he took out a pebble for each sheep. He knew the right number of sheep were in the pen when there were no more pebbles. If the shepherd had one pebble left, he knew a sheep was lost. The children like to play the same game with old pocket books and pebbles. They may take turns counting one another as they march around the room.

Later the teacher may continue the story by showing how the shepherd often had a very heavy pouch of pebbles to carry, until he finally thought of tallying the sheep by five as they went in and out of the fold. A child may hold the pouch and put the fifth pebble in it for every fifth child in the room. The children will see how much easier it is to carry the pouch with fewer pebbles in it.

During this demonstration the teacher should introduce the ordinal *fifth,* parallel with teaching the children to count by fives. As the children march she may reverse the procedure by having the keeper of the pouch take a pebble out of it for every five children that pass by him. This teaching should be reinforced by using objects and by counting by fives on the abacus.

Teaching Counting by Tens. After the value of zero as a place holder has been reviewed, the teacher may use objects to demonstrate counting by tens. The game of the shepherd boy may also be continued. Learning the names of the tens and counting by tens help to place the decades. This training should be done regularly in oral and written practice.

Presenting the Teens. Before presenting the teens, the teacher should give the class a thorough review of the numbers 1 through 10, and of zero as a place holder. The children must be helped to see that the numbers after the 9 are two-place numbers. They must understand that 11 is not just two ones side by side, but that 11 is made up of a 10 and a 1. Objects, counters and the abacus should be used to make the child comprehend the real meaning of 11. The child should handle these materials, as the kinesthetic and tactile senses help reinforce the memory.

Each separate *teen* should be taught in this manner. Comprehending the meaning of the teens is one of the most difficult feats the mentally retarded child must make in beginning numbers. If this concept is not established, the rest of the number system will remain a puzzle to him.

Understanding the Tens to One Hundred. Objects should be available for showing the numbers from 1 through 100. The abacus may be used, as it is easily handled. However, the actual handling and counting of objects provide better understanding in the beginning. The children may have a box of counting sticks and some rubber bands to make up bundles of ten sticks until they have ten bundles. As each one counts, he will become aware of the value of ten and of the number of tens it takes to make one hundred.

The teacher must be alert to devise different ways to present these concepts. One particularly slow child was unable to realize the meaning of the tens and hundreds until he was taken out of doors and allowed to collect pebbles by tens and put them in squares drawn on the ground with a stick. Tom drew ten squares and put ten pebbles in each square. This, for some unknown reason, was more understandable to him than putting 10 beans on top of ten squares drawn with chalk on the classroom floor.

The other children in the room became so intrigued with Tom's game that they played it too. The school yard was decorated for a long time with little mounds of pebbles arranged in tens. Tom's game makes an excellent experience for learning the values of hundreds to thousands, or for counting by 2's, 3's, or 5's.

During inclement weather a section of the floor in the classroom may be lined off and grains of corn used for counters. Large sheets of newsprint may be marked off into squares for counting by tens or hundreds. When ten such sheets are used, the children can readily see the hundreds that make the thousands.

Understanding for all will not come in one lesson or even in a dozen demonstrations; the teacher must be patient and repeat the lesson with new variations.

A game of fishing for numbers may be called "The Fish Bowl Game." This game is excellent for a review of recognizing the numbers. The directions for the game are simple.

The teacher may cut small fish from orange construction paper, tie a string through the head of the fish, put a number on each fish, and put the fish into a real fish bowl. The children take turns choosing a string to pull out a fish from the bowl. Each child who can say the number on the fish correctly keeps the fish for a score of 1. If he cannot say the number, he must put the fish back into the bowl.

Continuing Practice in Grouping. The children need continued practice in grouping and in quick recognition of quantities in groups. They will enjoy a card game that teaches *more, less, fewer,* and *greater.*

The teacher constructs the cards of lightweight cardboard about 3 x 6 inches in size on which are placed dots ranging from 1 through 10. The pupils play the game by comparing the groups of dots with a set the teacher presents to gain an understanding of the above terms.

The children may take turns in playing, as in any card game. One card is placed face up on the table; the rest are placed face down. Each child selects a card. If the face card has four dots, the first child to play compares his card with it. If his card has seven dots, he should say, "My card has more dots than four." He then keeps the card, which counts one point for him. He draws another card and the next child plays.

If this next child has a card with less dots than four, but calls them more than four, he puts the card on the bottom of the pile of cards in the center of the table, and draws another card.

The game should also be played using the terms *fewer* and *greater*. As the children's knowledge of number improves, more cards may be added until they have two complete sets of cards

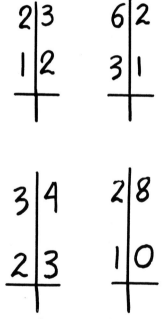

74.   Introducing two-place addition.

from which to choose. The scoring may be made more difficult as the pupils' ability improves.

Presenting Two-place Addition. The child whose mental age is around 8-0 may be ready for addition with two-place numbers, but with no carrying. In constructing examples, put the larger number at the top of the column and instruct the child to add down. He should be able to do partial counting. At first draw lines between the numbers in the units and tens column. The child can see the familiar examples he has been working with and will have confidence in his ability to find the sum.

After he has worked many pages of examples with this device, the guide lines should be left off the examples on part of the page and finally left off entirely. When the child has confidence in the above procedure, the teacher should then present subtraction in the same manner with two-place numbers, but with no borrowing.

Teaching about Borrowing and Carrying. The child must have a good understanding of the tens and the units values before the teacher starts to present carrying and borrowing. Here again it is more satisfactory to begin with addition and to teach carrying.

Pennies and dimes are excellent materials to use to teach the meaning of this process. The abacus is another good device for explaining units, tens, and hundreds. The teacher may use blocks, peg boards, or spool boards with the counters arranged in rows of tens to show how to carry in addition examples. After carrying in addition has been mastered, these same materials may be used to demonstrate borrowing in subtraction examples.

Only two addends should be used in two-place numbers in addition until after subtraction has been mastered for two-place numbers with borrowing. Then hundreds may be taught for addition and later for subtraction. The teacher should prepare simple examples at first, being sure that zero is included and is understood.

The three-place examples should have no borrowing or carrying until the children are secure in using the large numbers. The teacher will prepare examples beginning with the borrowing or carrying in the tens only. After they have become accustomed to this type of example, she presents the three-place examples with no carrying or borrowing in the tens but with carrying or borrowing in the hundreds. When they have mastered this process, the teacher presents three-place examples with borrowing and carrying in the units, tens, and hundreds.

Reading Larger Numbers. Extensive practice should be given in reading numbers from 1 through 1,000. The teacher should drill the children on the place values of numbers in the position of units, tens, hundreds, and thousands. She should not confuse the children by preparing drills in which the order of the place numbers has been scrambled, but should use the numbers in a manner that corresponds to reality in buying and selling.

Introducing Multiplication. Multiplication may be presented when the child has a mental age of about 8-6 to 9-0 years. The teacher may introduce multiplication first through pairs of objects, then by doubles of numbers, and by the use of addition combinations of doubles. These facts will be familiar to the children from other drills and games. The two's are usually quickly learned.

As understanding develops, the children are ready for a few new multiplication facts. These should be introduced gradually with ample demonstrations by the teacher and many class activities by the pupils. To insure understanding and retention will take many years, since other concepts in numbers are being developed at the same time.

When the child has become confident of his ability to multiply with one-place numbers, he is ready to be advanced to two-and three-place numbers with one multiplier and no carrying of tens, and is shown the use of zero in the units and tens place only after confidence has been gained in the process without carrying.

Introducing Division. Simple division with even numbers may be taught after comprehension and retention in the multiplication of simple numbers have been established. The division facts may be taught by using objects and by intensive drill. Division understanding progresses more slowly than multiplication. Most educable mentally retarded will gain little proficiency in division.

Presenting the Relationship of Numbers. After the child has some experience with addition, substraction, multiplication and division, a series of examples may be used to produce the same answers. This type of exercise will have meaning only for the

Relationship of Numbers

$0 + 6 = 6$ $6 - 0 = 6$

$1 + 5 = 6$ $2 \times 3 = 6$

$2 + 4 = 6$ $7 - 1 = 6$

$3 \times 2 = 6$

$3 + 3 = 6$ $8 - 2 = 6$

$1 \times 6 = 6$

$4 + 2 = 6$ $9 - 3 = 6$

$5 + 1 = 6$ $6 \times 1 = 6$

$10 - 4 = 6$

$6 + 0 = 6$

$12 \div 2 = 6$

75. Presenting the relationship of numbers.

children with the highest mental age in the group. The teacher should prepare the examples and go over them first with the children; then let the children ask questions about the examples.

If the children are unable to think of questions to ask regarding the relationship of numbers, the teacher may demonstrate the examples again. Then she may distribute examples without the answers for the children to solve. She should not be discouraged if she secures little progress in establishing this concept, because the educable mentally retarded will be able to work the simple problems that fulfill their needs without a complete understanding of the relationships of numbers.

14

ARITHMETIC—OTHER TOPICS

AT REGULAR intervals short units on other topics are taught. These should include money values, shapes, linear measurement, weights, dry and liquid measures, fractional parts, time, the calendar, the clock, the days of the week, the months of the year, the holidays, and the Roman numerals.

MONEY

Begin with real money to teach a child to make change. He will then have a correct image of the coins about which he is studying. After the correct concept has been established, use play money. Work with the child independently until he learns a few values. Then let him work in group activities with children who are about the same level of ability in handling money.

Teach the values of the one cent and the nickel concurrently with the study of the values of the numbers through five. When the child has learned the numbers from 6 through 10, teach him the value of the dime. Keep reviewing the cents and the nickel so that he will not forget them. *Go slowly.*

Present the larger values of money as the child matures and attains a readiness for them. Do not hurry this presentation, which should be started only after the concept of the corresponding number has been established. For example, present the quarter, 25c in change, and making change for a quarter only after the concept of the number 25 has been established.

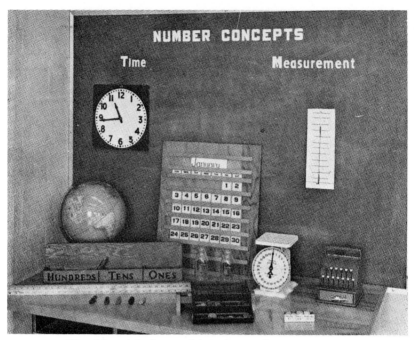

76.   Materials for teaching time and measurement.

When the child understands the number system up to 100, he is ready to learn the value of the dollar, the meaning of the decimal sign, the dollar sign, reading and writing the values of money in dollars and cents, and to solve practical problems about money.

The basic values are learned through individual instruction. The child will become proficient in recognizing money values and in making change through units of work about the grocery store, the post office, and other school activities.

The children should have practice in reading money values. This may be accomplished by writing amounts on the chalkboard, by allowing the class to practice reading them, and by pronouncing amounts to the children for them to write.

By the time the educable mentally retarded child is ready to leave the intermediate department he should be able to use money up to ten dollars in buying and selling at the school play store. Trading at the play store should be done with play money to avoid complications resulting from too much temptation.

Teach money values once or twice a week consistently so that

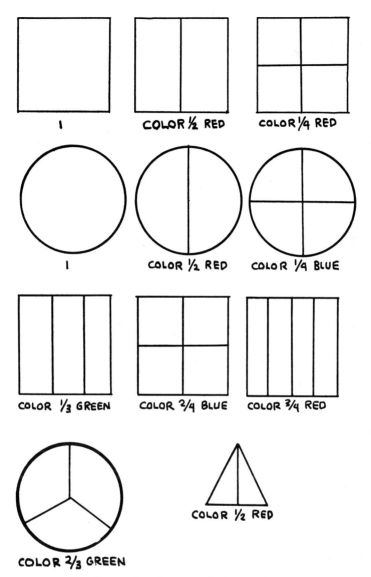

77. Presenting shapes and fractional parts.

the children will be competent and confident in handling money. Every teacher should encourage the children and be persistent in following through regularly in this process, because it is one of the valuable skills the child should attain for self-sufficiency.

SHAPES

Shapes should be incidentally taught to children from an early age at home. These are usually presented informally to the group of the primary age mentally retarded. Systematic instruction is started when the children arrive in the intermediate age group. Teach in this order the circle, square, triangle, rectangle, or oblong by using the following: stencils; forms to trace around; emery board cut-outs; forms drawn on the chalkboard or on paper to be colored solidly within the lines.

Show the pupils the circle, square, triangle, and rectangle forms that are to be found in the classroom. Ask the children to think of these forms and tell where they have been seen in other places. The entire presentation should not be hurried, but should cover about a two-year to three-year period.

The older retarded group should learn about the cube, cylinder, and sphere. These forms are used in everyday living in such items as food containers, balls, utensils, or as parts of our homes.

LINEAR MEASUREMENTS

The educable mentally retarded have great difficulty in recognizing distance. Since the idea of any linear measurement is vague and incomprehensible to them, things are usually referred to as far away, close, not very big, big, tall, not very tall. These concepts should be used as a basis for enlarging and extending the values of measurements.

The child becomes aware of the value of measurement and of the unit of the inch through being measured in the health clinic. When he demonstrates an interest in measurement, show him how to measure an inch and how to make a ruler one inch long. Make the ruler from a strip of inch-squared paper, which the pupil cuts into strips one-inch long. Linear measurement should be concurrently taught with learning the number system and with rote counting.

As the use of numbers increases, so will the concept of measurement. The pupil will learn the term *foot ruler* before he learns 12 inches. He can begin to measure in inches as soon as he learns to count one and one. This child must be shown the procedure to use in measuring a line. The teacher should talk to the child about the ruler and explain its use. She should show the child

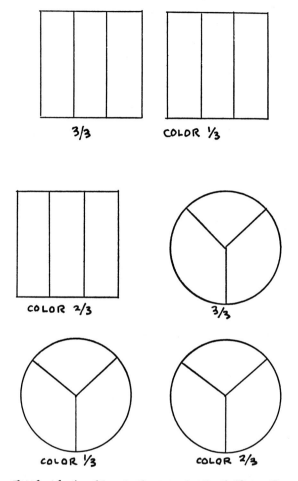

3/3 COLOR ⅓

COLOR ⅔ 3/3

COLOR ⅓ COLOR ⅔

THIS IS A SAMPLE OF ONE TYPE OF
WORK SHEET USED IN TEACHING FRACTIONAL PARTS.

78. Presenting shapes and fractional parts.

how to lay the ruler on the paper; how to hold the ruler to keep
it from wiggling; how to make a dot at the exact end of the ruler
and at the one-inch line; how to carefully draw between the dots
without moving the ruler.

As each child gains mastery of drawing the one-inch line, the
group may work together. The teacher may make a game of
giving the directions in a brief rhythmic tone as she moves among
the children and helps them to secure competency.

At a mental age of 7-0 to 7-6 years, the children may start to measure many things such as books, pencils, crayons, and desks. They may draw lines of stated length, or measure lines drawn on the chalkboard.

At the mental age of 7-6 to 8-0 years, the child may be expected to know the use of the foot ruler and the number of inches in a foot. He is now ready to be taught the use of the yardstick. He should learn that three feet make a yard, that 36 inches also make one yard, and that the yardstick is used to measure things that are larger than books and desks. He may measure the *length* of the room, the *width* of the hall, and learn to use those terms.

When the child attains a mental age of 8-6 or better, he should be taught about longer distances. To present the idea of a mile, instruct him to walk around the block three times, which is approximately one mile, according to the usual city block.

Discuss the length of time required to go various distances, as to the post office, to the grocery store, to school, to another city. Talk about how the trip was made, whether by car, by train, by plane, or by walking. The child should be made aware of measurement in everyday living.

WEIGHTS AND MEASURES

Until the educable mentally retarded child has a mental age of 7-6 to 8-0 years, he should not be expected to understand weights or measures. This, of course, depends upon his environment and experience.

Teach the *pound* first, as the child usually has some experience with a pound of coffee or a pound of butter. Give him some experience in handling weights of a pound, a half-pound, more than a pound, and less than a pound.

A small desk scale may be used to demonstrate how the pointer moves to indicate the various weights of articles. Stress the value of the pound through class activity such as the grocery store, the post office, or the market. Also, introduce through study of the post office or drug store the smaller unit of weight, the ounce.

Instruct the child with a mental age of 8-0 to 8-6 years about liquid measures, limiting the basic units of measure to a cup, a quart, a pint, and a gallon. Teach the dry measures of the quart, pint, and bushel at this time.

Collective units should also be introduced at this mental age. The terms pair, dozen and half-dozen should be taught through the use of gloves, shoes, shoe strings, and egg cartons.

Children with a mental age of 9-0 to 12-0 should be able to acquire a good working knowledge of the basic values in measurement.

FRACTIONAL PARTS

The child may know the term one-half when he starts to school, but still not have the concept that a half is one of two equal parts of a thing. At a mental age of 7-0 years, he is ready to be taught the meaning of the term.

There are commercial items available for teaching fractional parts. One item of value is a wooden fruit plate with three wooden fruits divided into fractional parts for demonstration purposes. Flannel boards with fuzzy circles and squares may be purchased or constructed by the teacher. All of these materials add interest and variety to the lessons on fractions.

Presenting One-Half. The teacher must use ingenuity in making games to present the idea of a fractional part. Children like to use things they can handle or even eat in class. Apples that are cut to show halves may be eaten at the close of the lesson. Small candy rolls may be used similarly by cutting some of them into halves and some into uneven parts. The children may choose matching halves. They may measure the piece chosen against a marker. If the piece chosen is a half, the child may keep the piece of candy.

Matching of halves may be done with sticks, straws, or other things of interest to the children. The ease of dividing accurately into the parts should be considered when selecting articles for demonstration. These lessons continue throughout the year at regular intervals, so that there is opportunity for review, and so that comprehension and retention will be maintained.

In addition to the above use of three-dimensional materials the teacher should also use forms cut from colored paper. This gives practice in following directions, in developing eye and hand coordination, and in extending the children's comprehension of the concept of one-half to include surface measurements.

A sample lesson is given which demonstrates the method of

presenting this concept. The procedure illustrates the detailed explanation and assistance which is necessary for the children's comprehension of simple directions.

Teacher: See this piece of red paper. What shape is this piece of red paper? Yes, it is round, it is a circle. We will call it a red circle. We are going to cut this red circle into two parts. We want each part to be the same size. We want the parts to be *equal. Equal* means the same size, or the same amount.

Each of you may pick up the red circle that is on your desk. Fold the paper together like this. (The teacher holds the red circle in both hands and folds the edges together.)

Be sure the edges are even. (She goes about among the children showing them what is meant by *edges* and *fold*.)

Hold the red paper tightly. Now, with thumb and finger of one hand, crease the red paper down the fold, like this. (The teacher goes from desk to desk, encouraging, helping, showing what is meant by a *crease*, and praising each child.)

Now, take the scissors and cut along the fold. (Some children will need help in cutting a straight line along the crease in the red paper.)

Put the pieces of paper on the desk. Put them side by side. How many pieces do you have? Into how many pieces did you cut the whole red circle? (Give the children time to look and to reply.)

Impress upon the children that a thing is only cut into halves when the cut pieces are of equal size. The children may paste the halves of the red circles into their arithmetic notebooks. The teacher should help them to write ½ under each part of the red circle.

Repeat this procedure many times using forms cut from colored paper and three-dimensional forms. Keep the directions simple. Do not confuse the children by naming the parts of the fraction— the denominator and numerator. Instead they may repeat, "The bottom number of the fraction tells into how many parts anything has been divided. The top number of the fraction shows how many of the parts were taken or were kept."

When combining ½ and ½, show the children that 1 and 1 make 2, and then that when 2 is over 2, it shows 2 equal parts or the whole apple or thing. Teach the word *halves* orally first for audi-

Addition of Fractions

$$\frac{1}{2}+\frac{1}{2}= \qquad \frac{2}{4}+\frac{1}{4}= \qquad \frac{1}{4}+\frac{2}{4}+\frac{1}{4}=$$

$$\frac{1}{4}+\frac{1}{4}= \qquad \frac{2}{4}+\frac{2}{4}= \qquad \frac{1}{4}+\frac{3}{4}=$$

$$\frac{1}{4}+\frac{1}{4}+\frac{1}{4}=$$

$$\frac{3}{4}+\frac{1}{4}= \qquad \frac{1}{3}+\frac{1}{3}=$$

$$\frac{1}{4}+\frac{1}{4}+\frac{1}{4}+\frac{1}{4}=$$

$$\frac{2}{3}+\frac{1}{3}= \qquad \frac{1}{3}+\frac{2}{3}=$$

79. Practice sheet for addition of fractions.

tory recognition of the word; then much later present it for visual recognition.

The teacher should instruct the children to count the parts of the apple, write the number 2, to draw a line *under* the 2, to count into how many parts the apple was cut, and to write down the number 2 *under* the line. She should say, "Now you have two halves. If the children do not appear to understand, she must repeat and reinforce the teaching; give further demonstrations; repeat the key questions and give the answers until the children show comprehension. Another process or step should not be started until this one is thoroughly understood.

Separating Groups into Fractions. The flannel board is a good device to use in demonstrating how to divide a group of things into fractions. The teacher should place two disks of contrasting color on the flannel board. Black disks on a white flannel board are stimulating to the children. The teacher talks to the children.

Teacher: How many black spots do you see?

Pupil: Two black spots.

Teacher: Tom, you may take away one of the black spots. You have taken away one-half of the black spots. Tom, how many black spots make one-half of two black spots?

Repeat this procedure many times, using other materials until the children understand without prompting that two is one-half of four. It may be further dramatized by using four children each with a real apple. The teacher separates the children into two groups. Each group keeps half of the apples.

Presenting One-fourth. The fractional part of one-fourth may be shown to the child when he has attained the mental age of 7-6 or better. The same techniques should be used as were outlined for teaching the concept one-half. Since one-fourth is more difficult to present than one-half, do not hurry, but continue through every step of the explanation to secure comprehension for this new concept.

Continue to drill with circles, squares, and fruits cut from paper. Use the flannel board and felt disks to demonstrate the fractional part of a group. Help the child to realize that four-fourths make a whole apple, or *one* of anything.

Presenting One-third. When the child has a mental age of 8-0 years or better, he is ready for the idea of thirds. Introduce in the same manner as one-half. After working for some time with ⅓, review ½ and ¼. Use small juice glasses marked with the fractional parts of ½, ¼, and ⅓ to test the child's knowledge of parts and wholes. Prepare stencils or make worksheets for the children to color the fractional part as named.

There should be practice on writing and naming the fractional parts, such as ½, ¼, and ⅓. As understanding develops, combine the fractional parts with similar denominators. A child with a mental age of 9-0 years will be able to add simple fractions with no sum greater than the whole, or *one*.

TIME, CALENDAR, CLOCK

Teaching the concept of time, as in other basic skills, requires a certain degree of maturity before understanding may be expected. The child needs to be conscious of time from the first day of school. Punctuality is a requirement for holding any position or job. The educable mentally retarded are seldom aware of the passage of time unless it is emphasized for them. This must be done with study and drill during their formative years.

The concepts about time that one may expect the educable mentally retarded to find useful are listed in the chapter with the Progress Chart with the approximate mental age at which the child should be able to comprehend and retain the material. The presentation of the material should be extended through a teaching period of about three years. At all mental ages children vary in their interests and ability to retain.

They may advance rapidly in one step of learning through the use of certain materials; again they may reach a plateau where more readiness must be given. The readiness must continue until they reach a stage of maturity where the next step of the learning process may be understood and absorbed. The teacher must be alert for these plateaus of learning, and for the period of readiness which usually follows after adequate preparation.

Presenting the Concept of Time. There are many devices available commercially for teaching time. However, devices may also be constructed in the classroom or shop. A large clock face may be made from plywood or heavy cardboard, with large numerals painted on the face. The hour and minute hands should be attached so that they turn to show the time.

A child who can tell time may be appointed as the clock monitor. He will keep the clock set for the next activity throughout the day. Each child should have an opportunity to be clock monitor.

A real clock should also be used for experience in telling time.

80.   Worksheet—sample clock faces for teaching the hour and half-hour.

81. Worksheet—sample clock faces for teaching the quarter-hour.

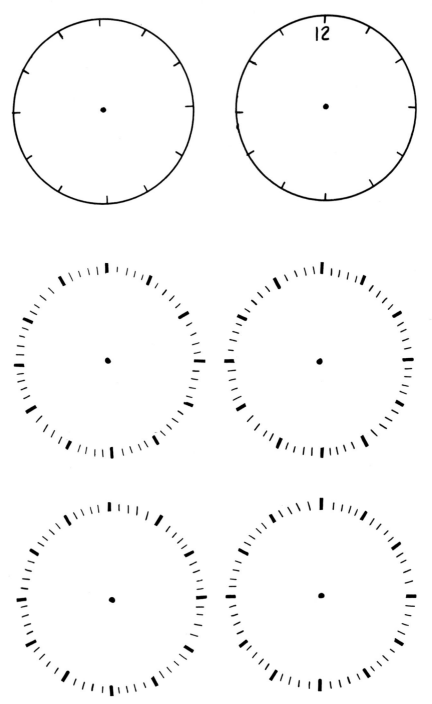

82. Worksheet—sample clock faces for teaching the minute and five minute intervals of time.

83.   Teaching aids for arithmetic.

An old clock serves the purpose of showing how the hands turn. The time values should be presented as outlined in the schedule as the child shows readiness. After explaining the meaning of the hours, half-hour, minutes, and quarter hour values, introduce the child to telling time by minutes.

The child should be shown the correct way to write time and how to read it. This can be done when the child can count by 5's to 55. He should be shown how to first write the hour, then the colon, and finally the minutes, as 2:35.

Prepare sheets for practice by stamping circles on ditto carbon sheets. The teacher should make sets of clock faces similar to the illustrations for each phase of presenting time. For the child who can count to five, she should use only those numerals he recognizes by sight, or from 1 through 5. The child should have sets of clock faces made for each number as he learns to recognize it and can count to it by rote.

The teacher should make up the same kind of sets of clock faces to show the half-hour through the use of the numbers 6 and 12.

Then she should add other numbers to show the hour hand at all positions.

The teacher should stress the position of the hands of the clock in telling time by the quarter-hour. The numbers on the clock face should be 12, 3, 6, and 9 for the first presentation. Then other numbers are added to show the hours, but the accent is on the quarter after the hour or the quarter before the hour. Counting by five may be started to establish the concept of fifteen minutes until, or fifteen minutes after the hour.

The child should have practice in drawing the hands on the clock faces to indicate the time as shown below the clock on a worksheet.

The teacher should prepare circles with heavy lines of color to mark the five-minute intervals instead of the numbers. The children learn to count from the top mark by fives. Then the number 12 is placed at the top of the clock face under the colored mark. The child continues the practice of counting by fives until this can be done correctly.

The next step is to make the minute intervals with a different color, diminishing the size of the markings as the child becomes secure in counting by fives and by ones to 60. Then use one color on all of the minute and hour marks on the clock face and finally put on all of the numbers. Drill should be continued for accuracy in telling time.

Presenting the Days of the Week. The educable mentally retarded need to learn the names of the days of the week, and to know them in sequence. Awareness of the days of the week and of the months of the year may be taught by using a mimeographed calendar form and a large wall calendar.

A calendar should be started the first day of school. The first period of the day is the best time for this activity. The teacher must be consistent in presenting this activity. She may ask the children for the name of the month, the day, the date, and the season of the year, which someone in the group will usually know. If no one does, the teacher will supply the information. After she has written the day of the week and the date, she will read it to the class. Then the children will read the information in unison.

The teacher should talk about the calendar, pointing out the day, the name of the month, and the date. Since the names of

Sun.	Mon.	Tues.	Wed.	Thurs.	Fri.	Sat.

84. Calendar form—for teaching months, weeks, and days.

the days on most calendars are abbreviated, the children should be taught to recognize them, as well as the entire name.

The children may keep a record of the weather on the small mimeographed calendar forms. They may use familiar symbols, such as a circle with rays for the sun, an umbrella for rain, and irregular forms for clouds. Keeping this record will make the children aware of many things concerning the weather which they have never noticed previously.

Along with the calendar exercises, discussions may be held concerning morning, afternoon, and dismissal time. The children become aware that noon is the time when morning ends and afternoon begins. Much later the teacher introduces evening, midnight, and then the letters that indicate morning and afternoon, A.M., and P.M.

Through imitation and repetition the children gradually learn to write time correctly. As the seasons change and the days become longer or shorter, the children become aware that the sun is shining when they get up in the morning, or that the sun does not shine until long after they have had breakfast. Even though they may not fully understand why this fact is true, they should be aware of the changes. They should also be made aware of the difference in the length of days and nights and of the seasons in other parts of the world than their home land.

A social studies unit is of value in teaching the differences in climate in the countries of the world. The educable mentally retarded are usually aware of other countries through the radio, television, pictures in newspapers, and through their contact with relatives in the armed services. Many teachers and visitors from other countries come to the schools almost daily to find out how the children are instructed in this country. They often contribute interesting information that helps the children realize something of the size of the world, and the variety of climate conditions of the world.

ROMAN NUMERALS

The teacher should tell the children about Roman numerals and explain and demonstrate the system from 1 through 20. The children will see these numerals on some clock faces and at the beginning of chapters in some books; therefore, they should be made aware of the meaning of the symbols. They may be interested to know the meaning of the I, V, X, and some of the combinations. There is no need to drill on learning the combinations; that is an unimportant item for the mentally retarded.

SOURCES OF CLASSROOM MATERIALS AND TEACHING AIDS

1. Allyn and Bacon, Publishers, Chicago: *Arithmetic in My World*, workbooks.
2. Beckley-Cardy Company, Chicago: Number games, counting devices.
3. Continental Press, Inc., Elizabethtown, Pa.: Number workbooks, ditto worksheets.
4. Educational Playthings, New York.
5. Eye Gate, Jamaica, N.Y.
6. Garrard Press, Champaign, Ill.: *Pay the Cashier* and other games.
7. Harr, Wagner Publishers, San Francisco: *Fundamentals in Arithmetic*, Books 1, 2, 3.
8. Houghton Mifflin Company, Boston: *Discovering Arithmetic*, Books 1, 2, Catherine Stern. *Structural Arithmetic Materials*.

9. Judy Company, Minneapolis, Minn.
10. Kenworthy Educational Service, Inc., Buffalo, N.Y.: *Number Readiness*, Ethel Savage.
11. The King Company, Chicago: Games, number materials.
12. D. C. Heath and Company, Chicago. *Learning to Use Arithmetic*, Readiness and Book 1, Agness G. Gunderson and George E. Hollister.
13. Hill-Godberson Company, Detroit: L-R Learning Aids; Pads of Want Ads; Pads of Application Blanks, Alice LeValli and Lillian Runge.
14. Laidlow Brothers, Chicago: *Numbers for Beginners*, A. L. Sanders.
15. Lyons and Carnahan, Chicago: *Number Friends*, Ruth L. Cole and Harry Karstans.
16. Milton Bradley, Springfield, Mass.: *Park and Shop, Easy Money*, and other number games.
17. Playskool Manufacturing Company, Chicago.
18. Row, Peterson and Company, Inc., Evanston, Ill.: *Row Peterson Arithmetic Workbooks*, Harry Grove Wheat, Geraldine Kauffman and Karl R. Douglas.
19. Silver Burdett Company, Morristown, N.J.: *Making Sure of Arithmetic*, Robert L. Morton, Merle Gray, Elizabeth Springstun, Wm. L. Schaaf. Myron F. Rosskopf. *Modern Arithmetic Through Discovery*, Robert L. Morton, Myron F. Rosskopf, H. Stewart Moredock, Merle Gray, Edward E. Sage, Wayne G. Collins, 1964.
20. Spitzer, Herbert F., and others: *Elementary Mathematics: Concepts, Properties, and Operations*. Grades k-6. Manchester, Mo., Webster, Division of McGraw-Hill, 1967.
21. Steck-Vaughn, Austin, Texas. *Working With Numbers, k-4*.
22. United States Armed Forces Institute, Madison, Wis.: Practical arithmetic and forms for study.
23. Watchmakers of Switzerland, Information Center, Inc., New York, N.Y.: Send for free unit and teaching aids on telling time. Ask for materials for the number of children in the class and for teachers' manual.

SUMMARY

The teacher of the educable mentally retarded has a great responsibility before her that will demand patience, persistence, endurance, love, and humility. She must realize that developing understanding within the damaged or malformed brain of these children requires gearing her activities and work plans for them to a slow repetitive pattern.

She should not allow the children's superficial ability to confuse her objectives. She must realize that true understanding is needed to make arithmetic useful, and that every small detail must be explained and demonstrated to secure the necessary comprehension. All of these skills and abilities should be taught with one purpose in mind—to produce happy, useful citizens.

REFERENCES

1. Allen, Amy, and Baker, Virginia: *Slow Learning Children in Ohio Schools*. Issued by E. E. Holt, Superintendent of Instruction, State Department of Education, Columbus, Ohio, 1962.
2. Bell, Peter: Mathematics for slow learners: Developing arithmetical skills. *Remedial Education, 3*(15), 1968.
3. Benoit, E. Paul, and Valene, Rita: Teaching retarded children to tell time. *Amer J Ment Defic, 59:*6, May 1962.
4. Burns, Paul C.: Arithmetic fundamentals for the educable mentally retarded. *Amer J Ment Defic, 66:*1, July 1961.
5. Carrison, D., and Werner, Heinz: Principles and methods of teaching arithmetic to mentally retarded children. *Amer J Ment Defic, 47:*4, January 1943.
6. Deans, Edwina: *Arithmetic Children Use*. Washington, D.C., Association for Childhood Education, 1954.
7. Descoeudres, Alice: *The Education of Mentally Defective Children*, translated from the second French edition by E. F. Ross. New York, D. C. Heath, 1928.
8. Feingold, Abraham: *Teaching Arithmetic to Slow Learners and Retarded*. New York, John Day, 1965.
9. Finley, C. J.: Arithmetic achievement in mentally retarded children. *Amer J Ment Defic, 67:*2, September 1962.
10. Glennon, Vincent J., and Callahan, LeRoy G.: *Elementary School Mathematics: A guide to Current Research*. Washington, D.C., ASCD, No. 611-17752.
11. Goldstein, Herbert, and Seigle, Dorothy: *Illinois Guide for Teachers of the Educable Mentally Handicapped*. Danville, Ill., Interstate Printers and Publishers, and Distributors for the Illinois Council for Mentally Retarded Children, 1958.
12. Ingram, Christine P.: *Education of the Slow Learning Child*, 3rd ed. New York, Ronald, 1960.

13. Johnson, G. Orville: *Education for the Slow Learners.* Englewood Cliffs, N.J., Prentice-Hall, 1963.
14. Kahn, Charles H., and others: *Measure Up.* Palo Alto, Fearon, 1968.
15. Kephart, Newell C.: *The Slow Learner in the Classroom.* Columbus, Ohio, Merrill, 1960.
16. Kirk, Samuel A.: *Early Education of the Mentally Retarded.* Urbana, Univ. of Illinois, 1960.
17. Martens, Elise H.: *A Guide to Curriculum Adjustments for Mentally Retarded Children,* rev. ed., Washington, D.C., United States Government Printing Office, 1962.
18. Marshall, J. J.: Mathematics for the slow learners: Modern mathematics for the older slow learner. *Remedial Education, 3*(24): 1, 1968.
19. Moore, Norman: Mathematics for slow learners: Teaching social arithmetic to slow learning children. *Remedial Education, 3*(19):1, 1968.
20. Morton, Robert Lee: *Teaching Children Arithmetic: Primary, Intermediate, Upper Grades.* New York, Silver Burdett, 1953.
21. Nicholls, R. H.: Mathematics for slow learners: A programmed preparation for number. *Remedial Education, 3*(1):11-14, 1968.
22. Nugent, Marion A.: *Home Training Manual.* Boston, Dept. of Mental Health, 1957.
23. Ohio, Hamilton County: *Guide for Slow Learners of Primary, Intermediate, Junior High and Senior High Levels.* Cincinnati, Office of the Superintendent of Hamilton County Public Schools, 1963.
24. Pollock, Morris, and Pollock, Miriam: *New Hope for the Retarded.* Boston, Porter Sargent, 1953.
25. Rosenzweig, Louis E., and Long, Julia: *Understanding and Teaching the Dependent Retarded Child.* Darien, Conn., Educational Pub. Corp., 1960.
26. Salvin, Sophia Tichnor, and Light, Beulah: *Curricula, Methods, and Habitation for the Multiply Handicapped.* Los Angeles, Univ. of Southern California, 1963.
27. Siegel, Ernest: *Helping the Brain Injured Child.* Great Neck, New York, Association for Brain-Injured Children, 1961.
28. Southwick, Selma: Some thoughts on modern math for the retarded child. *ETMR, CEC, 2*(33), 1967.

29. Strauss, Alfred A., and Lehtenin, Laura E.: *Psychopathology and the Education of the Brain-Injured Child: Volume I, Fundamentals and Treatment*. New York, Grune and Stratton, 1947.
30. Tansley, Albert E., and Gulliford, R.: *Education of Slow Learning Children*. New York, Humanities Press, 1962.
31. *Teaching of Arithmetic—Fiftieth Yearbook*, Part II. Chicago, NSSE, 1951.
32. Thresher, Janice M.: A problem for educators: Arithmetical concepts formation in the mentally retarded child. *Amer J Ment Defic, 66*:1, 1962.
33. Weber, Elmer W.: *Educable and Trainable Mentally Retarded Children*. Springfield, Thomas, 1962.
34. Wiley, Bertha Mae: *Time and Telling Time*. Palo Alto, Fearon, 1967.
35. Williams, Alec A.: Mathematics for slow learners: Organization and assessment. *Remedial Education, 3*(28):1, 1968.

15

AUDIO-VISUAL AND OTHER SENSORY TRAINING

PURPOSE OF THE PROGRAM

T HE mentally retarded child will learn more readily from audio-visual and sensory materials than he will from lectures or explanations. These children are not "word or thought" oriented. They are geared to handle an object, to see it, to hear it, to taste it, to smell it, in order to know and understand anything about it.

Kinds of Materials. Too often one thinks of sound films as being synonymous with audio-visual materials. However, other audio-visual materials assist in stimulating the interest, add to the field of information, and aid in retention.

There are many avenues to explore in this field. Among these are films, film-strips, slides, tape recorders, opaque projectors, photographs, paintings, magazines and books, charts, maps, dioramas, peep boxes, radio, television, phonograph records, field trips, materials brought into the classroom, dramatizations, puppet plays, shadow plays and games. The list is limited to the imagination and constructiveness of the teacher.

SELECTION OF MATERIALS

When selecting material to bring new experiences to children, the teacher should have in mind some of the basic values and aims in using the audio-visual materials. She should also consider the maturity and the abilities of the children who use them. The group must be ready for the material when it is presented. If it is on an interest level comparable with their chronological age, they will feel it is worthy of their attention. The materials, which must be simple, should recognize the dominant interest pertaining to the topic being studied.

Films. Films are the most frequently used of all audio-visual materials. They are prepared to teach certain facts, to assist in the understanding of definite skills, and to develop desirable attitudes. Sound films are available in color, as well as in black and white. The usual educational film for children runs for about eleven minutes. A short length film is better than a long one to retain the attention and interest of the educable mentally retarded.

Most school systems have their own film library or belong to a district or county exchange through which films, film-strips, and recordings may be requisitioned. The teachers are usually provided with lists of such materials.

Many films are also available for the cost of transportation. Some companies charge only for the return postage. The advertising in such films is usually inconspicuous and not at all objectionable.

If the school board does not furnish the needed records, films, and materials for the class, usually some civic group will help out with funds for renting and transporting them.

The film should be secured far enough ahead of the showing to preview it. Class preparation for the film may consist of the following steps: Explain why the film is being shown; ask the children to watch for particular things in the film in order to be prepared to discuss them after returning to the classroom.

It is a good plan to scatter the children about the room and if possible to have a vacant seat between each one. Best friends sitting side by side to view a film too often want to talk instead of look at the film.

After the children see the film, there should be a discussion period, during which a list of their comments is written on the chalkboard. Their thinking should be directed to bring out items that require emphasis for the subject under study and to correlate the new information with previous lessons. If possible, the film should be shown later to clear up misunderstandings or to emphasize certain points.

The same topic is often presented in several films at different interest levels. Most primary age educable mentally retarded understand the spoken language well enough to comprehend an intermediate age film on "Safety on the Bus," or "Taking Care of One's Things." An interesting language lesson might result from showing two films on the same topic at two levels. The older pupils could compare the presentation of the material.

Instructional Material Centers. A network of centers for instructional materials for special education teachers has been established throughout the United States. This network disseminates information about new materials and methods for all handicapped children. This service is for all teachers upon request. The headquarters may be visited to examine materials, or a telephone call will bring information. New materials are evaluated and suggestions are made for adapting materials for special requirements. Materials are loaned to the schools as from a library.

The address of the national headquarters of this center is: Coordinator, Instructional Materials Center Network for Handicapped Children and Youth, 1507 M Street N.W., Washington, D.C. 20005.

There are seventeen regional centers, and the plan is to open more centers as the facilities can be obtained and there is a need for them. Contact your State Education Director for information regarding your regional center, or the national coordinator at the above address in Washington, D.C.

An Instructional Materials Center for Handicapped Children and Youth has been established in Illinois under the direction of the Office of the Superintendent of Public Instruction. Services provided by the Center are concentrated on the instructional needs of all those associated with the programs of special education, except the visually impaired. The Center will loan materials to anyone connected professionally with exceptional children and youth. This Center is located at 726 South College St., Springfield, Illinois.

The Center at Springfield was established June, 1965, by the State of Illinois. In June, 1966, the U.S. Office of Education approved a three-year research and demonstration project by the Illinois State Department of Special Education. The Illinois Center is a member of the national network of Instructional Materials Centers for Handicapped Children and Youth. In the national network, Illinois was the first center to be included which had already been established under an official state agency of public instruction. All the other network centers at the time were university sponsored. The Illinois Center is also the first one to devise a unique mobile unit to improve instruction of handicapped children regardless of geographical location.

Illinois has a mandatory law which requires school districts to establish and maintain such education facilities as may be required for teaching all handicapped children. This mobile unit was provided to assist in the rapidly expanding services for the handicapped. The equipped mobile unit was obtained through Title VI, ESEA funds, while personnel and operating costs were provided through state and federal project funds.

FIELD TRIPS

To be effective, field trips need not be taken to far-away places. Every community has many interesting and helpful places available for school tours. A trip to a local store, post office, fire station, bakery, a near-by farm, museum, or library may be rewarding. The trip and the experience should meet the child's need.

The teacher should make careful preparation for a trip of this kind, whether it is for one hour to a local store or all day to a large museum. She should make plans far enough ahead to avoid confusion among either the children or their parents.

If the children are to leave the school grounds, parental permission should be obtained. A permit slip should be sent home to be signed for each trip. List the place to be visited, the mode of transportation, the hours of departure and return, and whether a lunch is to be taken or money to spend for souvenirs.

There is great concern for liability in case of an accident, so licensed carriers are recommended instead of parents' cars for transportation. The teacher should discuss carefully with the group the following procedure: the purpose of the trip; things they will see; possible questions they should ask; the kind of clothes they should wear; the kind of lunch to take; the place where the lunch will be eaten; the opportunities for getting a drink and for toileting; the time of departure and return; the amount of spending money allowed; courtesy; manners; and safety.

The teacher must insist that the group stay together so that there will be no rushing ahead to be first in line. The pupils should wait for the teacher to direct them in crossing streets, entering buildings, and viewing exhibits. After the field trip each pupil should be given an opportunity to relate his experiences. With the help of the teacher the children will write these stories to be used later in reading and review lessons. Words are selected from the stories for spelling and for writing lessons.

Some of the children will want to write their own stories. They may need some help with spelling. They will enjoy reading their own stories to the class.

Every child should have an opportunity to illustrate his story. Individual drawings may be put on the bulletin board. These usually depict a variety of scenes with whimsical forms and gay use of color. The older pupils will want to study the information they have collected, and evaluate their own abilities in terms of future jobs or leisure activities.

Training of the Senses. Mentally retarded children need special training of the senses. They will look off into the distance when the teacher is presenting a lesson on a chart or is writing on the board. Their listlessness and lack of attention are shown by their unwillingness to use a marker under a line of words. The teacher should insist upon its use, because it does focus their attention on the words.

These children must be taught to use their senses to help them retain an impression of the world in which they live. Games may be devised for training the visual, auditory, tactile, kinesthetic, taste, and olfactory senses to recognize things with which they come in contact.

The mentally retarded should be made aware of the meaning of these terms: hot, cold, warm, cool, sour, sweet, bitter, salt, pungent odors, high and low tones, smooth and rough surfaces, far and near, similar and different, colors and sounds.

TRAINING THE SENSES

1. Place some different articles in a box. They may be a plastic toy car, a red ribbon, a paper clip, and an eraser. Show the articles to the child for a minute and ask him what he saw. He may be able to name just one thing. Try again. Repeat this for several times each day until he is able to name all of the articles.

   If the child is very slow, use only two or three articles at first. Then increase the number of articles until he is able to name four or five things from a one minute glance. Change the contents of the box and continue this as long as it is effective.

2. Show the child different kinds of scraps of cloth. Allow him to handle them and become familiar with the names of such materials as cotton, linen, wool, velvet, and silk. This may take days or weeks before the names of the materials are established.

   Play a game using the cloth scraps. Place them in a bag and allow the child to feel the materials and select one at a time. Let him name the material before taking it from the bag. If he identifies it correctly, let him take a colored counter from a box for a tally. If he fails to give the correct name, tell him the name and put the material back in the bag. He can count the tallies and keep a record. If he is unable to write the number, the teacher may do it for him. This will provide motivation to learn to count and to make the numbers.

3. Cut construction paper of different colors into squares, triangles, circles, and oblongs. Paste small strips of felt or fuzzy paper to the backs of the strips. The child may then use the flannel board to group the shapes according to color, size, or form.

4. Games of lotto are excellent for matching. The teacher may buy commercial games, or she may, with the help of the pupils, prepare sets. The backs of tablets, suit boxes, or tagboard are good to use for the base of the game. Cut pictures or words from magazines in the category needed and paste them in orderly rows in squares on the cardboard. Paste the matching pictures or words on small squares to be used by the

children to mark their recognition of a word or picture. Build similar games for teaching units about foods, transportation, clothing, health, safety, animals, plants, the letters of the alphabet, and new words.

5. Make scrapbooks of pictures illustrating beginning sounds of words. Concentrate on one sound at a time. The preferable letter is the one being taught in writing or in phonics. The child should write the letter at the top of the page in the scrap book. Help him to find in an old magazine a picture that shows the beginning sound correctly. Let him paste the picture on the page under the letter of the alphabet. If you think he knows what to do or if he wants to work alone, let him try.

When the child has found a picture that he thinks belongs to the page, tell him to bring it to you to be checked *before* he pastes it in the scrap book. Have him say the word aloud before the picture is pasted in the books so that he experiences hearing the sound and associates it with the beginning letter of the word.

Have the child write the beginning letter under the picture, followed by a line to indicate there are more letters in the word, such as b—— under a picture of a ball.

6. Let the children construct a domino game of matching colors which involves drill with the use of the ruler and skill in using the pencil and crayons. Use lightweight cardboard for the dominoes. Draw across the cardboard lines forming rectangles 1½ x 3 inches. Cut the domino shapes apart, leaving two rectangles fastened end to end.

The children should color the dominoes with crayons. They may assign colors to the numbers from 0 to 5, as 0—black; 1—blue; 2—green; 3—yellow; 4—brown; 5—red. Lay out a set of real dominoes and help the children to see how many of each color are needed.

Play the game by matching the colors. Each child should name aloud the color he is matching. As soon as the names of the colors are learned, change to cards of different colors. For example, take out all of the green ones and add purple. Continue until the children recognize all of the colors.

7. Make another kind of matching game from old cloth swatch,

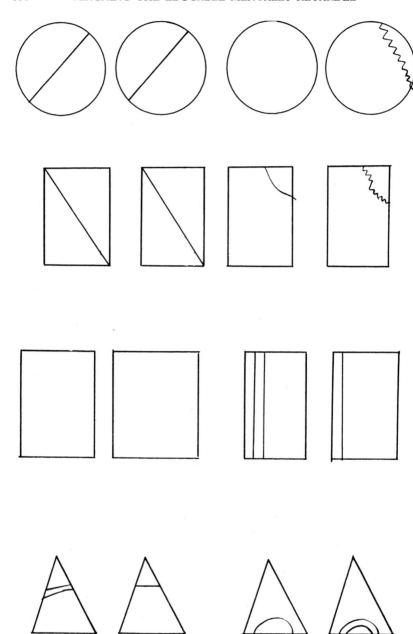

85.   Examples of designs for finding differences and likenesses.

or sample, cards, that may be secured from stores. Cut the cards into two pieces to be used for matching color, texture, and pattern.

8. Make cards to teach the opposites or comparisons. Use pictures from magazines or draw the illustrations for such words as big—little; more—less; black—white; rough—smooth. Show one card and let the child find the opposite.

Arrange the cards on two tables and let the child match them. Later clip the words to the cards. After the child gains confidence in matching the pictures and words, remove the pictures and match the words. Words meaning opposites and comparisons are difficult for the mentally retarded to remember and comprehend.

9. Take the children for a walk around the block, for the purpose of enabling them to draw pictures of something they have seen. This can be a seasonal activity, such as new leaves, the snow, or the birds' nests. The children's ability to observe, to tell what they saw, and to depict in drawings these things will improve after a few such walks.

10. Play games on the chalkboard to show likeness and differences. Draw circles, squares, ovals, oblongs, or triangles. Put lines or decorations on them in colored chalk to incite interest and to help the children observe more closely. The children choose teams to play a relay game. The teacher may appoint captains to keep the scores. Each member of the team has one chance to show the change that was made by the teacher on the drawing. The one who is *it* marks a tally on the board if he recognizes the change in the detail of the drawing, a zero if he does not identify it.

11. Make a game of watching for shapes in the clouds. Draw the shapes on blue paper with white chalk.

12. Give each child a leaf that has been picked from a tree or shrub on the playground. Match the leaf with another one from the playground. Learn to identify the trees and the shrubs by their leaves.

13. Train the hearing by learning to listen to voices, to the soft music of a phonograph, to the rhythm of singing voices, to people walking, to the wind in a tree, to the buzz of a bee or a fly, to the bounce of a ball, or to a bell being struck softly.

14. Teach the child to listen for directions and to pay attention while a direction is being completed; to listen to a message so that he will be able to deliver it promptly and correctly; or to read or to listen to a story for better comprehension and retention.

15. Train the olfactory sense by having the children sniff various odors from bottles or when walking on a tour, or arrange to cook some foods with distinctive odors. Odors for sniffing could be perfume, mints, vinegar; for cooking and smelling— chocolate, coffee, peanuts, popcorn, bacon.

16. Train the sense of taste by having "tasting parties." This may be used in connection with a study of foods in a nutrition unit. Intermediate age pupils especially enjoy this experience. Some pupils must be coaxed at first to sample new foods.

    Some ways to serve these foods at "tasting parties" follow: place a small amount of honey on a bite of bread; serve fresh fruit cut into cubes or wedges on toothpicks; serve different kinds of cheese in small cubes or bites on toothpicks; serve small portions of different kinds of bread; serve a few drops of vinegar, lemon juice, or syrup, in individual plastic spoons; serve a small portion of salt, sugar, or powdered alum in small plastic spoons.

    The junior high and senior high school pupils' interest in tasting will be stimulated by new food items used as refreshments for school parties, picnics, or dinners.

17. Peg boards are useful for training observation, and for improving coordination of the fine muscles of the hand. Start with the large size peg board, with the large round colored wooden sticks. When the child's coordination improves allow the use of the small six inch one hundred-hole peg board and the small pegs. The children enjoy using the plastic pegs with the knobs for color. Prepare a pattern of the one hundred holes of the boards according to size, and ditto off a supply. Draw patterns on these dots with colored pencils or felt tipped pens. Use a variety of simple lines for the pupils to duplicate with the pegs on the board. Each pupil works independently. Keep a record on each child's master set of patterns of his progress. This makes an interesting study. Be sure the pupil is making a copy of the pattern, not punch-

ing holes through the pattern. This is done sometimes at the beginning, but is more constructive if the child is able to learn to work alone. For example, pattern No. 1, begin with a blue line of dots down the left row of the ditto pattern. The child imitates this with the blue pegs in holes to match, so he has a row of blue pegs down the left side of his peg board. No. 2, a line of red dots across the top of the pattern. No. 3, a line of green dots down the right row of the pattern. No. 4, a line of orange dots across the bottom row of the pattern. No. 5, a square, use the same color dots on the lines as used previously. No. 6, offset the left row of dots in one row, change the color to purple, keep the other rows of dots and colors the same as before. No. 7, keep changing and adding to the complexity of the pattern. Later make simple forms to copy as, a house or a tree. Use all one color and repeat patterns.

18. When the child does not know color this is a good time to teach it. As he picks up the various colored sticks have him repeat, "a red stick," and later, "one red stick." Do not rush the counting. The color and the form are the important things to be learned first.

19. Recognizing and being able to draw common forms is important in giving the child self-confidence as he mingles with other children in many activities at home and at school. Many commercial kits are available with the square, triangle, circle, and rectangle or oblong, or the teacher may easily prepare one of each from cardboard. If the forms are cut out carefully, the space left may be used as a stencil.
Present the form to the child and say, "See the square." Try to get the child to say "square." Place the stencil over some paper and show the child how to trace around the inside of the stencil. Allow the child to color the square. Often the stencil should remain in place, so when it is lifted there will be a good outline of a square.
This must be repeated many times before the child is ready to try to draw a square without the stencil. He may try using the ruler, or cut away one side of the stencil and let him supply that line, then gradually remove another side. These are important steps and are to be carefully learned.

20. Another attention-holding method, that also improves eye-hand coordination, color discrimination, and space determination, is the use of colored self-adhering paper strips for sorting and pasting into patterns.

The first attempts at sorting should be with eight or ten pieces of the paper, of only two or three colors. As proficiency develops, the colors may be increased.

The next step is sorting and pasting onto another paper to follow a preset pattern. This could be simple at first with three or four strips already pasted, each on separate lines. The child finds the matching strips and pastes them along the appropriate lines. As the child becomes skilled, new colors and difficult shapes are introduced. These may represent stick animals, children, houses, boats, or flowers.

21. Other useful forms to use are artificial fruits, geometric shapes, puzzles, and quiet games like picture dominoes.

THE BULLETIN BOARD

Selection of Materials is Important. The teacher should carefully select the materials to be placed on the bulletin board, since it plays an important part in the teaching of mentally retarded children. It should be attractive with color, variety, and simple materials which stand out and invite attention. Glaring colors should be avoided. Use quiet backgrounds to avoid distraction.

86. Lettering and titles are important.

87.   Children's construction work should be displayed.

A large number of pictures and materials on display cause the children to ignore everything on the board. Materials should be changed frequently and brought back later if the teacher needs them for review.

Arrangement of Materials is Important. The bulletin board may be neatly divided into sections by using heavy cord or plastic tape. Each section should have a title or subtitle, and the children should be briefed on the meaning of every word used.

Lettering and Titles are Important. The titles should be in bold, eye-catching letters cut on simple lines. One color of paper is best for the letters of the titles, since a word cut from two or more colors is confusing to the vision. The word *Washington* cut with letters of red, white, and blue might not be recognizable as one word by the educable mentally retarded. The letters may be shadow cut by using one contrasting color under another or made more prominent by the use of a contrasting color for mounting purposes. The lettering should be kept in a straight line.

The letters may be given a three-dimensional appearance by raising them from the background on straight pins or loops of masking tape attached to the backs of the letters. Oblong blocks of paper may also be used and small circular or triangular contrasting pieces of paper may be pasted onto the oblongs to form the letters. Many kinds of materials may be used for letters, cloth, felt, wall paper, thin corrugated paper, or plastic.

Pictures should be Large. Pictures that are used on the bulletin board should be only those that can be plainly seen from any part of the school room. If a picture with much detail must be used, the teacher should be sure the children have an opportunity to look at it closely. Sometimes she should prepare a section of the bulletin board for humorous pictures just for fun for the children. Humorous animal pictures generally win a good response from the pupils. The teacher must remember that the humor of the mentally retarded is not subtle but is very practical and even rowdy.

Displays should be Changed Frequently. One section of the bulletin board may be reserved for material concerned with the current unit of study. The topic of the unit should be in a conspicuous place. The charts, maps, poster pictures, and exhibits should be changed from day to day as new material is introduced in the unit.

Display Material Should be Filed. Material for bulletin boards should be kept in some order to make it available for use when needed. Boxes from the clothing stores make excellent files. The large boxes that contained men's sweaters are a good size. The box should be wide enough and long enough to accommodate full page pictures with a mounting from magazines.

Trim the picture and if desired, mount it. If there is information concerning the picture which will be helpful when used in the classroom, attach it to the back of the mounting or clip it to the picture.

The pictures must be classified. Usually a special subject or topic can be selected and then a general classification. Attach these two titles to the upper-back part of the picture with the number of the picture and the number or title of the box in which the picture will be filed.

The cards used for the recording of the titles may be regular 3 x 5 cards. List the topics and their picture number at the top. List where the picture may be found in the center of the card with the other topic. A brief description of the picture may be typed under this to aid in finding a suitable picture for a bulletin board. File the cards alphabetically. File the boxes numerically.

Sources of Materials for Bulletin Boards.
1. Adhere-o-Learning Aids, Inc., Wilmette, Ill.
2. Fearon Publishers, Inc., San Francisco, Calif.
3. Hayes School Publishing Co., Wilkinsburg, Pa.
4. Mutual Aids, Los Angeles, Calif.

Displays should be Mounted. The displays should all be mounted to form an attractive picture. Small items may be grouped on a large card to form a pleasing arrangement. Then the teacher should walk about the room and view it from various places to judge its appeal and decide if there could be a more harmonious or effective placement. Three-dimensional displays are appealing. They are usually teacher-constructed in the primary, but are made by pupils in the older age classes.

Children's Contributions are Important. A space should be provided for the children's contributions. The teacher may place a large sheet of construction paper on the bulletin board and stick a few pins near it for attaching materials to the board. The children themselves put up the interesting items they bring and talk about their items during a sharing period.

Pupils' paintings, drawings, booklets, murals, and construction work in art and crafts should be displayed. Such material may be kept for only a day or two, but the pupils gain much satisfaction from seeing it exhibited. The pupils' contributions to the bulletin board should be discussed, and brought to the attention of the class.

If bulletin board space is limited, a corrugated box may be painted or papered and the sides used for display space, or part of the box may be cut away to form a show case. The raw edges may be taped and the box papered or painted. This will give space for items about the display. An easel type display board may be made from two heavy cardboards being tied together at the top and held apart by a string on each side a few inches from the bottom.

SUPPLEMENTARY MATERIALS TO THE BULLETIN BOARD

A table may be used as a supplement to the bulletin board for presenting materials used in connection with the unit being studied, such as reference books, or equipment. There should be other places about the room for such activities as cutting and pasting, clay modeling, painting, reading, science projects, storage for records and music, a phonograph, radio, and TV.

SUMMARY

The teacher must use every lesson and activity to train the eyes and the ears, and the other senses, which must do extra duty for the educable mentally retarded.

Properly used, the bulletin board with accessory displays assists in focusing the children's attention on the materials they are studying.

REFERENCES

1. Bowers, Melvyn K.: *Easy Bulletin Boards for the School Library.* New York and London, Scarecrow, 1966.
2. Chaney, Clara M., and Kephart, Newell C.: *Motoric Aids to Perceptual Training.* Columbus, Ohio, Merrill, 1968.
3. Chansky, Norman M., and Taylor, M.: Perceptual training with young mental retardates. *Amer J Ment Defic, 68:*4, 1964.
4. Dale, Edgar: *Audio-Visual Methods in Teaching,* rev. ed. New York, Dryden, 1954.
5. Fernald, Grace: *Remedial Techniques in Basic School Subjects.* New York, McGraw-Hill, 1943.
6. Freedman, Florence B., and Berg., Esther L.: *Classroom Teacher's Guide to Audio-Visual Material,* rev. ed. Philadelphia, Chilton Books, Education Division, 1961.
7. Frostig, Marianne, and Horne, David: *The Frostig Program for the Development of Visual Perception.* Chicago, Follett, 1964.
8. Goldstein, Edward: *Selective Audio-Visual Instruction for Mentally Retarded Pupils.* Springfield, Thomas, 1964.
9. Instructional Materials Center—Network for Handicapped Children and Youth. Coordinator: Instructional Center, Washington, D.C.
10. Kephart, Newell C.: *The Slow Learner in the Classroom.* Columbus, Ohio, Merrill, 1960.
11. Kingsley, Ronald F.: Associative learning ability in educable mentally retarded children. *Amer J Ment Defic, 73:*(1):5, 1968.
12. McCarthy, James J.: An overview of the IMC Network. *Exceptional Child, 25*(3):263, 1968.
13. Mental Retardation Film List. Arlington, Va., HEW, 1968.
14. Montessori, Maria: *Spontaneous Activity in Education,* translated by Florence Simmons. Cambridge, Mass., Bentley, 1964.
15. Scagotta, Edward G.: Tinker boards. A tactile kinesthetic approach to learning. *Exceptional Child 34*(2):129, 1967.
16. Tansley, Albert E., and Gulliford, R.: *Education of Slow Learning Children.* New York, Humanities, 1962.

17. Teaching Resources. An educational service of the *New York Times*. Boston.
18. Watkins, Harry L.: Visual perception training for the moderately retarded child. *Amer J Ment Defic, 61:4*, 1957.
19. Weber, Elmer W.: *Educable and Trainable Mentally Retarded Children.* Springfield, Thomas, 1962.
20. Weiner, Bluma, B.: Comment on textured illustrations—favorable. *Teaching Exceptional Children*, Nov. 1968, p. 20.
21. Witsen, Betty: *Perceptual Training Activities Handbook: TC Series in Special Education.* New York, Teachers College, 1967.

16

THE SOCIOGRAM

THE PURPOSE OF USING SOCIOGRAMS

T HE SOCIOGRAM is a useful instrument, when understood, and properly used, to determine interrelationships in the class, to locate individuals who may be causing friction, who may be isolates, or who may be potential leaders.

PROCEDURE

The teacher who is unfamiliar with the procedure of giving and evaluating a sociogram should study a text on the subject in order to secure the maximum benefit from the results of one. She can obtain adequate information, however, by preparing simple questions to ask each member of the group. These may be affirmative or negative questions or a combination of the two which may concern the relationships between pupils and their activities at school, at play, and at home.

The questions should not be presented to the entire group but be asked individually. There is a tendency by the pupils to look around the group and to make signals to each other or to ask questions, thereby revealing their choices which influence the answers of others. The teacher will find that this attempt will be made even though the questions are administered individually but with less influence on the results.

The teacher must maintain an objective and detached attitude toward the replies and encourage each child to answer each question, yet not to pressure him nor influence his reply.

The sociogram as presented here is simplified to be used to meet the teacher's every day situation in the classroom. These problems change from day to day, and sometimes from hour to hour, but frequently there is a situation that continues for days and the teacher wants to find out what is causing the friction.

New questions should be compiled to meet the new problems.

A form for the sociogram may be similar to the following list of affirmative and negative questions.

QUESTIONS FOR A SOCIOGRAM

1. If I could change my seat in school, I would like to sit by —————.
2. I would rather not sit by —————.
3. I would like to choose ————— for a partner in a game.
4. I would rather not have ————— for a partner in a game.
5. I would like to visit ————— in her/his home.
6. I would not care to have ————— visit me in my home.

The above set of questions concerns three different situations; the schoolroom; the playtime; the home. Three of the questions are negative, and three are affirmative. The teacher may make up a few questions and try them out with the pupils to test their reaction. Three wishes are often quite revealing of the child's personality. A few questions are better than a lengthy list.

Before the questions are asked, the teacher should have prepared a form sheet for recording the replies. List the pupils' names with a space after each name for an answer to each question. Number the spaces at the top of the column to correspond to the questions. This sheet presents all of the data in summary form for the teacher to evaluate.

Evaluating the Information. Draw a line across the center of a sheet of paper. In the upper right corner draw a circle as a symbol and label it "girls." In the upper left corner, draw a triangle and label it "boys." Write the number of the question used at the top of the page. Number the pupils and use the numbers instead of names when making the charts. Some teachers may

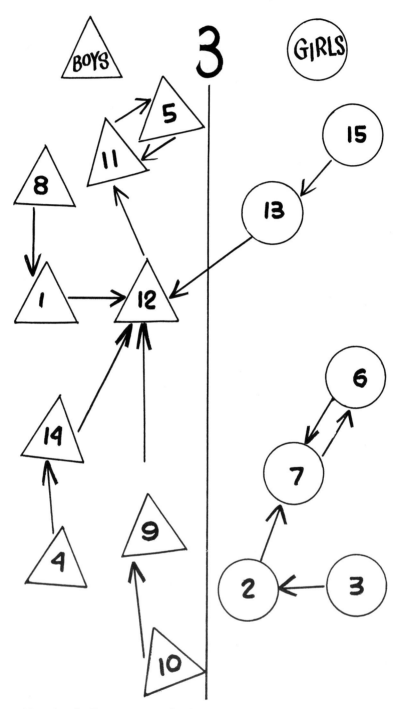

88. Graph illustrating results from one question on a sociogram.

prefer to use the pupils' names, but numbers lessen the chance of a child being recognized if the material should fall into unprofessional hands.

A typical evaluation chart is shown with this chapter. This is the result of asking the question, Whom would you like for a partner in a game? The responses of fifteen children are pictured. The chart shows some children were not chosen, others were chosen in a chain, while one boy, number 12, was chosen four times. He had not chosen any one of the group that had named him their choice. It would seem that boy number 12 was desirable for some reason as a partner.

There are two reciprocal choices: number 11 and 5; 7 and 6. There are chain choices: 4 to 14 to 12; 10 to 9 to 12; 8 to 1 to 12; 15 to 13 to 12; 3 to 2 to 7. The ones not chosen were numbers 8, 4, 10, 15, and 3.

The results of the sociogram may be shown in another way. The teacher may cut figures from colored paper or pictures from catalogs to represent the children. These figures or pictures may be pasted to a large cardboard on which colored lines may indicate the acceptance or rejection of each pupil. When all of the choices have been compiled in each category for each pupil, sometimes the teacher discovers a child who has not been accepted or rejected. This child has been ignored for some reason. He needs help and encouragement to become one of the group.

As the teacher works with this isolate she will study his records and may be able to discover some cause for this complete rejection. Perhaps this is a personal hygiene problem or an annoying habit. Whatever the problem, try to help him improve the situation. Try to discover some special ability or quality that will assist in minimizing the cause of rejection and build self-confidence so that he can begin to function more naturally.

The teacher may improve troubled spots in the classroom almost immediately by shifting the children's desks to different parts of the room. There is nothing to be gained by compelling two persons who actively dislike each other to sit side by side. Although children's habits are not quickly changed or formed, they may be gradually reformed by the teacher's patient, helpful direction into more desirable patterns.

A new sociogram may be given to the children when a problem is presented by unusual behavior. The questions should be changed in content to suit the conditions. Even if no problem appears, the teacher may give a sociogram several times during the year to compare the status of the pupils. A child who was previously considered a nonentity may mature socially and become a leader, while some other child may show many rejections. The teacher may avoid trouble among the pupils by recognizing these changes and by using skillful guidance and careful groupings for recitations and activities.

SUMMARY

The teacher may prepare and administer a sociogram to determine the interrelationships of the pupils. She should utilize this information to secure better grouping in activities, better seating arrangements, and better general social relationships.

REFERENCES

1. Akmann, J. Stanley: *Testing Student Achievements and Attitudes.* Washington, D.C., Center for Applied Research in Education, 1962.
2. Bills, R., Vance E., and McLean, O.: An index of adjustment of values. *J Abnorm Psychol, 51:*254-259, 1955.
3. Driscoll, Gertrude: *How to Study the Behavior of Children.* New York, Columbia Univ., 1954.
4. Gardner, Eric F., and Thompson, George C.: *Syracuse Scale of Social Relations, Elementary Level.* New York, Harcourt, Brace and World, 1959.
5. Gerberich, J. Raymond, Greene, Harry A., and Jorgensen, Albert N.: *Measurement and Evaluation in the Modern School.* New York, David McKay, 1962, pp. 145-148.
6. Green, John A.: *Teacher Made Tests.* New York, Harper and Row, 1963.
7. Gronlund, Norman E.: *Sociometry in the Classroom.* New York, Harper and Brothers, 1959.
8. Haring, Norris G., and Phillips, E. Larkin: Behavior rating scale. In *Educating Emotionally Disturbed Children.* New York, McGraw-Hill, 1962.
9. Hennings, Helen Hall: *Sociometry in Group Relations.* Washington, D.C., American Council on Education.

10. Horace Mann-Lincoln Institute Pamphlet: *How to Construct a Sociogram*, 7th ptg. New York, Bureau of Publications, Teachers College, Columbia Univ., 1954.

11. Jennings, Helen H.: *Sociometry in Group Relations*, 2nd ed. Washington, D.C., American Council on Education, 1959.

12. Johnson, G. Orville: A study of social position of mentally handicapped children in regular grades. *Amer J Ment Defic*, 55:60-89, 1950.

13. Kelman, Howard R.: Individualizing the social integration of the mentally retarded child. *Amer J Ment Defic*, 60:6, 1956.

14. Miller, Robert V.: Social status and socioempathic differences among mentally superior, mentally typical, and mentally retarded children. *Exceptional Child*, 23:114-119, 1956.

15. Noll, Victor H.: *Introduction to Educational Measurement*, 2nd ed. Boston, Houghton Mifflin, 1965.

16. Northway, Mary L.: *A Primer of Sociometry*. Toronto, Univ. of Toronto, 1952.

17. Northway, Mary L., and Weld, Lindsay: *Sociometry Testing: A Guide for Teachers*. Toronto, Univ. of Toronto, 1957.

INDEX